**Can we be sure
about anything?**

Can we be sure about anything?

SCIENCE, FAITH AND POSTMODERNISM

Edited by Denis Alexander

APOLLOS

APOLLOS (an imprint of Inter-Varsity Press)
38 De Montfort Street, Leicester LE1 7GP, England
Email: ivp@uccf.org.uk
Website: www.ivpbooks.com

First published 2005

British Library Cataloguing in Publication Data
A catalogue record for this book is available from the British Library.

ISBN–13:   978–1–84474–076–5
ISBN–10:   1–84474–076–5

Set in Monotype Garamond 11/13pt
Typeset in Great Britain by Servis Filmsetting Ltd, Manchester
Printed and bound in Great Britain by Creative Print and Design (Wales),
Ebbw Vale

*Inter-Varsity Press is the publishing division of the Universities and Colleges Christian
Fellowship (formerly the Inter-Varsity Fellowship), a student movement linking Christian
Unions in universities and colleges throughout Great Britain, and a member movement of the
International Fellowship of Evangelical Students. For more information about local and
national activities write to UCCF, 38 De Montfort Street, Leicester LE1 7GP, email us at
email@uccf.org.uk or visit the UCCF website at www.uccf.org.uk.*

CONTENTS

Contributors   7

Introduction: A multidisciplinary approach to
truth telling   9
Denis R. Alexander

1. A short introduction to postmodernism   13
   Dominic Smart

2. The Christian roots of scientific reasoning   30
   Roger Trigg

3. A biblical basis for the scientific enterprise   49
   Ernest Lucas

4. Christianity, science and the postmodern agenda   69
   John L. Taylor

5. The postmodern attack on scientific realism   92
   John L. Taylor

6. Maintaining scientific and Christian truths in
   a postmodern world   102
   D. A. Carson

7. Has science anything to do with human values?   126
   Colin A. Russell

8. The scientific community and the practice of
   science   140
   Denis R. Alexander

9. Quantum physics: a challenge to scientific
    objectivity?   165
    Peter J. Bussey

10. Truth in the geological sciences   187
    Robert S. White

11. Hawking, Dawkins and *The Matrix*: science and
    religion in the media   214
    David Wilkinson

12. BSE, MMR and GM: who's telling the truth?   237
    Derek Burke

CONTRIBUTORS

Denis Alexander is Head of the Laboratory of Lymphocyte Signalling and Development at The Babraham Institute, Fellow of St Edmund's College, Cambridge, and Editor of the journal *Science and Christian Belief*. He is the author of *Rebuilding the Matrix: Science and Faith in the Twenty-first Century* (Oxford: Lion, 2001).

Derek Burke was previously Vice-Chancellor of the University of East Anglia and former Chair of the UK Government's Advisory Committee on Novel Foods and Processes.

Peter Bussey is Reader in Physics at Glasgow University. He takes part in elementary particle experiments at the German DESY laboratory in Hamburg, and at the Fermi National Accelerator Laboratory near Chicago. He has an active interest in issues connected with the philosophy of quantum physics and the relationship between science and religious belief.

Don Carson is Research Professor of New Testament at Trinity Evangelical Divinity School, USA. His first degree was in chemistry. He is the author or editor of more than 45 books, including *The Gagging of God: Christianity Confronts Pluralism* (Grand Rapids: Zondervan, 1996).

Ernest Lucas has doctorates in both biochemistry and biblical studies. He is Vice-Principal and Tutor in Biblical Studies at Bristol Baptist College, an affiliated college of Bristol University, and author of *Science and the New Age Challenge* (Leicester: Apollos, 1996) and *Can we Believe Genesis Today?* (Leicester: IVP, 2001).

Colin Russell worked for many years in organic chemistry, and after moving into the history and philosophy of science is now Emeritus Professor at the Open University. His books include *Cross-Currents: Interactions between Science and Faith* (Leicester: IVP, 1985), revised and reprinted (London: Christian Impact, 1996), and *The Earth, Humanity and God* (London: UCL Press, 1994). He is a former president of Christians in Science.

Dominic Smart is the minister of Gilcomston South Church in the centre of Aberdeen. He is a regular speaker at conferences and universities and is a visiting tutor at the Highland Theological College. He has a science background and was surging rapidly towards a life in glaciology before becoming a minister.

John Taylor is Head of Physics and in charge of Philosophy at Rugby School, England. He is director of the Perspectives on Science project, which is responsible for the creation of a new AS level in the History, Philosophy and Ethics of Science.

Roger Trigg is Professor of Philosophy, University of Warwick, and co-edits the Ashgate series of monographs on science and religion. His most recent books are *Philosophy Matters* (Oxford: Blackwell, 2002) and *Morality Matters* (Oxford: Blackwell, 2004). He is writing a book on religion in public life for Oxford University Press.

Robert White FRS is Professor of Geophysics, Cambridge University, and Fellow of St Edmund's College, Cambridge. He leads a research team studying earthquakes, volcanoes and the structure of the earth's crust. Co-author with Denis Alexander of *Beyond Belief: Science, Faith and Ethical Challenges* (Oxford: Lion, 2004).

David Wilkinson is Wesley Research Lecturer in Theology and Science in the Department of Theology at the University of Durham, England. His background is research in theoretical astrophysics and his recent books include *The Message of Creation* (Leicester: IVP, 2002) and *God, Time and Stephen Hawking* (Crowborough: Monarch, 2001).

INTRODUCTION: A MULTIDISCIPLINARY APPROACH TO TRUTH TELLING

Denis R. Alexander

It is rare to find scientists, theologians, historians and philosophers engaging with each other seriously about the subject of postmodernism. This interdisciplinary volume of essays represents precisely such an unusual species. Whilst the 'culture wars' of the 1990s have to some extent faded from view, the background issues remain active and relevant, no less in the arts than in the sciences. In a world in which relativistic views of knowledge remain influential, is it really possible to know something? Or are all forms of human knowledge inevitably tentative and provisional? Too often the answers to those questions have been given by sniping across inter-disciplinary demarcation lines. Those in the humanities find scientists irritatingly arrogant as they display a high level of confidence in their latest scientific findings. Conversely scientists despair at the way in which those in the arts are so ready to tell them that what is true for one person might not be true for another, and vice versa. The writers in this volume point us to ways past this apparent impasse that are shaped by their common biblical world-view.

This volume was initiated by a day conference under the same title organized by Christians in Science and held in London on 29 September 2001. In fact six of the present chapters started life as talks given on that day, although some have been largely rewritten over the intervening period. In addition a further five chapters have been written especially for this volume, and a Templeton prize-winning paper (chapter 4) has also been incorporated from the journal *Science and Christian Belief*. No attempt has been made to enforce an artificial homogeneity upon the material. The authors come to the central questions from very different backgrounds and areas of expertise. Unsurprisingly there are differences of emphasis and opinion. Nevertheless the overall level of agreement between those from different disciplines is remarkable – something certainly not imposed by the editor of this collection!

Those who find postmodern jargon an alien and somewhat forbidding territory should find Dominic Smart's introductory chapter a useful overview. As the author points out, those with a scientific background often have very little idea as to what postmodernism is all about, or indeed may never have heard of the term. C. P. Snow's 'two cultures' are alive and well, each having their being in separate domains that (sadly) overlap only rarely.

In chapter 2 the philosopher Roger Trigg tackles the important question as to how scientific knowledge can be justified, arguing that science needs a metaphysical grounding if it is to be defensible, a grounding that can be located 'in the notion of an ordered creation, and a God-given rationality'.

The theologian Ernest Lucas then picks up the theological aspects of the same question in chapter 3, with a particular emphasis on the way in which biblical presuppositions contributed to the emergence of modern science.

The philosopher John Taylor in chapter 4 takes us back to recent developments in the philosophy of science with a focus on the writings of Thomas Kuhn. Taylor argues that in science it is perfectly possible to steer a sensible course between the Scylla of total relativism and the Charybdis of naïve realism.

Chapter 5 addresses in greater detail the philosophical incoherence implicit in phrases such as 'x is true for you but not for me'. As an analytical philosopher Taylor is well placed to carry out the dissection that follows carefully and persuasively.

In chapter 6 the theologian Don Carson goes deeper into the relationship between postmodern epistemology and Christian faith, arguing against the false antithesis often posed within post-modernity: that if we cannot know something absolutely and completely, then we must give up all claims to objective knowledge. The historian of science Colin Russell reflects in chapter 7 on the way in which cultural and historical contexts have impinged upon the development and even the content of scientific theories, yet in the final analysis theories are answerable to nature: they are never merely human constructs that can be detached from the properties of the world around us.

The social practices of the scientific community that give them confidence that they are constructing a body of reliable know-ledge are described further in chapter 8: it is argued that in practice virtually all scientists are 'critical realists' – they believe that there is a real world 'out there' which ultimately shapes their theories, but are well aware that their knowledge of that world is always partial. Two more scientists then focus on the possible ways in which postmodern thought impinges upon their respective disciplines.

The physicist Peter Bussey considers in chapter 9 the question as to whether quantum theory tends to undermine the objectivity of scientific knowledge, whilst the geophysicist Bob White in chapter 10 addresses the issue of how certain we can be about the kinds of data generated in the historical sciences such as geology, even when they relate to events that took place millions or even billions of years ago.

David Wilkinson in chapter 11 then discusses the way in which the media handle science, showing how postmodern thought per-colates into the assumptions made by radio and TV producers about the nature and practice of science.

Finally, and still concerned with the public domain, Derek Burke in chapter 12 draws on his long experience of chairing a Government advisory committee to discuss the public under-standing of science illustrated by the debate on topics such as BSE and genetic engineering.

All the contributors to this volume are Christians who believe that the question of truth is as critical in theology as it is in science. Several of the contributors draw attention to the shared epistemological space occupied by both Christians and scientists. For as the tide of realism has retreated and the postmodern waves of relativism have swept up the beach in its place, so scientists and Christians alike find themselves standing on what appears to be a very similar type of rock.

1. A SHORT INTRODUCTION TO POSTMODERNISM

Dominic Smart

A few years ago an acquaintance of mine, who is the head of a large biomedical research laboratory in Cambridge, decided to carry out an informal oral survey amongst the members of his research group. The aim of his survey was to determine what scientists thought about postmodernism. Here were the research elite – postdocs, PhD students and technicians, all focused on a life of academic research in the sciences, all in their twenties or early thirties, at an age when the impact of postmodernism might be expected to be quite dominant. Unfortunately, however, the survey did not get very far. For it quickly emerged that no-one in this research group had any particular views on postmodernism. But the problem ran deeper than that: no-one had even heard of the term and had no idea at all what it meant! And this despite the fact that their colleagues down the road in the English Department (for example) were grappling with the postmodern interpretation of texts as a normal part of their everyday lives. Ironically, of course, it is almost certain that these same scientists were deeply influenced by the tenets of postmodernism via the medium of films, music and popular culture. But they had never developed the intellectual tools necessary to cope with a cultural tide that impinged so deeply upon their daily lives.

This story illustrates, yet again, the yawning gulf that still remains between the arts and the sciences, and also underlines the need for this introductory chapter, which provides a brief overview of some of the central ideas of postmodernism. Readers from the humanities may wish to skip it, but if you have a science background or are unfamiliar with postmodern ideas, then you might be able to identify with the members of that Cambridge research group and therefore find such an introduction helpful.

The key to PoMo: there is no big story

The first thing to note is that the key to unlocking postmodernity is surprisingly simple: there is no big story. In 1979 the philosophy Professor Jean-François Lyotard wrote what has became a famous report for the Province of Quebec's *Conseil des Universitiés* (thankfully, it is available in English[1]). In this report he wrote, 'I define postmodern as incredulity toward metanarratives.'[2] He acknowledged that the definition is an extreme simplification, but it effectively takes us to the core of postmodernism. Incredulity is an unwillingness to believe – but what are metanarratives? Again it is a simple term: *meta* is Greek for 'above' or 'beyond'; narratives are the stories that tell our lives – what has happened to us, the world that we live in and our experience of it. Metanarratives are thus the big stories that contain the grand themes, the major plotlines and central characters that dominate our culture and by which we make sense of our own little stories.

If you want to understand postmodernism, you have to get a grip of this essential feature: there is no big story.

Naturally, the major big story that our society decreasingly believes is modernism. We would normally trace its development

---

1. Jean-François Lyotard, *The Postmodern Condition: A Report on Knowledge*, tr.
   Geoff Bennington and Brian Massumi (London: Methuen, 1984).
2. Ibid., p. xxiv.

back to 1637, when René Descartes published his *Discourse on Method*.[3] He split it into six parts, the fourth of which contains the (in)famous passage where Descartes wishes to determine what he can be certain about – what the foundation for knowledge is. He starts systematically to doubt everything in the world outside his mind, even his own body (this world forms the *res extendens* – the 'extended thing'), until he arrives at that which is going to provide him with certainty. What provides him with this is simply that he is thinking. He cannot doubt that for to doubt it would be to think. Rationality (*res cogitans*) provides his foundation; hence, 'I think; therefore I am.' (Of course, he need not have drawn that particular conclusion: he could have concluded, 'I think; therefore there is thought.') The rationalism that Descartes instigated became intertwined with what seems superficially to be its opposite: the inductive empiricism of the seventeenth-century philosopher Francis Bacon. Whilst Descartes looked inwards to alleviate doubt and arrive at a foundation, Bacon sought certainty in reading the book of nature, and together they provided the intellectual parentage for the big story of modernism, the story of reason, logic and rationality, a story that would have massive intellectual, political and cultural consequences. It has been claimed that its offspring include Western industrialization, imperial expansion, economic and political organization, large organizations structured along logical and rational lines, modern science and technological innovation.

But modernism is not the only metanarrative that framed Western society, and through it other societies. There have been other big stories. Another big story, romanticism, appeals to beauty. By the time we get to 1820, we read the romanticist metanarrative being expressed with concise poetic precision in John Keats's 'Ode on a Grecian Urn'. The last couplet reads, 'Beauty is truth. Truth beauty. / That is all ye know on earth and all ye need to know.' Neither reason nor observation gives the foundation for knowledge, but rather beauty. Marxism is another metanarrative; and capitalist democracy is a fourth.

---

3. René Descartes, *Discourse on Method*, tr. F. E. Sutcliffe (London: Penguin, 1968).

The reason why Lyotard's definition of postmodernism (PoMo) is so good is that it does not confine PoMo to being simply a movement away from modernism. PoMo is a movement away from belief in *any* single, dominant metanarrative. That means it is a movement away from metanarratives that come from other places; it is also a movement away from metanarratives that have been around since long before Descartes was even thought of.

Of course, Christians also have a metanarrative. We have a big story, not because we are the products of our culture, though we always are to some extent. We have a big story because it is given to us: our big story is God himself as he has revealed himself in his Word, the Bible, and principally by his Son. Therefore postmodern culture and thought are as uncomfortable with the Christian 'big story' as they are with the far more recent modernist story. Moreover, Christians ought to be uncomfortable, for they swim not only against the tide of these other metanarratives – Marxism, romanticism, capitalism and modernism – but also against the tide of postmodernity, for they are not disbelieving of their given metanarrative. They are not filled with incredulity regarding God and his Word.

How do metanarratives function?

Big stories function in six connected ways.

First, they make foundational claims: they tell you what you can be certain about. As we have seen, this was the whole reason for Descartes's programme of systematic doubt. He wanted to arrive at knowledge that is a foundation upon which everything else could be built. Unfortunately it proved to be the wrong foundation. Keats tried to establish a kind of foundational claim with romanticism: beauty is truth, and truth is beauty. That is all you know on earth and all you need to know. Marxism and capitalism are attempts to establish foundational frameworks of thought, in this case relating to the means of production and the economic structures of societies.

Second, they exert a dominant influence regarding what we might call the artefacts of our culture, the things that our culture produces. Through art, literature, music, cinema, theatre, language and the way it shifts and develops, political discourse and policy, architecture and design, the prevailing metanarrative expresses itself influentially. People who have never heard of Descartes, rationalism, modernism, or indeed any specialized philosophical jargon, are nonetheless shaped and framed by the big story. A social consensus is created.

Third, by making foundational claims and by pervading all aspects of culture, metanarratives provide a unifying system of thought into which all other ideas can be ordered. They provide a paradigm or matrix that enables other ideas to cohere. When you are arranging theories, ideas, facts, predictions and so on into an ordered system, you are not simply placing them in some sort of relation to the overall grand narrative: you are placing them in a more or less coherent relation to one another. The big story gives us a matrix into which we can fit our experiences, our interpretations of the world and of ourselves, a way in which we can bring together fragmentary human existence and try to make sense of it. It is the metanarratives that provide the skeleton upon which hang the intellectual muscle and the cultural skin.

Fourth, because of their foundational claims and their dominant and pervasive influence upon our culture, metanarratives define what is true and false for us. What is 'true' for a capitalist is not 'true' within a Marxist paradigm. The statement 'the acquisition of personal wealth is good' is true if you are a capitalist but false if you are a Marxist. Is it true that society advances through technological innovation? Keats would have said 'No!' But a thoroughly modern technocrat would say 'Yes!' Or again, is it true that words have meanings in themselves? Or do they only have meaning in relation to different words? The 'truthfulness' of your answers to these questions is decided by your metanarrative (or even by the lack of it). Big stories function by providing a means of assessing the truthfulness and the meaningfulness of everybody else's statements. Of course, the answers that are provided by the metanarrative for the true/false questions also apply to the value questions that define what is good and what is bad.

The fifth way in which metanarratives function is by providing a means of interpreting direction in history. If you have a big story, then you have some way of defining what is progress and what is regress. Thus, history is seen to be progressing in an entirely different way if you interpret it as a capitalist democrat from the way it is seen to be going if you are a Marxist. History is going in different ways, at different rates, if you are a rationalist or a romanticist. History is going in different ways if you are a Christian or an atheist. It is the big story that provides a sense of direction for history and defines progress.

These ways in which metanarratives function lead inevitably to the sixth: metanarratives (so say their critics[4]) provide a means of creating human identity, and therefore a means of social control, manipulation, oppression and marginalization.[5] You can define who is mad, bad or God in your society by their conformity or their non-conformity to the paradigm. If you are part of a group that holds to one particular big story, with its 'truth regime' (to use Michel Foucault's phrase[6]) and its direction for history, then you can decide that what others think is wrong and subversive. If you also have power, you can marginalize and silence your critics if they believe something fundamentally different from what you do. History – ancient and modern – is littered with examples of big stories providing the means of social control. Extreme and evil control in the recent past includes the pogroms, the holocaust and the Gulags. But postmodern thinkers would point to processes of

---

4. Among the best known is Michel Foucault. See his book *The Archaeology of Knowledge and Discourse on Language*, tr. A. M. Sheridan-Smith (New York: Pantheon, 1972).

5. It is interesting to note that Francis Bacon's main motive for developing his empiricism was social and arose from strong Christian convictions. He hoped for the improvement of society, rather than the mere control of it, but the practical uses of certain knowledge were at the forefront of his thinking, even though the applications of science did not in reality begin to make a major impact on society until the nineteenth century.

6. Foucault used the phrase in an interview with Alessandro Fontana and Pasquale Pasquino under the title of 'Truth and Power'. The transcript of this is in Colin Gordon (ed.), *Power/Knowledge: Selected Interviews and Other Writings 1972–77* (New York: Pantheon, 1981).

control that arise from a metanarrative and affect all of us, but that are exercised by social institutions and structures at a quieter, less obvious level. All metanarratives do this. Foucault's phrase 'truth regime' describes not only what modernism does, but also what Christians do in their churches. Christians, in this view, have their own versions of truth regimes by which they can exert social control within their churches, thereby defining who is subversive and who is not.

Why do metanarratives not work any more?

Why are we now *post*modern? Why could Lyotard talk about the postmodern condition being incredulity regarding metanarratives per se? Metanarratives do not work any more for (again) at least six reasons.

In the first place, big stories do not appeal to postmoderns because the one most familiar to them – modernism, with its 'techno-science' – has simply not delivered the goods, at least in the postmodern account of the situation. It promised heaven on earth and has given us something a lot more like hell in this view. Postmoderns look around and see a world that is heavily polluted, torn apart by war, riddled with social inequalities and injustice, and filled with lousy buildings. Where is the progress that the metanarratives guaranteed? We are in a mess! The big story has not worked, so who wants to commit themselves to it?

Second, there is no single big story because there are just so many stories to read nowadays. There is an immense heterogeneity in the variety of ways in which people around the globe view the world. We see on our TV screens the massive difference between non-Western cultures and our own, and can understand and embrace that difference better than our parents ever could. We do not simply see these vastly differing individual cultures around the world; we see the whole variety mixed together. In the twin-bladed big blender of global communications and the global consumer market, historically in no small measure due to the longer-term consequences of Christian global mission, we are in touch with a world that is massively varied and immediately accessible to us.

With commonplace technology we can go shopping in Seattle without setting foot outside our homes. In fact you do not need to go abroad any more – the other cultures are all around us within Britain. We live in one of the most culturally pluralistic, postmodern societies. We experience the effects not only of the big four metanarratives that have shaped the previous three centuries, but also other metanarratives that are much older from other parts of the world. People think differently in other places, and they think differently even though they occupy the same space.

The third reason that metanarratives do not work any more goes back to the truth regime of Michel Foucault: it is that metanarratives oppress. As a means of social control they are a means of exerting power. Thus the whole of history is just the story of power play. Truth is just a way of getting some people to do what you want them to do and marginalizing the ones who do not do what you want them to do. The same is true of virtue. Everything is a sham. What is really going on is that people want to be able to control other people by oppression. And because we do not want that, we do not want metanarratives.

Fourth, big stories have collapsed because of perspectival thinking. What shape is a piece of A4 paper? If you look at it one way, it is a very thin, straight line. Look at it from a different angle and it is a rectangle. It is your perspective that tells you what shape a piece of A4 paper is. Perspective is influenced by different elements: your paradigm, your thought world, affects what you see. Where you are in relation to particular big stories affects what you perceive and how you perceive and interpret it, both in the world and in yourself.

If your paradigm shapes your perspective, your person also does the same. Who you are affects what you see. We bring to our observation of the world our ability to commit ourselves to it and listen to it: to try to understand it as it is and as it would shape our thinking about it. Alternatively we can bring to our observation of the world our pre-set, concrete-like ideas of what it should be and fail to understand it. The philosophical basis of the rationalism and empiricism that lie behind modernism has been thoroughly critiqued by scientists and philosophers of science themselves. In the latter third of last century, Thomas Kuhn, Paul Feyerabend,

Michael Polanyi, Harold Brown and many others broke the modernist metanarrative from within its greatest venture – science. They did so by radically rethinking the epistemological role of the person who does science.[7] Other writers in this volume pursue the implications for science of this critique in greater detail.

Your paradigm shapes your perspective. So does your personality. Some people will look through prison bars – some see bars, some see stars. Most importantly in the articulation of postmodernism, what you have in your life, your 'phenomena', also shapes your perspective. Have you had a painful childhood? That shapes your perspective on, say, the word 'father'. When you look at the world around you, you see it from within the horizons of your own world, whether those horizons are linguistic, emotional, social, artistic, intellectual or whatever. Whether it is a text in a book, a glacier or the person you are married to – whatever you try to understand, you bring to it all that is contained within the horizons of your own understanding. Yet the text, the glacier, the spouse have their own 'worlds' with their horizons. Our ability to perceive and understand is affected by the things in our horizon and by what we do with them. Some would argue that when we, say, look at a text, we should try to put aside what is in our horizon and try to understand the horizon of the text and its author;[8] then we can let the text reshape our horizon as we fuse the two horizons together. Others would argue that the horizons of the text or the author are inaccessible, and only what you can see within your own horizon gives any meaning to, say, a passage of Scripture.

---

7. See Thomas S. Kuhn, *The Structure of Scientific Revolutions* (2nd edn; Chicago: University of Chicago Press, 1970). Also, e.g., Paul K. Feyerabend, *Against Method* (London: Verso, 1978); Michael Polanyi, *Personal Knowledge: Towards a Post-Critical Philosophy* (London: Routledge & Kegan Paul, 1958); Harold I. Brown, *Perception, Theory and Commitment: The New Philosophy of Science* (Chicago: University of Chicago Press, 1977).

8. See for instance Hans-Georg Gadamer, *Philosophical Hermeneutics* (Berkeley: University of California Press, 1976). Also Anthony C. Thistleton, *The Two Horizons* (Exeter: Paternoster Press, 1980).

So in the postmodern view everything is a matter of perspective: it just depends on how you look at it. It depends on what kind of person you are. It just depends on that matrix that is functioning in your mind. It depends on what has gone on in your life. Is God good? The postmodernist would say, 'It depends which way you look at it. It depends what kind of life you've had.' What you cannot say is that 'God is good' in any absolute sense. It just depends.

Now the answer to the question 'What shape is an A4 piece of paper?' that I just asked (answer: 'it depends on your perspective') represents one postmodern view. There is a more sophisticated postmodern answer, and this is the fifth reason why metanarratives do not function too well any more. It is because we construct our reality. The more sophisticated postmodern answer to the question 'what shape is a piece of paper?' is 'shape is just a construct of your mind. It isn't one shape or the other: shape is just a construct. Shape is just something that you have got in your head that you impose upon what is outside you. So you construct reality.' In fact this view would go further and claim that we inevitably construct our own reality. You cannot jump outside your own skin in order to see yourself. Similarly, you cannot jump outside your knowledge, language and perception of the world in order to test them. So all the time you are in fact constructing your own reality. Legoland and Disneyland are excellent icons of a postmodern world. As Richard Middleton and Brian Walsh comment:

> To the postmodernist mind . . . we have no access to something called 'reality' apart from that which we 'represent' as reality in our concepts, language and discourse. Richard Rorty says that since we never encounter reality 'except under a chosen description,' we are denied the luxury or pretence of claiming naive, immediate access to the world. We can never get outside our knowledge to check its accuracy against objective reality. Our access is always mediated by our own linguistic and conceptual constructions.[9]

---

9. From J. Richard Middleton and Brian J. Walsh, 'Facing the Postmodern Scalpel', in Timothy R. Philips and Dennis L. Okham (eds.), *Christian Apologetics in the Postmodern World* (Downers Grove: InterVarsity Press,

'Reality' is what you make it, what you want it to be. There is no big story to tell you what it is or ought to be, says postmodernism.

Sixth, we no longer think of ourselves as simply reading; we are now and always have been interpreting. Much of the influential thinking in postmodernism has come from the world of literary theory – how we interpret texts, what words are and how they work, what's going on in the activities of reading and writing. The general umbrella term for this area of thought is hermeneutics and the importance of debates within this area – which touches on so many others – cannot be overstressed. You and I do hermeneutics even though we might hardly be aware of it. We try to make sense of our newspapers and magazines, the results from the last experiment, the instructions of our research supervisor, the Bible, body language, the rules and regulations of the sports we play, the instructions for the DVD player; even this paragraph! Making sense of what we see and hear – any kind of 'text' – is a basic human activity.

Postmodernity and hermeneutics

It might seem that hermeneutics is a tiresome irrelevance to scientists, who after all deal with plain observations, hard facts and unequivocal numbers; but no-one with his or her eyes and ears even half open does much science for very long before realizing the fallacy of this notion. What's happening to hermeneutics in postmodern culture? Remember that the metanarratives purport to define what is true, what is false and how you decide it. The metanarratives tell us what is acceptable and where it fits in with everything else. By providing a context the big story also provides meaning. But meaning and how you interpret it have changed in two ways. The first is a cultural way. Hermeneutics has changed

---

1995), p. 134. The quote from Rorty is from Richard Rorty, 'Pragmatism and Philosophy', in Kenneth Baynes, James Bohman and Thomas McCarthy (eds.), *After Philosophy: End or Transformation?* (Cambridge, MA: MIT Press, 1987), p. 57.

because the 'big story' was once understood and accepted by a significant number of people engaged in a significant spread of cultural and personal activities. The big story created a unifying consensus about what things mean and what words might mean. In the postmodern world, that unifying consensus of ideas and values is vanishing.

Here is a trivial illustration. Imagine a contemporary living room in which tasteful decoration brings together twentieth-century prints by Ben Nicholson and Paul Klee together with imitation Byzantine icons. Anybody who thinks like Ben Nicholson or Paul Klee does not think like the Byzantine artists who produced the icons. The people who produced the icons believed in particular ways, and had a particular shared content to their belief in God. The iconic image functioned as a sign, to point believers to God. By contrast, the works of Nicholson and Klee point to a supposedly pure human rationality and logical order (Nicholson) or the world of human dreams and imagination (Klee). But because the icons have been taken away from their generative context of shared belief in God and shared beliefs about God, they can hang in the same room as Nicholson's and Klee's work, and nobody – even if he or she recognizes the paintings – bats an eyelid. The cohabiting young postmoderns who decorated their room simply thought they looked quite nice together: a bit of diversity, a bit of variety. They 'do something' for them. But the original meanings are unknown, even unknowable: irrelevant and lost in the incoherence of postmodernity.

Because our culture no longer appeals to a commonly acknowledged big story, the meaning of a picture or a landscape or a set of results or a poem or a passage in Scripture ceases to be a matter for consensus. It becomes only what it means to me now. Meaning becomes localized. It becomes individualized and privatized. Even at its most communal, it is only a matter of sporadic or momentarily orchestrated individualism.

The second way in which hermeneutics has changed has more to do with literary theory about words and how they work. Again, this might seem far removed from the world of science, but the interrelatedness of academic disciplines lies at the heart of postmodernity. The classical view of language, which normally we trace back to Plato, was that meaning is contained in the words themselves. Meaning comes from the fact that words name ideas about the things they are used for, and these ideas express the essence of the things. Thus we use the word 'dog' because it expresses the idea of real, essential dogness.

The shift towards postmodern hermeneutics began with the French-speaking Swiss philosopher Ferdinand de Saussure. According to Saussure, rather than meaning lying in the words themselves and their 'essence', meaning comes from the hidden, assumed, tacit relation of one word to another in a language system, a relation that is primarily one of difference: 'in language, there are only differences'.[10] Thus we use 'dog' because it is not 'bog', 'cog', 'fog', 'log' and so on. We use it to describe canines merely by convention. Words are therefore fairly arbitrary signs. As signs, words are both present (the word on the page or in one's ears) and absent (the link with the thing signified is a hidden, unseen and unheard link). Saussure also made a radical move that points the reader/interpreter away from what a word means in some other language system from other times. Both the underlying relations between words and the conventions of the system are always contemporary. The historical cause of the word – the ety-mology – is less important than its use now in its immediate context. Further, the 'original meaning' of a historical text like the Bible is not the determining factor for its meaning now.

The underlying relations that give words meaning were, for Saussure, the deep structures of thought, convention and culture – the products of a metanarrative. Saussure used the game of chess as a limited illustration. What makes the game work is not the actual shape of the pieces in the chess set. You can buy extremely minimalist stainless steel chess sets, or intricately carved wooden sets in which the queen looks like one and the castle has finely detailed parapets and a drawbridge. The shape of the piece is arbitrary, as long as the queens look different from the castles or the bishops or the pawns and so on. With either set you play the

---

10. From his *Course in General Linguistics*, tr. Wade Baskin (New York: McGraw-Hill, 1966), p. 120.

same game, since chess works because of the hidden rules and the nature of the board.

The approach that Saussure established is called 'structuralism'. One thinker who developed his ideas further was Roland Barthes. Barthes saw clearly that we read in a very different way if we are a structuralist from the way in which we read if we are a classical reader. In particular, structuralism disengages itself from the historical world that generated the text – the historical world of the author. Since the locus of meaning no longer lies in the intentions of the author, literature can have many meanings, not just one. In fact any kind of 'text' can have many meanings. The meanings come from the world of each 'reader'. Thus structuralism hastened what Barthes termed the 'death of the author' and the 'birth of the reader'.

But the structuralism of Saussure and Barthes was taken even further by the post-structuralist Jacques Derrida. Derrida's move beyond structuralism involved several radical rethinks about words and meaning. He considered the appeal to deep, hidden structures to be little more than a piece of power play. The criticism belongs to that same post-structuralist family of disparate authors that Foucault, with his 'truth regime', belonged to. Who says that there are deep hidden structures? And why them? How can they exert such an influence? Why should others succumb to it?

To describe the way that he sees texts working, Derrida coined the term *differance*. (You have to say it with a French accent – it is a play on the French *différence* – diversity, contrast, difference.) Differance has two parts. First, words and texts do have a relational component to their meaning, and (*à la* Saussure – remember that *post-* does not mean *anti-*) that relation is one of difference. The second part to 'differance' is that meaning is deferred. It does not come from the author's mind straight to us via the subsequent choosing of an appropriate word. Intended meaning does not produce words but is rather the other way round. The words that an author uses are mere traces of what was going through his mind, not the actual intended, pre-formulated meaning of the author's thoughts. Derrida argues therefore for the primacy of the word.

This might intuitively seem incoherent. But in fact a close parallel can be found to what Derrida is describing in the process of drawing. It is not until I begin to draw that I know what the picture is really going to be like. The first pencil line suggests the next, and so on – the picture and the intention form *by* drawing, not *before* drawing. In fact the process of drawing is, for the artist, not the process of recording, but of discovering. The artist discovers meanings and interpretations that he or she never intended. The line has primacy. Thus, going back to words, if you want to know what a text means, you are really wasting your time trying to unearth authorial intent. Instead, the words create their own meanings in the mind of you the reader. In fact, you can take the author right out of the process of constructing the meaning of a text or previous readings of a text. A text must be allowed to have endless fresh meanings as it is changed and played with. In this context it should be said that Derrida's aim was not to destroy texts, but to revitalize 'dead' texts – texts that have been given particular meanings, fixed to their author's intentions, and that have thus ceased to be living texts. In Derrida's view, therefore, there is no determinative reading of a text: meaning is deferred as meanings are passed on from reader to reader.

This is Derrida's deconstructionism, or better, post-structuralism. Peel away the sediments of authorial intent, or even of authorial existence. Dismantle the appeal to the world in which a text was written to or the etymology of the words. Break away from the customary and previously 'right' readings of a text. The text means what you, with your own particular 'sediments', want it to mean. (This incidentally prevents an author from claiming that he or she has been misunderstood. It is ironic that Derrida was an author: at least he could not accuse us of *mis*construing him!)

Meaning – like postmodern culture generally – is therefore endlessly fresh and contemporary. As Don Carson writes in *The Gagging of God*, 'In academic biblical studies, postmodernism links with the "new" literary criticism to create endless "fresh" readings, many of them clever, and parts of them insightful, even if, taken as a whole, their insight is more and more removed from reasoned and defensible anchorage in the text.'[11] Thus words on a page

---

11. D. A. Carson, *The Gagging of God* (Leicester: Apollos, 1996), p. 29.

cease to function as a text that communicates meaning from author to reader: they become only what each reader makes of them. Is there a text in this Church, or General Assembly, or Divinity seminar? According to this form of reader-response hermeneutics, the answer is 'No'. Meaning therefore becomes not only endlessly contemporary, but endlessly individualistic.

Even the 'interpretive communities' of Stanley Fish barely break free from the post-structuralist world. Fish sought to account for the fact that in reality there are not as many interpretations of a text as there are interpreters. We do not have just one reading, but neither do we have *any* number of readings. There are shared readings. Thus a text will draw certain communal readings – the communities are not created independently of the text before coming to examine it; instead the text creates its own groupings. Thus you can have a post-feminist, gay, conservative evangelical, Marxist or American reading of Paul's letter to the Romans (though probably not one that would encompass all five of the above!) as the text draws together those who share particular ways of looking at the world. But they might not read the sports pages of a newspaper or the *Financial Times* with the same communal responses. Two women who happen to be conservative evangelicals and read Romans in roughly the same way, might not support the same football team or share the same views about the role of the Bank of England in exchange rate mechanisms. Fish still maintains that meaning is produced by readers not authors. 'The reader's response is not *to* the meaning, it *is* the meaning.'[12]

All of this represents a massive mind-shift that has taken place, whether it happens in the world of academic hermeneutics or at a popular level. The question 'what does this passage mean?' becomes redundant, replaced by the question 'what does it do for me?'

---

12. Stanley Fish, *Is There a Text in This Class?* (Cambridge, MA: Harvard University Press, 1980), p. 3.

Science and postmodernity

Culturally, as highlighted at the beginning of this chapter, the younger segment, at least, of the scientific community in the West is deeply immersed in the assumptions of postmodernity. Intellectually, however, scientists operate with a different set of assumptions that work well in the laboratory. It is perhaps a tribute to the influence of postmodernity that the tension between the two world-views is rarely recognized or explored within the scientific community itself. It is to address this deficit that we now turn to the various ways in which scientists, theologians and philosophers perceive the challenges of postmodernity to scientific and Christian ways of thinking.

2. THE CHRISTIAN ROOTS OF SCIENTIFIC REASONING

Roger Trigg

Why trust science?

Modern science prides itself on its independence from any form of religious dogma. It considers that it is part of its very nature to investigate facts about the physical world without any preconceptions, let alone any religious commitment. The facts will speak for themselves, and will be the same for an atheist as for a theist. Science is the epitome of human rationality. It is dispassionate, detached and objective, untainted by particular viewpoints, unsullied by prejudice. Indeed, it has often been thought to provide the only hope for human progress, previously held back by battles, real and intellectual, between different religious communities.

This was essentially the picture encouraged by the later Enlightenment in the eighteenth century. It focused on human reason and its capabilities, and discouraged appeals to metaphysics, which appeared to be insoluble. It stressed the crucial role of human experience, and helped to spread the philosophical doctrine of empiricism, according to which reality is a construct of what human beings can experience. We start with our experience, rather than with the nature of the world we are investigating. Instead of talking about reality, we concentrate on reality as it can be known by us. In other words, the emphasis has swung from the character of what there is to the way in which it can be known. After all, it may be asked, how can we decide to talk about the world as it is, instead of our knowledge of it? Being absorbed with what we do not know, rather than with what we do, does not seem a very productive way of living. We are then being guided by ignorance, not knowledge, or as some would unkindly put it, by faith and not science. It is significant that in the English language, 'science' has acquired a much narrower meaning than the Latin *scientia*, or even the contemporary German *Wissenschaft*. It means empirical knowledge, arrived at by a distinctive method, rather than human knowledge as such. Many have for a long time stopped distinguishing the two.

However, the distinction between the way the world is, and whether, and how, we can know it, is a crucial one. Concentrating on what appears to be human knowledge may seem very sensible, but it raises the question as to how we can be sure it is well founded. Philosophical arguments about whether we can know anything may make those imbued with 'common sense' impatient, but it is vital that we question the basis of our knowledge. Reality and our knowledge of it are very far from being the same thing. As Socrates was fond of pointing out, to the annoyance of his contemporaries, many people think that they know when in fact they do not. When this point is applied to modern science, it means that it is foolhardy to take it at face value. Just because science appears to 'work' does not remove from us the obligation to consider why. What is the justification for our trust in science? This is not an idle question, since many in our society are openly questioning whether science should set the standard for everything – or indeed for anything. Whereas once the growth of science seemed to be synonymous with human progress, now it all too often seems a threat to some, while so-called postmodernists openly question its right to claim truth.

All this means that the questions of whether physical reality can be known, and whether human minds are able properly to grasp its nature, are important. Some philosophers have echoed John

Locke's belief in the seventeenth century that they should merely follow in the footsteps of master-builders such as Boyle and Newton. Locke famously regarded himself as a mere 'under-labourer in clearing ground a little and removing some of the rubbish that lies in the way to knowledge'.[1] Philosophy, it seems, is the servant, not the master, of science. It is easy to see why an empiricist philosopher should think this, because of an insistence on the priority of experience. Clearly, scientists are particularly in the business of gathering, ordering, and systematizing human experience. Scientific method is built on the idea of empirical investigation. Yet Locke himself realized that this raised questions about the nature of the world that is being investigated. Why should we assume that it is ordered and not chaotic, intelligible to the human mind and not an impenetrable mystery?

Locke made no secret of the fact that he was writing as a Christian philosopher, and on such issues as the 'coherence and continuity of the parts of matter' he says unambiguously that 'we cannot but ascribe them to the arbitrary will and good pleasure of the Wise Architect'.[2] God was free to create the world as he wished, so pure reason could not discover its necessary nature. We have to look and see, experiment and test, to discover how in fact it is. In other words, a belief in the contingent nature of the world was combined with a view of reality as intrinsically ordered, with an inherent rationality, endowed by the Creator. The answer to the further question as to how mere humans can hope to understand this through their experience comes from a conception of reason as itself having its source in God. Locke did not believe we were born with any innate ideas, but he did accept that reason came from the Creator. It was, in a phrase much loved in the seven-teenth century, the 'candle of the Lord'. This was used by Locke, but was in fact the slogan of the Cambridge Platonists, who stressed the role of reason, and its origin in God. It gives a theo-logical underpinning to the idea of reason in general, and to

1. John Locke, *An Essay Concerning Human Understanding*, ed. P. H. Nidditch (Oxford: Oxford University Press, 1975), p. 10.
2. Ibid., p. 500.

empirical science in particular. At the same time, it warns us that reason may only give us a flickering and partial light with which to see into the nature of things. The world is seen in the pale glow of a candle, and we do not attain the bright certainty given by a world illuminated by a powerful searchlight.

The 'Cambridge Platonists' were active in Cambridge at the time of the English Civil War, and influenced the outlook of such scientists as Newton and Boyle. They were to be found amongst the founders of the Royal Society. No doubt they looked to reason as a way of resolving the horrendous disputes and violence of the time they were living through. Most certainly they can lay claim to being amongst the founders of the European Enlightenment. The significant fact, however, is that this was not a secular view of reason, inclining people to the materialism of the French Enlightenment in the eighteenth century. Instead it suggested that science was only possible because of a belief in an orderliness in the physical world that could be relied on because a rational Creator had made it like that. Science was only able to read the Book of Nature because it had a heavenly Author, who was the ultimate source of the laws of nature.

Science without religion

The success of science made it all too easy to forget the theistic assumptions that made it possible. This was at a philosophical price, as the work of David Hume illustrates. He stressed the role of experience in building up a scientific view of the world, but gave up the theistic setting that gave it sense and purpose. As a result, even induction, the generalizing from one time or place to another on the basis of observed instances, can no longer be given a justification. It is just something that, as humans, we are accustomed to do. There is then no longer any way of giving an intellectual grounding to science.

Empiricists try to avoid this problem by stressing that order is discovered in the world. The uniformity of nature is the result of a picture built up by empirical science, rather than the very presupposition that makes science possible. Hume himself, however, had the honesty to see that this was too easy a solution. At any given point, whatever uniformity and order there appears to be, we have to face the problem as to why it should be typical of the whole. Why should future discoveries follow the same pattern? How can we be sure that the whole universe behaves in the same regular way? However much we have discovered, we will always be haunted by the problem that the future may not be like the past, the unseen may not conform to the seen, 'there' may not be like 'here'. Without a metaphysics that governs our expectations we must always be floundering.

Analogous difficulties have always accompanied those who wish to put their philosophical trust wholly in the empirical outcomes delivered by science. In the twentieth century, when logical positivism proclaimed that all problems, which could be meaningfully formulated, were soluble by science, it produced the 'verification principle'. According to this, statements gained their meaning through the empirical methods by which they could be verified. By definition we could not understand what was said, if we did not know how to go about testing it. This conveniently ruled out at a stroke all metaphysical and theological claims. The position had many flaws, but the most glaring one was the status of the verification principle itself. Where were verificationists standing in order to make such claims?

Like all such global views about science, people have to be making such assertions from beyond science. A scientist cannot claim that science can explain everything, as this is a statement about science. It cannot be made from within science. It is a global, metaphysical claim, not something that can be checked through experience. 'Everything' will always by definition outstrip the experience of all of us. A. J. Ayer, one of the central figures of twentieth-century positivism, suggested that the verification principle could be treated as an axiom, but axioms do not have to be adopted, and he was still left with having to explain why this particular axiom was a necessary one, especially when it ruled out much that humans find valuable. Moral and aesthetic statements were in as much difficulty as any piece of metaphysics.

Ayer himself confronted the issue of the 'uniformity of nature' as an underpinning for induction in his classic *Language, Truth and*

Logic, first published in 1936. He interpreted the principle not as a metaphysical one about the order inherent in the physical world, but as a statement about experience. He thought it amounted to the claim that 'past experience is a reliable guide to the future'. As this is a restatement of induction, he himself pointed out that it merely begs the question. Ayer's conclusion was that there is therefore no possible way of solving the problem of induction. In this he was following in the footsteps of Hume, although he went further than Hume in saying that it was not a genuine issue. He claimed that the problem of induction 'is a fictitious problem, since all genuine problems are at least theoretically capable of being solved'[3] Since the only genuine solutions were for Ayer empirical ones, this also begs a very large question. It is easy to dismiss philosophical views about the relation of reality to experience because they are not the result of experience. This however assumes that experience is our sole source of knowledge, which is the very point at issue. It is also all too easy to dismiss difficult problems as fictitious, merely because a proper answer to them requires recourse to assumptions which a blinkered empiricist cannot make.

Ayer went on to provide a reason for still trusting scientific method, without any philosophical basis for doing so. It is probably the most popular one that tends to be given, namely 'success in practice'. He said that 'we are entitled to have faith in our procedure just so long as it does the work it is designed to do – that is, enables us to predict future experience, and so control our environment'.[4] This is also the argument of the pragmatist, and many are content with it. Science 'works'. Ayer admitted that we cannot have any reason for trusting that this will continue, apart from experience. We have no right to rely on the physical world, beyond stumbling on in the unjustifiable hope that things will continue in the way that they have turned out so far. As a basis for human exploration into the nature of things, it seems sadly insubstantial. We *have been* successful, so we probably *will* be. Why, though, should

---

3. A. J. Ayer, *Language, Truth and Logic* (2nd ed.; London: Gollancz, 1946), p. 50.
4. Ibid.

this be? What is the character of the physical world that allows us to acquire reliable knowledge in this way? Why is the world ordered? Ayer's response was to say that, because we cannot give a ready answer, or an answer he would welcome, we must forget the question, and even pretend we cannot understand it. It is perhaps not surprising that in the ensuing generations positivism has been challenged, and the underlying issue keeps reappearing.

Empiricists, such as Ayer, have always preferred to start with the fact of human experience. Their philosophy is explicitly anthropocentric, and can never make assumptions about the character of reality. That is always viewed as something constructed by humans through their experience. As a result, general claims going beyond human experience are impossible. A theist, however, is in a position to make wide-ranging assumptions about the nature of the physical world before it is investigated empirically. If God created the world, it can be assumed that his rationality is reflected in that world. Indeed this justifies our expectation that it makes sense to make scientific observations and experiments. We can discover regularities and can generalize from them. This is not a matter of blind faith but follows from the very nature of God. Theism can underpin and justify inductions about the nature of the physical world. We can rely on its regularity, order and consistency in ways that can justify generalizing going from here to there and now to then. The nature of the physical is not going to change arbitrarily in major ways, since God is to be trusted.

Theism and the world

Despite the chill winds of logical positivism, and the prevailing atheism of much of twentieth-century philosophy, voices could still be heard at intervals through the century, pointing to a need for a more substantial basis for science. For example, in 1934 M. B. Foster wrote a seminal article relating Christianity to the rise of modern natural science. He claimed, 'The method of natural science depends upon the presuppositions which are held about nature, and the presuppositions about nature in turn upon the doctrine of God.'[5] Empirical observations can only be made and correlated on the assumption that they typically sample what physical reality is like. We can only keep to a belief in the stability and orderliness of nature by supposing that its order is not a chance, local occurrence. The world has been made like that.

Some twenty years later, a leading physicist wrote:

> That common search for a common truth, that unexamined belief that facts are correlatable, i.e. stand in relation to one another and cohere in a scheme: that unprovable assumption that there is an order and constancy in Nature . . . all of it is a legacy from religious conviction.[6]

Science was, in other words, able to progress, because it had absorbed in its infancy in the modern era theistic assumptions about the nature of the world. A world created by God could be taken to be reliable, rationally structured, and put together in a coherent way. All this is so taken for granted by contemporary science that it all seems obvious that this is the way things are. Perhaps, as the anthropic principle in physics has indicated, we could not have existed in any other type of world. Yet that does not explain why we do exist. Put like that, it is plain that questions about the foundations of science are very likely to be traversing the same ground as religious issues.

These issues have not gone away in the second half of the twentieth century. Yet science has not gone unchallenged itself. One of the most striking movements has been a reaction against so-called 'modern' views of rationality, as expressed in science. The result has been that science has been called upon to justify itself. The very fact of science's origins in a theistic view of the world has been used as an argument against its conception of the world and of reasoning about the world. Richard Rorty was one of the first to attack the idea that the physical world somehow had a

---

5. M. B. Foster, 'The Christian Doctrine of Creation and the Rise of Modern Natural Science', *Mind* 43 (1934), pp. 446–468 (463).

6. C. A. Coulson, *Science and Christian Belief* (London: Oxford University Press, 1955), p. 55.

fixed nature, waiting to be understood by means of human ration-ality. He wrote:

> The very idea that the world or self has an intrinsic nature . . . is a remnant of the idea that the world is a divine creation, the work of someone who had something in mind . . . To drop the idea of languages as representation, and to be thoroughly Wittgensteinian in our approach to language, would be to de-divinize the world.[7]

This is postmodernism, a view that challenges the so-called 'Enlightenment' view of reason. Indeed, Rorty is quite right to see that the roots of that view lay in a belief that the world was a product of a divine mind. It had been made in a particular way, and we, made in the image of the Creator, had the ability to see that. There is a structured reality, which has its own nature, regard-less of how it is conceived by anyone. Nevertheless human reason had the God-given ability to inquire into its nature. Scepticism about the possibility of human knowledge could therefore be ruled out. Many in the modern era, like Ayer, and other empiricists and pragmatists, have chosen to ignore these roots of science. If they have been acknowledged, it has been only to dismiss them as intellectually irrelevant. They may have provided the occasion for the rise of science, just as the political aftermath of the English Civil War no doubt had something to do with the establishment of the Royal Society under Charles II. That may make an interesting historical footnote, but it can have nothing, it will be claimed, to do with the inner character of science.

Postmodernists have seen the matter differently. They them-selves have not been writing from a religious standpoint. Indeed, as the usual conclusion of what they say has been that there can be no 'grand narrative', no claim to global truth, they are removing the very basis of theism. The trouble, though, is that any rational basis for science itself has been thoroughly challenged. It becomes just one amongst many perspectives, and there can in principle be

---

7. Richard Rorty, *Contingency, Irony and Solidarity* (Cambridge: Cambridge University Press, 1989), p. 21.

no reason for adopting it. 'Reason' itself becomes something rooted in time and place. In fact it becomes a creature of the Enlightenment, historically situated, and limited to one particular historical context. Science itself can all too easily be defined merely as 'Western science', one amongst many possible ways of looking at the world.

Postmodernism glories in diversity, and extols pluralism. It typically moves attention away from the nature of reality. As we have seen from Rorty, the idea that there is such a thing is to be dismissed. We are no longer to be thought in the business of forming beliefs about entities that have their fixed characteristics, and exist independently of the way we think about them. Such 'realism' is exposed as having its roots in theology. Indeed, this is a theme that itself has surfaced regularly since the time of Nietzsche, so that the very idea of objective truth is dismissed as being theological in origin. This is far too extreme a reaction, as without such a notion there can be no distinction between a thing's being the case and its not being the case. Even the difference between atheism and theism cannot be expressed without an appeal to the difference between there being a God and there not being one. Although there is plenty of room for dispute over what precisely is at issue in that debate, it may seem a little quick to maintain that the very possibility of the objective truth of atheism shows there must be a God as the ground of the distinction between truth and falsity.

There are those, like Rorty, however, who associate so strongly the idea of an objective, structured, world with a theological origin, that they are quite ready to dispense with any distinction between truth and falsity, or fact and fiction. Everything becomes a matter of 'story' or 'narrative', historically situated and contextually bound. The alleged universality of reason is derided, as itself a belief that arose in the context of the European Enlightenment. Difference and variety is extolled at the expense of any 'totalizing' (even totalitarian) view of a truth that is the same for everyone everywhere. In fact, what happens is that our attention is deliberately moved from the object of our inquiry or the content of our beliefs. Rorty complains that language should not be thought of as representational. It is not 'about' anything, let alone holding up a mirror to an independently existing world. His reference to the later Wittgenstein shows his eagerness to look at how language is used in different contexts, not the way it labels 'things'. Yet the result of that is to focus on the fact of different human practices, or to stress the fact that people have certain beliefs, which go to make up a way of life. Religion is then viewed as a social practice to be judged in its own terms, in a way that can insulate it from any criticism or onslaught from bodies of belief beyond it. Similarly, science can no longer be thought of as a body of knowledge about the world, built up carefully and cumulatively through the generations. Instead, it is what scientists do. It is hardly surprising that, in the eyes of some sociologists of science, the activities of scientists are a similar object of study to the practices of remote tribes. Indeed, since there are very few tribes so remote that they are untouched by contemporary life (or out of reach of satellite television), sociologists and anthropologists may well find scientists a more rewarding focus for their theories.

Postmodernism and relativism

Sometimes theorists about religion are themselves seduced by postmodernism. They use a postmodern critique of modernity to attack any idea of objective truth, or universal rationality. They see such views as products of the Enlightenment, all too often serving to legitimize science at the expense of religion. It seems reassuring to deny science any chance of dismissing religion by claiming a monopoly of truth for itself. If nothing can be objectively true, then science can be in no better position than any religion. To quote one religious studies writer, postmodernism has not only dislodged the autonomous subject, but 'it has also undermined the false claims of a disinterested objectivity'.[8] In other words, we cannot claim a rationality that can lay claims that should apply to everyone. We cannot claim objective truth, it seems, although it is

---

8. Ursula King, 'Is There a Future for Religious Studies as We know It? Some Post-modern, Feminist and Spiritual Challenges', *Journal of the American Academy of Religion* 70 (2002), p. 371.

interesting that in the same sentence the writer is able to assert that such claims are (objectively) false.

We cannot, it is alleged, subtract ourselves sufficiently from our social context to talk about what is true, as opposed to what we are conditioned to think as a result of our gender, or our social situation. Such claims to truth merely reflect, in particular, the patriarchical structures in society, under which the interests of males are pursued. The same writer continues that 'today such an outlook has given way to a constructionist outlook whereby the certainty of knowledge is replaced by an ongoing process of interpretation'.[9] As a result there are no final and definitive positions. Instead, she says, 'all are open to revision, to further development and dynamic change'.[10] In one sense, this could be perfectly acceptable. Those who saw reason as a small candle, and not a great burst of light, realized only too well that what passes for human knowledge is provisional and tentative. Science itself forgets this at its peril, as genuine progress often involves the reappraisal of apparently well-established theories. In religion, a comparison of the finite nature of human minds with the infinite nature of God must always give us a genuine humility.

A stress on the partial and tentative nature of all human knowledge is one thing. Removing the whole possibility of any knowledge is quite another. Once we arrive at this point, we are immersed in the muddy waters of relativism. Religion and science appear merely to be constituted by typical practices. Neither is characterized by beliefs about an independently existing world. They are not the kind of thing that could be true or false, nor do they need any form of justification or grounding. It follows that there can be no pretence that they grow out of common roots, or that they have anything in common. There is nothing against which they can both be calibrated. The 'world' as seen from the perspective of one need have nothing in common with that of the other. In fact, it is no exaggeration to say that, according to this view, religious people and scientists live in different worlds. It

---

9. Ibid.
10. Ibid.

ought to be embarrassing to views like this that the same person can be a scientist and a religious believer, but it would be held that such people just switch practices and perspectives. There is no contradiction in a cricketer also playing golf. Wittgenstein's own example of seeing a 'duck-rabbit' drawn first as a duck and then as a rabbit offers another parallel.[11] We can perceive different aspects of the same picture. It can be seen in different ways, but there is no answer to the question as to what it really is.

In this case, of course, the ambiguous drawing can provide a common point of reference. The true relativist will see everything as internal to the practice or body of belief in question. Nothing can be agreed as forming a common starting point. There is no 'world', waiting to be interpreted. An interpretation, and the 'object' of interpretation, cannot be prised apart. The postmodernist will not allow any idea of an uninterpreted world. It follows that all references to reality are to be seen as the construction, or projection, of those set in particular social contexts at a particular time. Truth can then never be objective, or have a universal claim. It is associated with what sets of people happen to believe at a particular time. Since, by definition, there is nothing beyond the beliefs against which they can be judged, the mere fact that they are held becomes a sufficient guarantee of their truth. Agreement and convention constitute truth.

It is, however, from a traditional viewpoint, an odd kind of truth, since the beliefs can only be 'true for' those who hold them. In other words, talking of the truth of a belief is just another way of saying that it is held. There can be no question of giving reasons why it should be held or of justifying it to others. The norm for belief is the collective agreement of the social group to which one belongs. The only reason for doing science is that scientists agree about the character and methods of their practices. The analogy with games holds. Cricket is ultimately defined by the collective agreement of those playing the game as to what the rules should be. There is no cosmic justification of the game. Even the

---

11. L. Wittgenstein, *Philosophical Investigations*, tr. G. E. M. Anscombe (Oxford: Basil Blackwell, 1963), II.xi, p. 194.

most ardent cricket lover would hesitate to suggest that the character of the game reflects some ultimate facet of reality, or that playing the game can be justified because the particular beliefs underlying it are true.

The great problem is that once a 'constructionist' view has been adopted, and 'dynamic change' becomes the norm, the question arises why anyone should change their views or reinterpret their position. If all is interpretation, any interpretation is as good (or bad) as any other. There is nothing against which it can be judged, nor indeed any reason for making a judgment. Everyone is immersed in the prejudices and presuppositions of a particular society. Nothing can be true, and nothing false. The exploitation of women by men may be a feature of a particular society, or even of all societies, but there would seem nowhere for anyone to stand to make a rational protest, or even to describe the situation dispassionately. Even the academic study of social differences has to be ruled out, because it presupposes that academics can detach themselves from their own surroundings sufficiently to make dispassionate and unprejudiced judgments about the way a society works. The sociology of science becomes a contradictory exercise. Either science is a rational pursuit of knowledge of the truth or it is not. If it cannot be, the sociologist cannot pretend that he is capable of what the physical scientist is not, namely of investigating an independently existing reality. If physicists are caught up with the prejudices of their society, and cannot talk of reality as it is, so must be the sociologist. The latter cannot talk disinterestedly about a social reality without conceding that the former can do so about a physical reality.

Postmodernism cannot escape the charge of relativism, and, since the time of Plato, relativists have been accused of incoherence. All arguments and assertions have to presuppose the idea of truth, since otherwise they would be unable to distinguish between what is and is not the case. This is bound to apply equally to 'second order' statements about the status of other statements and beliefs. Saying that truth is not an objective matter, but is relative to the believer, is bound itself to be a claim to truth. Unless it is a claim to objective truth, which demands universal acceptance, it can make no impact, but would be a mere autobiographical, or ethnocentric, remark. The remark quoted earlier about 'the false claims of a disinterested objectivity' is typical. In espousing relativism, it simultaneously denies it. The remark only has cogency if is being maintained that such claims are objectively false (for everyone). It only deserves respect if it is intended itself as a 'disinterested' remark, as opposed to the dogmatic claim of invincible prejudice. All relativists find themselves eventually in the embarrassing situation of saying implicitly, or explicitly, that it is objectively true that there is no such thing as objective truth.

A grounding for science

In addition to the issue of its internal incoherence, relativism in its contemporary forms removes all possibility of providing an intellectual basis for science. This is largely because it prohibits any reference to any reality existing independently of the way 'it' is judged or interpreted. Any idea of an objective world, with its own characteristics, has to be discarded, and all we are left with is an ongoing flux of opinions and beliefs. Yet because they no longer have any clear focus outside themselves, there is no way of providing them with any justification. None can be said to be better than any others. Any scientific belief is as good as any other, and any practice can be as good as 'Western' science. There seems little point in doing science, and no way of defending it against its detractors. It might be said to be just there, as a 'social fact', except that no postmodernist can consistently talk of social facts apart from particular interpretations. In such an intellectual climate, science can no doubt survive for a time, as an ongoing practice. Since, however, it is denied the rational resources to defend itself, or to justify itself, it may find its position increasingly insecure. It will be at the mercy of the fickle winds of arbitrary fashion.

Another facet of relativism, and of all similar views which stress the separate identity of different practices, and forms of life, is that the comparison of different views becomes impossible. They each set their own internal standards, but have by definition no external point of reference. This becomes of particular importance when the relationship of science and religion is raised. Each sets its own criteria, and just, it seems, as science cannot be judged according to the demands of religious faith, so the latter need not conform to the standards of the physical sciences. It has always been a problem of what counts as a practice. Should we think of physics, or science in general? Should we talk vaguely of religion, or specifically of Christianity? Indeed, the issue of the relationship of the sciences with each other becomes problematic if they cannot be understood as being about the same reality, and thus have to tell a consistent story about it. The relationship of the different religions is equally a crucial question, and relativism becomes particularly attractive to those who refuse to accept that one might have greater validity than another.

Beyond these issues, however, is the temptation to keep religion and science separate so that each has to be understood by its own criteria, and cannot impinge on the other. This can be an explicitly relativist programme, but it need not be. Indeed, more than a generation ago C. A. Coulson imported from quantum physics the idea of 'complementarity' to describe what he saw as their relationship. He referred to how Niels Bohr applied his notion more widely than in its original context in physics, in dealing with quantum phenomena as both waves and particles. He further claimed that many intellectual struggles should be seen as examples of this kind of duality. Bohr's use of the idea of complementarity involves the use of contrasting pictures that are incompatible with each other, but each seems to say something true. It is just that they cannot be combined. As Coulson says of this kind of case, 'both are right, but they have no contact with each other'.[12] It is easy to see how this analysis could apply to debates between science and religion. Each deals with different kinds of issues, and thus is never in a position to contradict the other. To put it simply, one might say that science tells us 'how', and religion 'why', physical events occur.

This is a constant temptation. Followers of Wittgenstein are likely to talk of religion and science as different forms of life and, very recently, the late Stephen Jay Gould argued powerfully that

12. Coulson, *Science and Christian Belief*, p. 72.

science and religion form what he called 'non-overlapping magis-teria'. He insisted that 'they remain logically distinct and fully separate in styles of inquiry'.[13] Enlarging on this, he said, 'The net, or magisterium, of science covers the empirical realm: what is the universe made of (fact), and why does it work in this way (theory). The magisterium of religion extends over questions of ultimate meaning and moral value. These magisteria do not overlap.'[14] Such an account can be attractive to those who want to appear tolerant of religion, without allowing it actually to affect anything. It suits the traditional American separation of church and state, so that religion can be left to the private sphere, and science can dominate the public arena. It can fit in with an old-fashioned positivist agenda regarding facts as the province of science. 'Subjective' values can then be left to the province of religion.

The trouble with this stance is that it either becomes relativist (and even subjectivist), or it gives pride of place to science. 'Real' explanations are then to be regarded as scientific, and religion is left with people's personal attitudes. Science is about truth, and religion can be left with issues about 'meaning'. The latter may seem important, but all too often what is being claimed is that science has a monopoly of insights into the nature of reality, leaving religion with individual decisions about how to view life. Science then has no need to imagine any conflict with religion, since it has by definition claimed the high ground, and is able to have the last word on the nature of the world. Religion has to be content with whatever is left (and that is not in fact very much). Thus an apparent relativism, stressing the different kinds of cri-teria appropriate in different domains, can become inverted into what looks like an old-fashioned materialism, stressing the role of scientific method in defining the nature of reality. Unless we are satisfied with the incipient epistemological anarchy encouraged by postmodernism, the temptation will always be to stress the differences between scientific and religious ways of thinking in a manner that ultimately downgrades religion.

---

13. S. J. Gould, *Rocks of Ages* (New York: Ballantine, 1999), p. 58.
14. Ibid., p. 6.

Relativism and contemporary forms of materialism appear to offer the main choices for those who want to make sense of the relations between science and religion.[15] Faced with those who simply take it for granted that science can explain everything, it is perhaps not surprising that some would-be defenders of religion retreat to postmodernism. The latter may stop science claiming truth at the expense of religion, but only by destroying any idea of objective truth. Without the right to claim truth, any religion has itself been eviscerated. Yet there is a serious problem for science as well. Obviously any science that is stopped from making claims about reality cannot justify itself, and relapses into being one social practice amongst many.

What is, however, often not appreciated is that the strong 'materialist' view of science as the sole source of knowledge has to face the same criticism. How can science be a justifiable practice? This is a philosophical question demanding a philosophical, and even metaphysical, answer, which can transcend science, and put it into a wider context. Being given a scientific answer to questions about the very legitimacy of science merely begs the question at issue. Why can human science, the vehicle of human reason, uncover the secrets of the universe? Appealing to evolution as the source of our mental capacities, by saying that we could not have survived and flourished without them, calls into play a scientific theory. Yet the status of all scientific theories (of which the theory of evolution through natural selection is one) is being challenged. What is at stake is the capability of human rationality to recognize and understand the workings of the physical world. Our ability to conceive of evolution is as much in question as anything else.

We are thus brought full circle to the assumptions made by many of the founders of modern science in the seventeenth century. They were not relativists, nor materialists, and they believed that their attempts to explain the workings of the material world rested on an ability to understand the regularities and orderliness given the world by a Creator, who had also given them the

---

15. See my *Philosophy Matters* (Oxford: Blackwell, 2002) for a further discussion of contemporary forms of materialism and relativism.

pale, but adequate, light of reason. For them, rationality was not a human construction, but a God-given gift. As such, it was not surprising that it provided the means of finding intelligible the created world. The subsequent success of science enabled many to forget the intellectual sources from which it had come. By so doing, however, all science has left itself vulnerable to challenge. Unless one blindly accepted it and made it the only source of truth by definition (as the positivists did), there has seemed no way of giving it any legitimation.

The empirical success of science led many to despise metaphysics in general, and theology in particular. Yet that left no grounding for science, and no way of defending it. The doctrines of Christianity have provided fertile soil for the growth of science. Many postmodernists, following thinkers such as Nietzsche, have concluded that without Christianity, notions of objective truth must be discarded. Perhaps an alternative argument might be that the idea of truth is but one of several crucial notions for the successful pursuit of empirical science, which all derive from Christian doctrine. Perhaps rather than being in retreat from the onward march of science, Christian doctrine itself is indispensable to it. Certainly, without the idea of an ordered creation, and a God-given rationality, it is difficult to see how science can be provided with the metaphysical grounding it so clearly needs.[16]

---

16. This chapter was first published as 'A Christian Basis for Science', *Science and Christian Belief* 15 (2003), pp. 3–15.

3. A BIBLICAL BASIS FOR THE SCIENTIFIC ENTERPRISE

Ernest Lucas

In the twentieth century some historians of science grappled with the question 'Why did modern science arise in late medieval Europe and not in some other culture at some other time?' After all, some major advances in particular areas of science or technology, or both, were made in several different cultures at different times. The answer arrived at was that *in part* this was due to the Christian world view which prevailed in Europe at that time. This world view had its roots in the Bible.

The 'conflict thesis'

This answer was somewhat surprising in view of the 'conflict thesis' that had arisen in the last few decades of the nineteenth century. In Britain this was promoted by Thomas Huxley and a group of associates.[1] It was popularized by two influential books,

---

1. C. A. Russell, 'The Conflict Metaphor and its Social Origins', *Science and*

History of the Conflict between Religion and Science[2] and *A History of the Warfare of Science with Theology in Christendom*.[3] The 'thesis' was that the history of the relationship between science and religion had essentially been one of conflict ever since the early Christian centuries. Of course the proponents of the 'conflict thesis' had to account for the fact that modern science had arisen within Christendom. One way of doing this was to argue that science arose when the Greek learning rediscovered at the time of the Renaissance broke the grip that theology had on people's thinking. This explanation sounds odd to anyone who had read much in the writings of the early modern scientists, because some of them inveigh with considerable animosity against 'the philosopher' and his followers. The person who is in their sights is the Greek philosopher Aristotle. His teachings, at least as promulgated in the centres of learning of the time, were seen as a stumbling block to the advance of science by these pioneers of modern science. Robert Boyle complained that 'In about two thousand years since Aristotle's time the adorers of his physics, at least by virtue of his peculiar principles, seem to have done little more than wrangle.'[4]

The demise of the 'conflict thesis'

As early as 1883 Ernst Mach sounded a note of caution about the emphasis on 'the conflict between science and theology'. He saw it as very misleading because, in his view, many of the conceptions 'which completely dominate modern physics' actually 'arose under the influence of theological ideas'.[5] At the time his was a voice

Christian Belief 1 (1988), pp. 3–26.

2. J. W. Draper, London, 1875.
3. A. D. White, New York, 1896.
4. R. Boyle, *Considerations and Experiments Touching the Origin of Qualities and Forms*, in *Collected Works*, vol. 3 (1772), p. 75.
5. E. Mach, *Science of Mechanics*, tr. T. J. McCormack (LaSalle, IL: Open Court, 1942), pp. 542, 551–552.

crying in the wilderness. It was not until 1926 that a more influential voice was heard. The philosopher A. N. Whitehead in his book *Science and the Modern World*[6] argued for the importance of Christian beliefs in the development of Newtonian science. In the mid-1930s the same case was argued in some detail in two lucid articles by Michael Foster,[7] though it was a decade or more before they began to get the attention they deserved. Meanwhile E. Zilsel published an important paper, in which he showed that the concept of physical law 'was virtually unknown to antiquity and the middle ages and that it did not arise before the middle of the seventeenth century'.[8] He showed that when it did arise in the time of Descartes, Hooke, Boyle and Newton a major root of the concept was the Old Testament teaching about God as the Creator who gave moral laws to his people and who also established laws in the physical realm. When faced with the question why this root did not give flower, so to speak, until the seventeenth century, Zilsel suggested that a significant factor was a sociopolitical one, the rise of 'a state with rational statute law and fully developed central sovereignty'.[9] F. Oakley showed the weakness of this second part of Zilsel's thesis.[10] He argued that what allowed the biblical root to begin to flourish was the breaking of the stranglehold of Aristotelian philosophy on Christian theology following the condemnation of a list of philosophical propositions as contrary to the Christian faith in 1277. The condemnation was issued formally by Etienne Tempier, Bishop of Paris, and Robert Kilwardby, Archbishop of Canterbury. This marked the beginning

---

6. Cambridge: Cambridge University Press, 1930.

7. M. Foster, 'The Christian Doctrine of Creation and the Rise of Modern Natural Science', *Mind* 43 (1934), pp. 446–468; 'Christian Theology and the Modern Science of Nature', *Mind* 45 (1936), pp. 1–28.

8. E. Zilsel, 'The Genesis of the Concept of Physical Law', *Philosophical Review* 51 (1942), p. 245.

9. Ibid., p. 279.

10. F. Oakley, 'Christian Theology and the Newtonian Science: The Rise of the Concept of the Laws of Nature', *Church History* 30 (1961), pp. 433–457.

of a theological reaction that emphasized the freedom and omnip-
otence of the transcendent Creator God of the Judaeo-Christian
Scriptures. Oakley charts how this led first of all to the rise of the
concept of natural law, in the moral sense, as something imposed
on the creation from outside by God. Then, prompted by certain
biblical texts, it led in turn to the concept of natural physical laws.
What is more, this concept arose within the context of belief in
God's freedom to impose whatever state of order he chose.
Therefore it was necessary to study the created world in order to
discover what laws had actually been imposed on it. In 1945 R. G.
Collingwood stressed the importance of Christian beliefs for the
development of modern science.[11] In a separate essay he wrote,
'The presuppositions that go to make up this "Catholic faith", pre-
served for many centuries by the religious institutions of
Christendom, have as a matter of historical fact been the main or
fundamental presuppositions of natural science ever since.'[12]

Following further studies C. A. Russell was able to stand the
position advocated by proponents of the 'conflict thesis' on its
head and argue that the evidence showed that 'science arose in the
West, not when Christian theology was submerged by Greek
rationalism, but rather when Greek and other "pagan" ideas of
nature were shown to be inadequate in the new climate of biblical
awareness brought about at the Reformation'.[13] In the 1930s historians began to take note of the fact that Protestants, and Puritans in
particular, were represented in the ranks of seventeenth-century
scientists out of all proportion to their numbers in society at large.[14]

---

11. R. G. Collingwood, *Idea of Nature* (Oxford: Oxford University Press,
    1945).

12. R. G. Collingwood, *An Essay on Metaphysics* (Oxford: Oxford University
    Press, 1947), p. 127.

13. C. A. Russell, *Cross-Currents: Interactions between Science and Faith* (Leicester:
    IVP, 1985), p. 55.

14. D. Stimson, 'Puritanism and the New Philosophy in 17th century
    England', *Bulletin of the Institute of the History of Medicine* 3 (1935), pp.
    321–324; R. K. Merton, 'Puritanism, Pietism, and Science', *Sociological
    Review* 28 (1936), pp. 1–30.

A number of hypotheses have been put forward to explain this. Most recently P. Harrison has argued that the explanation is to be found in the Protestant Reformers' approach to interpreting the Bible.[15] They rejected the allegorizing of texts (a method borrowed from pre-Christian Greek scholars) that had been common in medieval times and insisted on the primacy of the 'natural sense' of texts, the grammatical meaning of the text in its historical context. The medieval allegorizing of texts encouraged the allegorizing of nature. Animals and plants were looked at primarily as symbols of moral and spiritual truth. Harrison argues that the Protestant stress on the 'literal' meaning of texts led to a new, non-symbolic, approach to nature. 'As an inevitable consequence of this way of reading texts nature would lose its meaning, and the vacuum created by this loss of intelligibility was gradually to be occupied by alternative accounts of the significance of natural things – those explanations which we regard as scientific.'[16]

The presuppositions of modern science

The 'presuppositions' to which Collingwood referred are wider than the concept of natural law. R. Trigg sums them up when he says of the founders of modern science in the seventeenth century, 'they believed that their attempts to explain the workings of the material world rested on an ability to understand the regularities and orderliness given the world by a Creator, who had also given them the pale, but adequate, light of reason'.[17]

The position that has been reached, then, is the recognition by historians of science that a set of Christian beliefs played a significant part in the rise of modern science. In summary, these can be set out as follows.

---

15. P. Harrison, *The Bible, Protestantism, and the Rise of Natural Science* (Cambridge: Cambridge University Press, 1998).

16. Ibid., p. 114.

17. R. Trigg, 'A Christian Basis for Science', *Science and Christian Belief* 15 (2003), p. 15; and chapter 2, p. 47, in this volume.

1. A theistic view of the God–world relationship, in which God is self-existent and the sole source of all that exists outside himself. The world is therefore dependent on God for its existence.
2. The belief that the creation is an ordered cosmos, with God as the originator and faithful sustainer of that order.
3. The belief that humans are created in the image and likeness of God, and so able, at least in some measure, to recognize and understand the order inherent in the world.
4. As the sovereign Creator, God was free to create whatever kind of world he willed; therefore it is necessary to investigate it to find out what kind of world it actually is.
5. The command to exercise dominion and rule over the world given to humankind by God (Genesis 1:26–30) lays on humans the responsibility to understand the world and its creatures in order to be able to fulfil this command properly. Moreover, since it is now a fallen world, humans must play their part in seeking to ameliorate or overcome the effects of the fall.

The following quotations from the writings of some early modern scientists provide a flavour of how these beliefs influenced their thinking.

> I began to be annoyed that the philosophers . . . had discovered no sure scheme for the movements of the machinery of the world, which has been built for us by the best and most orderly workman of all.[18]

> We copy the sin of our first parents . . . They wished to be like God, but their posterity wish to be even greater. For we create worlds, we direct and domineer over nature, we will have it that all things are as in our folly we think they should be, not as seems fittest to the divine wisdom, or as they are found to be in fact . . . we clearly impress the stamp of our own image on the creatures and works of God, instead of carefully examining and recognising in them the stamp of the Creator himself.[19]

---

18. N. Copernicus, *De revolutionibus orbium coelestium*, 1543, author's preface.
19. F. Bacon, *The Advancement of Learning*, 1605, bk 1.

Geometry existed before the creation, is co-eternal with God, is God himself (what exists in God that is not God himself?). Geometry provided God with a model for the creation and was implanted into man, together with God's own likeness – and not merely converged to his mind through the eyes.[20]

Man by the Fall fell at the same time from his state of innocence and from his dominion over nature. Both of these losses, however, can even in this life be in some part repaired; the former by religion and faith, the latter by the arts and sciences.[21]

Thus the universe being once framed by God and the laws of motion settled and all upheld by his perpetual concourse and general providence, the same philosophy teaches, that the phenomena of the world are physically produced by the mechanical properties of the parts of matter, and that they operate upon one another according to mechanical laws.[22]

Most of the early modern scientists were not biblical scholars, and in their day the Bible was read in what is now described as a 'pre-critical' way, without the use of the analytical approaches that have been developed over the last two centuries or so. It is therefore worth re-examining the biblical basis of the presuppositions listed above to see what difference, if any, a 'critical' approach makes.

The God–world relationship

The doctrine of *creatio ex nihilo* was developed by early Christian theologians as a way of distinguishing theism from two other world views that were current in the early Christian era: pantheism and dualism. The Stoic philosophy that was fairly popular in the Graeco-Roman world was pantheistic in its world view. Pantheism

---

20. J. Kepler, *Harmonice mundi*, 1618, bk 4, ch. 1.
21. F. Bacon, *Novum organum scientiorum*, 1620, bk 2, aphorism 52.
22. R. Boyle, *The Excellency and Grounds of the Mechanical Hypothesis*, 1674, introduction.

identifies God with the world. God might be seen as the 'soul' of the world and/or as the 'rational principle' that gives the world its structure. In this view God is immanent in the world but not transcendent over it. God and the world are dependent on each other, and neither can exist without the other. This was seen as incompatible with the biblical picture of the God–world relationship, and the doctrine of *creatio ex nihilo* ruled it out by asserting that God brought the world into being and that, while God can exist without the world, without God's creating and sustaining of it, the world would not exist.

Dualism is the world view that there are two eternally existing entities that are opposed to each other. An extreme form of it is Zoroastrianism, with its belief in a good god and an evil god, eternally at war with each other. For aeons at a time one or the other is dominant. At the end of each cycle the world is destroyed in a great conflagration and another comes into existence. A modified form of dualism was part of the Neoplatonism that was popular in the early Christian centuries. It taught a dualism of spirit–mind and matter–body. The true God was pure spirit and the realm of the spirit was seen as the realm of changeless perfection. Matter, like God, is eternal but the realm of matter is the realm of change and imperfection. God can have no direct contact with matter, so the creator god was viewed as an inferior being who shaped matter into the imperfect world in which we live. This view, too, was seen as incompatible with the biblical picture of the God–world relationship, and the doctrine of *creation ex nihilo* ruled it out by asserting that matter is not an eternally self-existent entity, but owes its existence to God.

It is important to recognize that the doctrine of *creatio ex nihilo* was always primarily a statement about the ontological relationship between God and the world. It asserts that the world exists only because God gave it existence, and maintains it in existence. It does not specify *how* or *when* God created the world. It is as compatible with the 'continuous creation' cosmology put forward by Sir Fred Hoyle and others in the 1950s as with the 'big bang' cosmology that superseded it. There is nothing in the theological doctrine that requires that the world God created should, from the view of those within it, have a dateable origin. For this reason, Stephen Hawking's comment that because his version of the 'big bang' cosmology removes any dateable 'beginning' it leaves no room for a Creator God is a misunderstanding of the doctrine of *creatio ex nihilo*.[23]

There are three biblical verses that have traditionally been appealed to as support for the doctrine of *creatio ex nihilo*. Until recently Genesis 1:1–2a has been translated as 'In the beginning God created the heavens and the earth. The earth was without form and void.' This has been taken to imply an *ex nihilo* creation, with the initial result being a formless and empty earth. However, it is possible to construe the Hebrew as meaning, 'When God began to create the heavens and the earth, the earth was without form and void.' In this case the story begins with an existing formless and empty earth, which God then 'creates' by shaping it and filling it with creatures. The main reason for adopting this meaning is that it gives a good parallel with the opening sentence of other ancient Near Eastern creation stories. An argument against it is that when the verb 'to create' (*bārā'*) is used elsewhere in the Old Testament with God as the subject, there is never any mention of a pre-existing 'substance' out of which something is created.[24] Perhaps the most we can safely conclude is that *creatio ex nihilo* is a possible understanding of Genesis 1:1–2a.

The first clear statement of *creatio ex nihilo* in the Judaeo-Christian tradition is in 2 Maccabees, a book accepted into the Roman Catholic, but not the Protestant, canon of Scripture. In 2

---

23. S. W. Hawking, *A Brief History of Time* (London: Bantam, 1988), p. 141.

24. There are a few texts where this may be debatable. Isaiah 43:1 is about the creation of the nation of Israel. Probably the covenant-making at Sinai is seen as creating a new relationship *ex nihilo* in the sense that it did not exist before in that form. The covenant with Abraham was a very different kind of covenant, which was made with an individual and renewed with individuals (Isaac and Jacob). In Amos 4:13 and Psalm 104:29–30 the issue is how the ancient Hebrews would have understood the physical phenomena involved. Did they understand the wind as the movement of pre-existing air, or as an *ex nihilo* creation? Did they regard the conception of new creatures as in some way an *ex nihilo* creation? The very hazy picture of pre-natal life in Psalm 139:13–16 allows this possibility.

Maccabees 7:28 a mother exhorts her son to 'look at the heaven and the earth and see everything that is in them, and recognize that God did not make them out of things that existed'.[25] In the New Testament Hebrews 11:3 seems to express the same understanding of creation, 'By faith we understand that the world was created by the word of God, so that what is seen was made out of things which do not appear'.

Outside Genesis 1 – 2 references to God as Creator are most numerous in Isaiah 40 – 55. Two verses in these chapters are worthy of note. Isaiah 43:10 says:

'You are my witnesses,' says the LORD,
  'and my servant whom I have chosen,
that you may know and believe me
  and understand that I am He.
Before me no god was formed,
  nor shall there be any after me.'

This clearly rules out any dualism in which there are two co-eternal gods. Isaiah 45:7 is probably a specific rejection of Zoroastrian dualism. The verse comes at the end of a prophetic oracle addressed to the Persian emperor Cyrus. By that time Zoroastrianism was probably a prominent religion in Persia, even if it was not yet the official religion. In Zoroastrianism the 'good god' is identified with light and the 'evil god' with darkness. Isaiah 45:7 totally rejects this dualism. Echoing Genesis 1:1–5, it asserts that both light and darkness are 'creatures' created by the God of Israel, not gods.

Dualism in which matter is co-eternal with God may be ruled out by Isaiah 48:12b–13:

I am He, I am the first,
  and I am the last.
My hand laid the foundation of the earth,
  and my right hand spread out the heavens;

---

25. Unless stated otherwise, all Bible quotations in this chapter are from the Revised Standard Version.

when I call to them,
they stand forth together.

The New Testament references to Christ as the one through whom everything was created (Colossians 1:15–17; Hebrews 1:2–3) are notable for their stress on Christ as the one who continually holds all created things in being. Colossians 1:16b–17 can also be taken as implying *creatio ex nihilo*, 'all things were created through him and for him. He is before all things, and in him all things hold together.'

An ordered cosmos

According to Zilsel, the biblical verses particularly important in the development of the concept of 'laws of nature' were those that use the Hebrew word *ḥôq* (decree, statute), or the related verb *ḥāqaq* (to inscribe, decree), with reference to the natural world.[26] The English equivalent of this word is italicized in the following quotations.

> He has *described* [or 'decreed'] a circle upon the face of the waters / at the boundary between light and darkness.[27]

> he made a *decree* for the rain, / and a way for the lightning of the thunder . . .[28]

> [I] prescribed *bounds* [lit. 'my decree'] for it [the sea], / and set bars and doors, / and said, 'Thus far you shall come, and no farther, / and here shall your proud waves be stayed.'[29]

> when he [God] assigned to the sea its *limit* [or 'decree'], / so that the

---

26. Zilsel, 'Genesis of the Concept', pp. 247–249. He used the transliteration *chok* for the Hebrew noun.

27. Job 26:10.

28. Job 28:26.

29. Job 38:10–11.

waters might not transgress his command, / when he *marked out* [or
'decreed'] the foundations of the earth, / then I [wisdom] was beside
him, like a master workman . . .[30]

I [God] placed the sand as the bound for the sea, / a perpetual *barrier* [or
'decree'] which it cannot pass . . .[31]

Presumably it was the absence of any specific mention of
'decree' or 'law' which meant that appeal was not made to the
promise in Genesis 8:22, 'While the earth remains, seedtime and
harvest, cold and heat, summer and winter, day and night, shall not
cease.' This asserts God's upholding of the regular cycle of the
seasons. Interestingly, in Psalm 19 the 'glory' of God is seen in
the regular motion of the sun, and this is then put in parallel with
the moral law.

Scholars recognize that behind the New Testament references
to Christ as creator and sustainer of the universe lies reflection
during the intertestamental period on the role of wisdom in creation in Proverbs 3:19–20; 8:22–31. The implication of these
passages is that God's creation of the world is planned and
ordered, and this is in line with the picture of it provided in
Genesis 1:1 – 2:4a.

The image of God

During the Middle Ages there was a strong tendency to identify
the 'image of God' with human rationality. This, after all, is one of
the most obvious differences between humans and other animals.
It also fitted in with the emphasis on rationality in much Greek
philosophy. It was this understanding of the 'image of God' in
humans that supported the belief that humans are able to understand the order that God has put into the created world. In the
quotation from *Harmonice mundi* given above, Kepler explains what

---

30. Proverbs 8:29–30a.
31. Jeremiah 5:22b.

gave him the confidence to keep searching for five years for a geometrical shape that would fit the data he had for the orbit of Mars. If the word 'geometry' in the quotation is replaced by 'wisdom' it can be seen to be a paraphrase of Proverbs 8:23, 30 combined with Genesis 1:26–27.

Since the beginning of the twentieth century or so there has been much debate about what is meant by the 'image of God' in Genesis 1:26–28.[32] There has been a move away from trying to identify it with any single human attribute or ability. One reason for this has been the inability of scholars to agree on what that attribute might be, though rationality and moral sense have been front runners down the centuries. Another reason has been the recognition that in Genesis 1:26–28 the making of humans in (or maybe 'as') the image of God is combined with the giving to them of dominion over the rest of the creatures. Linked to this is the fact that in the ancient Near East rulers are sometimes regarded as the representative, or image, of the national deity. In the Old Testament this is expressed by saying that the king of the Davidic line is God's 'son' (Psalm 2:7 – children resemble their parents). Therefore there has been a growing consensus that the 'image of God' should be understood in a 'holistic' way. Humans are given responsibility as God's vice-regents over creation because human nature is so constituted that it reflects, in its limited finitude, something of the nature of God. Like God, humans can display wisdom, love, understanding, justice, compassion and so on.

This wider understanding of the 'image of God' in no way invalidates the belief that gave the early modern scientists the confidence that they would be able to discern and understand the 'laws of nature' that God had imposed on the creation. It simply incorporates it as part of a wider understanding. Some further support for that belief is provided by a fresh understanding of the story of Adam's naming the animals (Genesis 2:18–20).

---

32. D. Cairns, *The Image of God in Man* (rev. ed.; London: Fontana, 1973), provides a good survey of the discussion of this topic by theologians up to the time of its publication. G. Wenham, *Genesis 1–15* (Waco, TX: Word, 1987), summarizes the discussions by biblical scholars.

Traditionally this has been understood in the light of the assumption that 'naming' in the Old Testament is an exercise of power, a gaining of control over what is named. However, a careful study by G. Ramsey of all the 'name-givings' in the Old Testament has shown that this is wrong.[33] He points out that some 'name-givings' happen at just the point where there is loss of power or control over what is named. A notable example is Isaac's naming of the wells at Gerar as 'enmity' and 'contention' when he had to give them up to the Philistines (Genesis 26:17–22). Ramsey shows that the one thing that all the 'name-givings' have in common is an act of discernment of the situation or of the nature of what is named. This makes good sense of Genesis 2:18–20. The point of this story is that Adam discerns the nature of each animal and so discovers that none of them is 'a helper fit for him'. In this way he is prepared to receive Eve as the companion he needs. He therefore welcomes her with the words 'At last!' (Genesis 2:23).

If humans are made in God's image so that they can act as God's vice-regents, they need to be able to obtain reliable knowledge about the created order and the creatures for which they have responsibility. Knowledge about the physical world can only be obtained by the use of our physical senses. The assumption, therefore, has to be that this sense data is reliable. From what evidence we have this seems to have been the assumption of the biblical writers. It is clearly expressed in 1 John 1:1, 'We declare to you what was from the beginning, what we have heard, what we have seen with our eyes, what we have looked at and touched with our hands, concerning the word of life' (NRSV).

The reference here is to the incarnation of the divine Word in Jesus. Harrison shows that the allegorizing of natural things led to a downplaying, even sometimes a disparaging, of knowledge based on sense data about nature in favour of knowledge gained by purely mental contemplation of things.[34] Interestingly, he goes on to argue that the new emphasis placed on the physical incarnation

---

33. G. Ramsey, 'Is Name-Giving an Act of Domination in Genesis 2:23 and Elsewhere?' *Catholic Biblical Quarterly* 50 (1974), pp. 24–35.

34. Harrison, *Rise of Natural Science*, pp. 30–33.

of Christ following the publication of Anselm's book *Cur deus homo* (1098), which became one of the standard theological texts of the Middle Ages, led to fresh appreciation of the importance of sense data.[35] He quotes Hildegard of Bingen, who wrote, 'we can know the whole world through our sight, understand through our hearing, distinguish it by our sense of smell . . . dominate it by our touch, and in this way come to know the true God, author of all creation'.[36]

In the Bible there is the recognition that human knowledge has limitations. It is limited because we are both finite and fallen. Two places where these limitations are expressed clearly are Isaiah 55:8–9 and Romans 1:18–21. The former, perhaps, puts the emphasis on human finitude:

> For my thoughts are not your thoughts,
>   neither are your ways my ways, says the LORD.
> For as the heavens are higher than the earth,
>   so are my ways higher than your ways
>   and my thoughts than your thoughts.

In Romans the apostle Paul speaks of the sinful human tendency to 'suppress the truth'. Neither of these limitations vitiates the reality of human knowledge and understanding. They are countered by God's 'common grace' (Romans 2:14–16 gives an example of this in terms of moral knowledge) and his initiative of revelation (Isaiah 55:10–11 goes on to speak of this). John Calvin summed up (1559) the implication of this when he wrote, 'If we hold the Spirit of God to be the only source of truth, we will neither reject nor despise the truth, wherever it may reveal itself, lest we offend the Spirit of God.'[37] He goes on to say that the discovery and understanding of the truth is not restricted to Christians and that 'those men whom Scripture calls "natural men"' are 'sharp and penetrating' in their investigation of the

---

35. Ibid., pp. 36–38.
36. Ibid., p. 37.
37. J. Calvin, *Institutes of the Christian Religion* (London: SCM, 1960), 2.2.15.

truth about the world. This belief that, by God's common grace, all humans do have access to 'genuine' truth despite our finitude and fallenness has sometimes been supported by reference to John 1:4, 9, which speak of Christ as the Word that is the 'true light, which enlightens everyone'.

A 'perfectly free' Creator

In the preface to the second edition of Newton's *Philosophae naturalis principia mathematica* Roger Cotes expresses the opinion that the true business of natural philosophy is

> to inquire after those laws on which the Great Creator actually chose to found this most beautiful Frame of the World, not those by which he might have done the same had he pleased . . . Without all doubt this world . . . could arise from nothing but the perfectly free Will of God directing and presiding over all. From this Fountain it is that those laws, which we call the laws of Nature, have flowed, in which there appear many traces indeed of the most wise contrivance but not the least shadow of necessity.[38]

What he is reacting against here is the 'necessitarianism' that marked much Greek philosophy which saw the world as having a form that was logically necessary. In Platonic thought the world had to be created in accordance with the Eternal Forms and the human mind could, by contemplation, intuit these forms. Therefore observation and experiment were unnecessary. As Oakley points out, this metaphysical necessitarianism began to be challenged by the listing of philosophical propositions that were condemned as contrary to the Christian faith in 1277. They were condemned because they could not be squared with the biblical teaching that God is the sovereign Lord of both nature and history. This understanding of God was deeply rooted in Israel's faith and celebrated in her worship. Psalms 104 and 105 form a

---

38. Quoted in Oakley, 'Christian Theology', p. 437.

'diptych' that celebrates God as Lord of *nature* (Psalm 104) and *history* (Psalm 105). Because the early modern scientists shared this understanding of God they realized that the necessity did not lie with God, who had to create the world according to certain patterns that they might then be able to intuit, but with them. They needed to go out to observe and study the world to find which patterns God had in fact imposed on it according to his free choice. Zilsel suggests that certain biblical references to God's giving things their 'measure' and 'weight' also encouraged this outlook.[39]

It is interesting to reflect on the fact that this insight that the world did not have to be the way it is has come to the fore in a new way in the debate about the 'anthropic principle', or as it is sometimes put, the fact that the universe seems to be 'fine-tuned for life'. There are cosmologists who are unhappy to accept the fact that the exact value of certain fundamental constants is crucially important for the existence of carbon-based life as a contingent fact. Some hope that eventually a 'theory of everything' will be found which will show that the values of these constants are logically necessary. Others adopt the 'many worlds' hypothesis: that our universe is only one of a multitude of possible universes that have come into being, each with a different set of fundamental constants. Of necessity it is the one in which this set makes conscious life possible. At present both of these options are 'faith positions'. Both are fully consonant with a Christian belief in God being 'perfectly free' to create whatever kind of universe he wills in whatever way he wills to do so.

The 'creation mandate'

Christians often refer to Genesis 1:28 as the 'creation mandate' or the 'cultural mandate'. It certainly provided some of the early modern scientists with an important motivation for their work, as

---

39. Zilsel, 'Genesis of the Concept', p. 248, n. 3. He refers to Job 28:25; 38:5. One can add to these verses Isaiah 40:12.

the quotation from Bacon's *Novum organum scientiorum* shows. Although given before the fall, after it, as Bacon points out, it takes on an even greater significance. In the light of this mandate the scientific enterprise can be seen as an important enterprise in which Christians should be involved.

In recent times the 'creation mandate' has come under fire from some environmental activists. Commenting on it in *Design with Nature*, Ian McHarg wrote, 'If one seeks licence for those who would increase radio-activity, create canals and harbours with atomic bombs, employ poisons without constraint, or give consent to the bulldozer mentality, there could be no better injunction than this text.'[40] His comments are rather extreme, but his assertion that Christianity inevitably encourages environmentally harmful attitudes, is quite widely held by environmental activists. This view, however, rests on a misunderstanding of the mandate as giving humans the licence to exploit the rest of creation in any way they wish for their own selfish ends.

One reason why Ian McHarg, and other environmentalists, react strongly to Genesis 1:26–28 is the use in these verses of the words 'subdue' and 'have dominion over'. These words are used elsewhere in the Old Testament of harsh, violent actions. However, it is a basic rule in semantics that 'words mean what they mean in context'. Careful attention to the contexts in which these words occur in the Old Testament shows that the 'harshness' of the meaning comes from the context and is not inherent in the 'core' meaning of the words themselves (in Leviticus 25:43 ff. the 'dominion' is specifically said not to be 'harsh'). Taken in context, it is quite wrong to see in Genesis 1:28 a licence to exploit and ravage the earth. Several times in Genesis 1 God declares that his creation is 'good'. Surely he would not then command humans to despoil and ravage it! Moreover, as we have seen above, the command to subdue and rule over it is given to humans because we are made in the 'image' of God. Whatever else that means, it expresses the truth that we are meant to do things in the way that God would do them, displaying aspects of his character. We are

---

40. I. McHarg, 'Design with Nature', *Natural History* (1969), p. 26.

not to rule as selfish despots, but as stewards who look after God's property in the same manner that God would. In other words, our rule over creation should display wisdom, justice, and loving care. John Calvin, a contemporary of Copernicus, expressed a true biblical understanding of the implications of this mandate:

The Earth was given to man with this condition, that he should occupy himself in its cultivation . . . The custody of the garden was given in charge to Adam, to show that we possess the things that God has committed to our hands, on the condition, that being content with a frugal and moderate use of them, we should take care of what shall remain . . . Let everyone regard himself as a steward of God in all things which he possesses. Then will he neither conduct himself dissolutely, nor corrupt by abuse those things which God requires to be preserved.[41]

One could hardly want a more 'ecologically sound' comment relevant to the twenty-first century! The 'creation mandate' still provides Christians with a motivation and general framework for involvement in the scientific enterprise.

Conclusion

This re-examination, in the light of recent biblical scholarship and some current debates, of the presuppositions that influenced the early modern scientists shows that their roots are indeed firmly biblical. They still provide a Christian basis for the scientific enterprise. Indeed, since the success of science has led to a neglect, or conscious rejection, of metaphysics, secular practitioners of science at present have little or no grounding for what they do apart from the assertion that 'it works'. This is becoming a somewhat unstable grounding in the face of a growing disenchantment with some of the 'works' of science and technology and of the attacks of 'postmodernists' on the idea that there is any such thing as 'objective truth' of the kind that most scientists think they are

---

41. J. Calvin, *Commentary on Genesis* (London: Banner of Truth, 1965), p. 125.

searching for. Rediscovering its theological roots would be helpful to science on both fronts. Judaeo-Christian values, such as those expressed by Calvin, would provide a framework for a more acceptable deployment of scientific and technological resources and applications. Over against postmodernism, the biblical presuppositions assert that there is a rationally understandable reality 'out there' which is the object of scientific study. Because of human finitude and fallenness our grasp on it will always be provisional and open to critical challenge and change. However, the knowledge gained by doing science is 'real discovery', not just a 'consensual construct'.

4. CHRISTIANITY, SCIENCE AND THE POSTMODERN AGENDA

John L. Taylor

Modernism and postmodernism

Philosophy of science in its modernist phase held that science was an objective, truth-seeking discipline, in which scientists communicated in a shared language and assessed theories according to the rules of a logical method held to be equally binding on all scientists. This method told them to aim steadfastly at a single goal, namely, *the truth*, and encouraged them (by reminding them of past successes) that if they played by the rules, they could reasonably expect to make progress towards it.

Science, in the eyes of the modernist, had an exalted position. The modernist picture of science presented it as an exemplar of the process of the rational, objective pursuit of truth. Modernists were so impressed by the successes of scientific methodology that it came to seem that the only rational method for attaining knowledge of the nature of the world was by application of scientific techniques. The expressions 'rational' and 'scientific' came to seem equivalent in the popular mind.

The enthronement of scientific method as the arbiter of what is rational meant a corresponding downgrading of non-scientific systems of belief. In particular, it seemed to the modernist that the blinding light of science had exposed the poverty of the rational credentials of religious belief. The scientific method had been proven to yield a steadily increasing amount of knowledge concerning the physical world. By contrast, there seemed to be no indication of progress towards agreement within the domain of religious belief. For the modernist, the failure of religious belief to match up to the criteria provided by scientific methodology (namely, that beliefs should be confirmed by experimental testing) indicated the fundamentally irrational nature of religious belief.

To be postmodern is to reject some, or all, of modernism's characteristic doctrines. The postmodernist rejects modernism's elevation of science above other possible perspectives on the world. Western science, western religion, primitive magic, eastern mystical world views – each of these different systems of thought have their own, internal standards of what it is reasonable to believe. The modernist supposed that all belief systems should be measured against a single set of 'rational' standards, embodied in scientific method. The postmodernist allows that what is rational varies according to one's perspective, and that Western science is simply one such perspective among many. As Feyerabend puts it, 'We can only speak of what does, or does not, seem appropriate when viewed from a particular and restricted point of view, different views, temperaments, attitudes giving rise to different judgements and different methods of approach.'[1]

To the religious believer who feels the oppressive force of modernism's rejection of the rationality of religious belief, this postmodern openness will come as a great relief. From the postmodern standpoint, religious belief is a permissible world view. Believers need not retain their religious commitments at the expense of a commitment to a scientific world view. Religion and science are independent of each other and can therefore coexist,

---

1. P. Feyerabend, 'Against Method: Outline of an Anarchistic Theory of Knowledge', *Minnesota Studies in the Philosophy of Science* 4 (1970), p. 21.

since the tests for the acceptability of a religious doctrine or a scientific theory are entirely internal to these respective systems.

This emphasis on the compatibility of religion and science appears to be a welcome feature of postmodernism. Yet there remain questions about the general acceptability of postmodern perspectives. Is religion simply one belief system amongst many others? If so, how can it be recommended to the unbeliever as a 'rational' choice for a world view? To make such an appeal is to assume, against the postmodernist, that there are standards of rationality that are independent of particular systems of belief, and that can be applied to make a rational choice amongst world-view options.

A further question concerns the concept of truth. For the modernist, truth has an objective character. Truth is not simply a matter of human agreement, but depends upon how things are, in a reality that exists independently of human beliefs and concepts. Postmodernists tend to assert, however, that truth is not objective in this way. There are many different belief systems, all of which are equally valid. In place of the idea that one system may be objectively correct, the postmodernist will prefer to speak of world-view options as true in a relative sense. One religious system may be true (or acceptable) for one community of religious believers, whereas another system may be true relative to a different community.

For the postmodernist, science may come to be treated as merely one option on the world-view shelf alongside various options such as occultic, mystical or magical world views. We may judge that a scientific world view contains more truth than the folklore of primitive tribes, but this judgment is simply being made from a Western perspective. There is no objective sense in which a scientific outlook contains more truth.

For the Christian, postmodernist approaches to science have both appealing and objectionable aspects. There is thus a challenge to be faced by the Christian who seeks to make a discerning response to postmodernity. The following question must be addressed: how is it possible to accept the postmodernist critique of the excesses of modernism (in particular, the modernist exaltation of scientific method as the only means for forming a rational world-view) without lapsing into the relativism that characterizes much of postmodern thought?

In this chapter the nature of the transition from modernist to postmodernist philosophy of science will be examined. This transition will be traced out by reference to the work of Thomas Kuhn, whose writings contain the materials for a powerful critique of modernist assumptions about science. The manner in which Kuhn's work tends towards an objectionable relativism will be examined. Finally, it will be argued that Kuhn's work can be reinterpreted in a non-relativist framework. This reading of Kuhn suggests a partially postmodern philosophy of science, which succeeds in retaining the postmodern openness towards religion, without lapsing into a denial of the possibility of objective truth.

Kuhn's philosophy of science

There is an appealing picture of scientific progress that, prior to Kuhn, many philosophers would have found acceptable. This is the theory of *convergent realism*: science aims at the truth, and the progress of science has consisted in a steady development of theories towards the truth. Scientific progress is made possible by scientific method, which consists of a rule-governed system for assessing the theory that, given the available data, is most likely to be true. When scientists are guided by this method, they are exemplifying rationality. With its commitment to objective truth as science's goal, together with the assumption of a binding scientific methodology that enshrines the canons of rational theory choice, convergent realism fits neatly into a modernist framework.

It was the opinion of Thomas Kuhn that the convergent realist image of science appears defensible only because philosophers of science focus their attention predominantly upon the finished products of scientific enquiry, namely mature theories.[2] But the

---

2. For exposition of Kuhn's work see T. S. Kuhn, *The Structure of Scientific Revolutions* (2nd ed.; Chicago : University of Chicago Press,1970). See also Kuhn's 'Reflections on my Critics', in I. Lakatos and A. Musgrave,

exposition of theories in the textbooks of science, Kuhn noted, betrayed a mischievous tendency on the part of scientists to rewrite scientific history, portraying it as a smooth progression towards the favoured theories of contemporary science. Kuhn's important work on scientific revolutions is an explicit attack on the notion of a steady progression towards objective scientific truth.

Kuhn drew attention to the fact that science is a human activity. Instead of simply considering the polished products of scientific enquiry found in the textbooks, he addressed himself to science as an institution. Scientists operate, in the normal phase of scientific enquiry, under the guidance of a paradigm. The paradigm is the disciplinary matrix. The term is used by Kuhn in a slightly loose fashion to point towards all that binds a group of scientists together – the theories they hold to, the model solutions to past problems, shared values and metaphysical principles. In ordinary research, the paradigm dominates. It directs the researcher's attention to particular puzzles – places where the paradigm doesn't quite fit nature – and suggests methods to guide them in puzzle solving.

All this may sound quite amenable from the standpoint of the convergent realist. But Kuhn's work became much more contentious with the introduction of the idea of scientific revolutions. Kuhn observed that, from time to time, scientists find that puzzles resist solution by the methods countenanced by the reigning paradigm. The puzzle becomes an anomaly, perhaps gaining attention by leading workers in the field. If the anomaly proves particularly recalcitrant, the discipline enters a crisis phase, since the legitimacy of its paradigm is now being called into question. The agreement that characterized normal science comes under threat, as various modifications, or relaxations, of the rules enshrined in the paradigm are advocated.

The crisis in the discipline becomes acute if, in this period of instability, a novel paradigm is articulated that offers to resolve the anomalies of the existing paradigm, as well as offering the discipline the promise of a fertile new approach. If a sufficiently large

Criticism and the Growth of Knowledge (Cambridge : Cambridge University Press, 1970), pp. 231–278.

number of scientists are disaffected with the existing paradigm, they may transfer their allegiance to the new one – a process Kuhn calls a scientific revolution.

Kuhn is quite consciously using a political metaphor to describe this phase of theory choice. Political revolutions occur in a social context of deep dissatisfaction with existing structures. The very institutions within which normal political debate and decision take place are themselves called into question, so that revolution tends to be a deeply disturbing, violent affair, in which the direction of future political activity is determined, not by any process of rational political debate, but rather by such factors as which side can muster most force. Kuhn suggests that there is a comparable breakdown in rationality during scientific revolutions:

> As in political revolution, so in paradigm choice – there is no standard higher than the assent of the relevant community. To discover how scientific revolutions are effected, we shall therefore have to examine not only the impact of nature and of logic, but also the techniques of persuasive argumentation effective within the quite special groups that constitute the community of scientists.[3]

We might like to read Kuhn as simply saying that, alongside rational considerations, non-rational factors enter the actual process of theory choice during revolutions. Yet Kuhn seems to be making a much stronger claim, namely that there is no possibility of rational comparison between paradigms. Rival paradigms are, to use his technical term, *incommensurable*: 'The normal-scientific tradition that emerges from a scientific revolution is not only incompatible but often actually incommensurable with that which has gone before.'[4] The term 'incommensurability' means simply that rational choice between paradigms is not possible; different paradigms cannot be rationally 'co-measured'.

Kuhn has a number of reasons for his claim that paradigms are incommensurable. In the first instance, it is simply the corollary of

---

3. Kuhn, *Scientific Revolutions*, p. 94.
4. Ibid., p. 102.

the emphasis he places upon the normative role of paradigms in normal science. It is the role of the paradigm under which a scientist works to provide guidance in the process of theory choice – to tell the scientist what a good theory looks like. Indeed, the paradigm itself should contain an exemplary model of a solved problem, which the scientist can examine and employ when he or she attempts to solve novel puzzles. But if the paradigm itself supplies the rules for theory choice, to what can a scientist appeal when seeking to rationalize a choice of paradigm? As Kuhn notes, there is here a problem of circularity: a scientist's conception of what makes for a good theory is so determined by the paradigm into which he has been inculcated that any attempt at rational debate between proponents of different paradigms would find both sides arguing in a question-begging manner.[5]

Clearly, if there is incommensurability due to the paradigm dependence of the standards for theory choice, the prospects for the convergent realist interpretation of scientific progress are dim. For the claim of the convergent realist is that, if scientists adhere to the canons of rational theory choice, they will select theories that come steadily nearer to the truth about nature. But this presupposes that there are such canons – that there are principles to which the scientist may appeal, when faced with a choice between paradigms, that will guide him towards the paradigm most likely to contain truth. If, however, Kuhn's claim is correct, there are no 'paradigm independent' canons to guide the theorist in the critical, revolutionary phases of science. We are reduced to a situation in which assessments of the value of a paradigm are themselves paradigm-relative.

The first source of incommensurability is the argument that the values which guide theory choice are themselves paradigm-dependent, so that there is no neutral basis for comparing two paradigms. But Kuhn claimed that there were further obstacles in the path of the convergent realist. The second source of incommensurability is connected to considerations about meaning.

Kuhn adopted a theory of meaning according to which the

-----

5. Ibid., p. 108.

meaning of a theoretical term, such as 'mass', was determined by the role the term played in the paradigm to which it belonged. But it follows from this 'holistic' approach to meaning that a change in paradigm implies a change in the meanings of theoretical terms. This seems to imply a new threat of incommensurability, for if theorists operating in different paradigms do not even mean the same when they speak of concepts such as mass, how can they engage in rational debate about the merits of their respective paradigms? As Kuhn puts it:

> In the transition from one theory to the next words change their meanings or conditions of applicability in subtle ways. Though most of the same signs are used before and after a revolution – e.g. force, mass, element, compound, cell – the ways in which some of them attach to nature has somehow changed. Successive theories are thus, we say, incommensurable.[6]

The two sources of incommensurability do not, by themselves, imply that there is no such thing as scientific truth. It remains possible that there is a single paradigm which accurately characterizes the way the world is. However, the impossibility of rational comparison between paradigms implies that there is no basis for the claim that science is steadily progressing closer to the truth. We are left in a situation of scepticism – we are unable to know whether any paradigm's success indicates that it is more likely to be true than a rival. Yet, for all that, the notion of a single true paradigm remains.

However, Kuhn has further arguments against the idea of objective scientific truth. The classical version of an objective theory of truth is provided by the correspondence theory, according to which truth is a matter of correspondence between a theory, and a world that exists in some independent sense. Kuhn considers that this theory of truth is untenable. For we have no access to the way the world is in itself, so to speak – all that we may speak of is the world as described by the paradigm we adopt:

---

6. Kuhn, 'Reflections on my Critics', p. 266.

One often hears that successive theories grow ever closer to, or approximate more and more closely to, the truth. Apparently generalizations like that refer not to the puzzle-solutions and the concrete predictions derived from a theory but rather to its ontology, to the match, that is, between the entities with which the theory populates nature and what is 'really there' . . .

Perhaps there is some other way of salvaging the notion of 'truth' for application to whole theories, but this one will not do. There is, I think, no theory-independent way to reconstruct phrases like 'really there'; the notion of match between the ontology of a theory and its 'real' counterpart in nature now seems to me illusive in principle.[7]

This denial of any clear notion of an objective world commits Kuhn to a strongly relativist position. There is no such thing as 'the way the world is', independently of how we believe it to be. In some sense, the nature of the world is determined by our beliefs about it. This radical relativism makes sense of one of Kuhn's most notorious observations, namely that, when a scientist changes paradigm, his entire world changes:

In a sense that I am unable to explicate further, the proponents of competing paradigms practise their trades in different worlds. One contains constrained bodies that fall slowly, the other pendulums that repeat their motion again and again. In one, solutions are compounds, in the other mixtures. One is embedded in a flat, the other in a curved, matrix of space. Practising in different worlds, the two groups of scientists see different things when they look from the same point in the same direction.[8]

Kuhnian relativism finds its most vivid expression in what Kuhn has to say about perception. Prior to Kuhn, philosophers had hoped to establish a language for reporting observational data that made no theoretical commitments. Such a theory-neutral language was thought to be required if observation was to play the

---

7. Kuhn, *Scientific Revolutions*, p. 206.
8. Ibid., p. 150.

decisive role in theory choice that classical philosophy of science considered it to have. If all reports of observation presuppose some theory, it would seem that observation could not provide the ultimate grounds for belief in theory. Philosophers toyed with the suggestion that it would be possible to describe the results of experiments in terms that enshrined no commitments to any theory whatsoever. An example of such a 'neutral' language was the language of 'sense-data', which simply reported on the nature of sensations.

The work of Kuhn challenged the assumption that there could be such a language. According to Kuhn, the language scientists use to report their observations is 'theory-laden'. That is, the observational language embodies some theoretical commitments. Scientists operating in different paradigms will accordingly conceptualize what they see in different ways. It is in this sense that the contents of their perceptual experience will differ. Where an Aristotelian would see a constrained object falling slowly, Galileo would see a pendulum.

Kuhn illustrated this strong claim of theory-ladenness by comparing the process to the manner in which visual images such as the duck/rabbit could be seen first as a duck, and then as a rabbit. It is not simply a matter of having a single visual experience and entertaining two different interpretations of it – a change in paradigm induces a change in the very nature of what is seen. This is the import, at the perceptual level, of Kuhn's idea that the world itself changes with a change in paradigm.

Postmodern aspects of Kuhn's critique of realism

Kuhn's work embodies a substantial challenge to the image of science portrayed by the convergent realist. Two central tenets of that image – the idea that scientific history may be seen as a rational progression from one paradigm to the next, and the idea that this progress is directed towards the goal of an objectively true description of nature – are both under threat. In place of convergent realism, Kuhn substitutes an image of science as a human, political institution, without any especially rational canons for theory choice, and without any 'extra-theoretic' objective truth as its goal. Realism has been supplanted by relativism, and rationality by sociology. The generally postmodern flavour of Kuhn's philosophy of science is evident. The modernist liked to think that there was something 'special' about science – that it was an activity governed by a method which was, in a distinctive fashion, ideally rational. In place of this exalted conception of scientific rationality, Kuhn suggests that, at critical moments in scientific development, rationality is no more a part of decision-making than it is during political revolutions. Instead of looking for a 'logical' account of the nature of theory choice, it would be more appropriate to investigate the sociological factors that influence scientists (i.e. which paradigm is backed by the strongest propaganda?). Scientific rationality is demoted from its modernist pedestal.

There is another respect in which Kuhn's critique of realism may be termed 'postmodern'. The convergent realist, in claiming that science is a rational enterprise, was not committed to claiming that scientists always act rationally. The claim was rather that there are canons which guide scientists – a scientific method – that, when followed carefully, will yield progress towards truth. The convergent realist wishes to show that it is at least possible to provide a reconstruction of the historical development of science which brings out its rational character. For the realist, this amounts to a demonstration of a steady progression towards truth in the course of scientific history.

Convergent realism is offering an interpretation of the activity of science by setting it within a particular philosophical context that specifies truth as the goal, and a rational method as the means of achieving that goal. Postmodernism, in general, rejects this tendency of philosophers to attempt to 'stand outside' an activity in order to offer a philosophical 'legitimation' or 'justification' of it. In J.-F. Lyotard's terms, postmodernism can be defined as 'incredulity toward meta-narratives'.[9] The

---

9. See Jean-François Lyotard, *The Post-Modern Condition: A Report on Knowledge*, tr. G. Bennington and B. Massumi (Manchester: Manchester University Press, 1985), p. xxiv.

postmodernist will argue that, contra the convergent realist, we have no need of a general interpretation, or rational reconstruction, of science. Instead of attempting to interpret science using philosophical notions of rationality and truth, we should be content simply with the narratives of science itself. Instead of asking whether there is some truth 'outside' the paradigm, we should simply adopt the view of the world given to us in our current paradigms, and explicate scientific rationality in terms suggested by this paradigm.[10]

Kuhn's philosophy of science encourages a postmodern restriction of vision to the view from within the paradigm. Indeed, following Kuhn's lead, sociologists of science proposed that it should be possible to understand scientific development in purely sociological terms, without any reference to concepts such as truth or reason.[11] Scientists are influenced, when choosing theories, not by factors that may be taken as reliable indicators of truth, but instead by 'extrinsic' considerations such as which theory is supported by the most eminent proponents, which theory will attract most funding, and so on. This so-called 'strong programme' represents a bold rejection of convergent realism, more severe than that countenanced by Kuhn himself. It illustrates the harsh face of postmodernity – its radical rejection of the role of rationality, and its abdication of any notion of truth.

The postmodern flavour of Kuhn's philosophy of science also

---

10. In this respect, Arthur Fine's rejection of realism in favour of what he terms the *natural ontological attitude* (or NOA) could be deemed postmodern. Fine comments that 'NOA urges us not to undertake the construction of teleological frameworks in which to set science. It suggests the subversive idea that perhaps there is no need for authority (outer or inner), nor for general authenticating. NOA whispers the thought that maybe we can actually get along without extra attachments to science at all ...' See Fine, 'Unnatural Attitudes: Realist and Instrumentalist Attachments to Science', *Mind* 95 (1986), p. 172.

11. See, e.g., B. Barnes, *Interests and the Growth of Knowledge* (London: Routledge & Kegan Paul, 1977); and D. Bloor, *Knowledge and Social Imagery* (London: Routledge & Kegan Paul, 1976).

emerges with his suggestion that, in some sense, a change in paradigm brings with it a change in the very nature of the world. This makes reality dependent upon our beliefs about it. Such a thought is at home in a postmodern context, which stresses the 'social construction' of reality. Instead of saying, as the convergent realist would, that the history of science has consisted in a succession of theories which are progressing steadily closer towards an objectively correct account of nature, Kuhn presents us with a vision of science as a 'world-changing' activity, in which the conceptual transformations that accompany paradigm shifts may be said to lead scientists into a new reality. The thought that there is a theory-independent reality which theories aim to describe seems to be lost at this point.

Reworking Kuhn

Kuhn himself was disturbed when the relativist, irrationalist implications of his theory of the incommensurability of scientific paradigms were pointed out. In a significant postscript to *Structures of Scientific Revolutions*, he aimed to clarify the meaning of certain critical claims, especially those surrounding the notion of incommensurability.[12] It was not his intent, he claimed, to reject the notion of scientific rationality, nor to dispense with (as the social constructivists might wish) the notion of truth. Kuhn makes significant modifications to the picture of science described above, in a direction that makes it less hostile (although still challenging) to convergent realism.

In the first place, the critical argument for incommensurability due to the paradigm-dependence of standards is qualified significantly. Kuhn does not return to the 'modernist' ideal of characterizing scientific method via a uniquely binding set of rules. He does, however, point to the existence of a number of *values*, or *theoretical virtues*, which are paradigm-independent, in the sense that all scientists agree that these are good features for a paradigm to

---

12. The postscript is in the second edition.

possess. The possession by a theory of qualities such as accuracy, scope, simplicity and fruitfulness provides good reason for belief in that theory.[13]

What then is the import of his claim that successive paradigms are incommensurable? It is not, Kuhn says, that rational debate is impossible. Rather, his point is that there is no logical, rule-governed decision procedure available to adjudicate decisively between paradigms during revolutions:

> What I am denying then is neither the existence of good reasons nor that these reasons are of the sort usually described. I am, however, insisting that such reasons constitute values to be used in making choices rather than rules of choice. Scientists who share them may nevertheless make different choices in the same concrete situations.[14]

A helpful analogy can be made at this point with wine-tasting.[15] There is no rule-governed decision procedure to which appeal can be made when seeking to judge the relative merits of a pair of wines. It does not follow, however, that all wines are equally good. There is such a thing as the quality of a wine. Many of us can judge at a primitive level whether one wine is better than another. There are cases in which we are not competent to judge, but would be prepared to defer to the decisions of specialists, who have been trained to recognize the various characteristics that make a good wine. Similarly, although philosophers of science would now tend to agree that there is no rule-governed procedure which can be used to tell us which scientific theories are the best, it does not follow that all theories are equally good. We all know that some theories are poor (geocentrism, phlogiston, caloric theory), and in other cases we defer to the judgment of the relevant experts,

---

13. Kuhn, 'Reflections on my Critics', p. 261.

14. Ibid., p. 262.

15. For the wine-tasting analogy, see W. H. Newton-Smith, *The Rationality of Science* (London: Routledge & Kegan Paul, 1981), p. 234. Newton-Smith's work provides a powerful defence of realism in science, and the rationality of theory choice.

whose experience and training enables them to make judgments concerning theoretical value at a sophisticated level.

Abandoning the hope for a rule-governed procedure in favour of the idea of shared theoretical virtues does represent a significant concession by the realist. There may be shared values – but it does not follow that these values will always be interpreted in the same way by all scientists (the concept of theoretical 'simplicity' is a notoriously difficult one). Moreover, the problem of underdetermination presents itself. Just as there can be cases of seemingly irresoluble disagreement between wine-tasters as to which of a pair of wines is 'best', we can envisage cases in which a pair of theories may equally well 'fit with the available data'. The philosopher of science will be concerned to examine the possibility that underdetermination may obtain, even in the limiting case that all experimentation has been done. A further question may also be asked, namely why it is that we should suppose that the subjective preferences of scientists concerning matters such as simplicity, coherence and elegance should be taken to indicate truth reliably. Why should we suppose that the 'loveliest' theories are the 'likeliest' to be true?[16]

The realist, then, is not out of the woods. But at least there seems to be a promising route to take away from entanglement in Kuhnian relativism. Emphasizing the values that scientists do share (values that will typically be taken to be reliable guides in the task of seeking out truth), helps to restore confidence in the workability of the notion of scientific objectivity. The strongly modernist flavour of pre-Kuhnian realism has been tempered by Kuhn's emphasis on sociological considerations. But we are not

---

16. For the Christian, there is a tempting line of argument at this point. The fact that our judgments about the apparent virtues of scientific theories provide us with reliable insight into theoretical truth is well explained by supposing that God, in his benevolence, ordained a harmonious relation between the order of the natural world and the human intellect. For a development of this argument, see the final chapter of R. Walker, *The Coherence Theory of Truth* (London: Routledge & Kegan Paul, 1989).

obliged to dispense entirely with realism as an ingredient in a desirable philosophy of science.

This moral is borne out by reflecting on the question of the meanings of theoretical terms. Kuhn argued that one source of incommensurability was the fact that theoretical terms are assigned different meanings in different paradigms. The realist may concede that paradigm change does induce a change in the meanings of theoretical terms, yet question whether this implies a complete breakdown in communication. Why not simply allow that meanings do vary, but translation is a possibility? Kuhn does not argue against this, and indeed, in his more temperate comments, suggests that he never intended to claim that total communication breakdown occurs during revolutions.[17] The relativistic nature of his comments about rationality had been overstressed and his comments about meaning had been similarly misappropriated.

Allowing translation between paradigms is a significant concession in favour of the realist. The radical, relativistic interpretation of Kuhn suggests an image of scientists locked into isolated worlds, constituted by their differing paradigms. The discontinuity between paradigms is so great that a scientist is not able even to render intelligible the sentences uttered by rivals in another paradigm. On the less radical, non-relativist reading of Kuhn being proposed here, we are left with a more plausible scenario in which the meanings of theoretical terms do vary, so that there may on occasion be difficulties of communication, but such difficulties may be resolved by attention to the task of translation.

In place of the radically relativist picture of Kuhn that the postmodernist will be tempted to paint, a more modest picture is emerging. This is a picture, inspired by Kuhn's philosophy of science, that is not ultimately inimical to convergent realism. It allows for interparadigm communication, and holds that there is at least the possibility that this communication will take the form of rational debate, being guided by the values shared by all scientists.

It would not be fair to Kuhn to claim that his philosophy of

---

17. Kuhn, 'Reflections on my Critics', pp. 266–278.

science can be given an interpretation that poses no threats to the realist. Although his concessions on the questions of rationality and meaning make the Kuhnian picture more amenable to the friends of realism, Kuhn never retracted his more relativistic pronouncements about truth and the nature of the reality. He remained hostile to a conception of truth as correspondence with a theory-independent world.

The correspondence theory of truth states that truth is a relation of correspondence between sentences and facts. This theory is not without philosophical problems.[18] However, defenders of the correspondence theory are concerned to defend something that is important about the concept of truth, namely its objectivity. The correspondence theory embodies one way of expressing a commitment to the thought that truth and falsity have to do with how things lie in a world which exists independently of ourselves.

In place of this emphasis on the objectivity of truth, Kuhn speaks about paradigm shifts being 'world-changing'. This strongly suggests that he would adhere to a relativist analysis of truth in terms of human agreement. Whilst it would seem too simple-minded to equate truth with what humans believe to be true, the relativist will, in some sense, assert that truth depends upon the existence of a community who agree about certain things. If there are communities with fundamentally different beliefs (such as two groups of scientists working in incommensurable paradigms), then what is true for the one community will differ from what is true for the other. This is a conclusion that concurs with Kuhn's metaphor of 'world-changing' paradigm shifts.

The realist will object that relativism is an inadequate analysis of the concept of truth. Against the relativist, the realist will urge that what is true cannot be dependent upon the existence of human

---

18. The central problem is that it has proved hard to give illuminating accounts of either the nature of facts, or of the relation of correspondence. Rorty comments that 'several hundred years of effort have failed to make interesting sense of the notion of "correspondence" (either of thoughts to things or of words to things)' (R. Rorty, *Consequences of Pragmatism* [Brighton: Harvester, 1982], p. xvii).

agreement. For it is consistent to suppose that a theory could be true, even if I (or, for that matter, my community, or human beings in general) had never existed. Truth cannot therefore be dependent upon the existence of communities of shared belief, as the relativist supposes.

Against the relativist's attempt to ground truth on human agreement, the realist insists that what is true and what is false is a matter of how things lie, in a world that exists independently from us. From the basis of this resilient resistance to the relativization of truth to systems of belief the realist may address some critical comments to Kuhn's talk about 'world-changes'. It will seem to the realist that there is a clear sense in which the world itself does not change during paradigm shifts. The essential nature of the sun did not change when scientists moved from a geocentric paradigm to a heliocentric view. In a clear sense, both Kepler and Brahe, when they looked at the sun, saw the same object, and thus had the same experience, albeit that they went on to offer differing interpretations of this experience.

The realist's verdict on talk about 'world-changes' will be that Kuhn has been swept away by the power of his own metaphor. To liken scientific activity to a political process was a novel, fruitful proposal. Kuhn has helped us to see science as a human institution, thereby helping to moderate the exalted position to which modernism had raised scientific rationality. But though we may learn from Kuhn's sociological perspective on science, we are not obliged to follow Kuhn's more radical, relativistic pronouncements. By refusing to be carried along by the force of the metaphor of world-changing paradigm shifts, it is possible to learn from Kuhn's most salient points whilst still not abandoning the role of the notion of objective truth in understanding science.

Christianity as a paradigm

This chapter opened with a problem, namely the question of how it is possible to appropriate a 'postmodern' openness to the rational acceptability of non-scientific belief systems, without thereby buying into postmodern relativism. By way of conclusion, we may note that the 'non-relativist' interpretation (or perhaps 'reinterpretation') of Kuhn which this chapter has advocated provides a way to resolve this difficulty.

We have seen that it is possible to accept much of what Kuhn has to say about the role of paradigms in science without endorsing his view that there is no such thing as objective scientific truth. Building on Kuhn, the general structure of a philosophy of science has been developed that makes space for the idea of rational comparison of paradigms, and which endorses the realist belief that scientific theories aim at describing the nature of a paradigm-independent reality. By retaining the possibility of rational comparison of paradigms, and an objective notion of truth, this approach succeeds in avoiding the negative assessment of rationality and objectivity that can be found in the more radical of postmodern philosophies of science.

Whilst allowing for the rationality of science, this approach does not fall into the modernist trap of equating rationality with scientific method. Science may be a rational activity, but it is not the sole exemplar of rationality, as modernists tended to suppose. This emerges most clearly when we note that the account proposed in this chapter of the possibility of rational choice between paradigms is applicable in more general contexts. In particular, it would seem that a choice of a religious belief system such as Christianity may be rational in much the way that a scientist's choice of paradigm is rational.

We have seen that scientific paradigm choice is informed by a set of values that all scientists share. Scientists seek theories that possess such virtues as accuracy, scope, simplicity and fruitfulness. In the absence of logically compelling reasons for choosing one paradigm over another, the individual scientist must make a judgment, in the light of these values, as to which paradigm makes best sense of the available data. Being guided by these values, the judgment may be rational, but it will not be one that is logically demonstrably correct.

Unresolved anomalies persist, even in science. A new paradigm clears up some difficulties, but will have other difficulties of its own. There are points of tension, where it is not clear how different parts of a theory may be rendered consistent. Again, this means that to choose between paradigms requires an exercise of judgment. On balance, does the value of the paradigm in making good sense of a wide range of the data outweigh the weaknesses due to data that cannot be explained, or the fact that there are points where it is hard for the paradigm to escape contradiction?

The situation is not, in principle, different when someone faces the choice of whether or not to embrace Christianity. There is a distinctively Christian paradigm, a set of principles and convictions that constitutes the Christian world view, and provides the way in which Christians make sense of their experience of the world. According to the Christian paradigm, our inquiry into the world proceeds from the belief that the world was created by an all-powerful, loving, Personal Being, who sustains his creation and reveals himself in it, in both general and special ways. The analogy with scientific paradigms suggests to us that we should not expect to find a knock-down argument for this view. The inquirer will need to assess the individual pieces of evidence that comprise the cumulative case for Christianity – the evidence of design, the evidence of revelation, of individual religious experience and so on. They will need to weigh this against the counter-evidence provided by the existence of evil, and consider the adequacy of Christian efforts to cope with this tension in their world view. They will eventually have to make an act of judgment in deciding whether or not, on balance, the Christian scheme makes best sense of the available data of experience (which will include their personal experience).

The parallel between the process of paradigm choice in science and the process of religious conversion is striking. Kuhn himself noted the parallel, although his use of the term 'conversion' was intended to reflect upon the irrational element in scientific paradigm choice.[19] Yet we have seen that a choice of scientific paradigm may be rationally justified by appeal to values such as simplicity, accuracy and so on. Accordingly, there is the possibility of rationally defending the Christian world view as a system of beliefs that exemplifies similar values.

---

19. See Kuhn, *Scientific Revolutions*, p. 151.

Christianity offers a 'religious paradigm'. It can be rationally defended by arguments demonstrating the simplicity, coherence and accuracy of the explanation of experience that it provides. We may thus invert Kuhn's analogy. Instead of viewing both scientific revolutions and the adoption of a religious belief system as processes of irrational conversion, we can conclude that the choice of a religious belief system may be rational in much the way that choice of a scientific paradigm may be rational.[20]

The analogy between Christianity and a scientific paradigm thus leads us to conclude, against the modernist, that rational justification for religious belief is possible. In one respect, this is a postmodern conclusion, since it represents a rejection of the modernist doctrine of the irrational nature of religion. Yet this conclusion also runs counter to the relativism that is part of much postmodern thought. Postmodernists are inclined to proclaim the incommensurability of different world views. The view that one could compare different religious paradigms in an effort to discern which system is rationally preferable is not one to which the postmodernist will incline. If the views defended in this chapter are to be thought of as postmodern, I stress that this is simply because they diverge from modernism by allowing that the domain of reason is not restricted to purely scientific matters.

The postmodern relativist will, like Kuhn, be sceptical about the concept of objective truth. Yet we have seen that it is possible to appropriate much of Kuhn's analysis whilst retaining an insistence on the objectivity of truth. The relativist grounding of the concept of truth upon human agreement seems inadequate. Realists are on solid philosophical grounds when they defiantly insist that objective truth is a viable concept, and indeed, that the goal for the scientific enterprise is an objectively true account of nature.

---

20. For discussion of this approach to the justification of religious belief, see B. Mitchell, *The Justification of Religious Belief* (London: Macmillan, 1973), and M. Banner, *The Justification of Science and the Rationality of Religious Belief* (Oxford: Oxford University Press, 1990). For a detailed defence of theism as the best explanation of a range of data, see R. Swinburne, *The Existence of God* (Oxford: Clarendon, 1979).

Traditionally, Christian faith has been proclaimed as an objectively true account of the ultimate nature of things. In a postmodern era, it is tempting to endorse relativism as an interpretation of the nature of religion. To do so would be to reject the concept of objective truth in the religious domain. For the postmodernist, Christianity should not be recommended on the basis that there are good reasons for supposing it true (in an objective sense). Instead, when Christians assert that their belief system is true, they should be taken as reporting their subjective preference for the Christian perspective.

It is not the purpose of this chapter to engage fully with an argument against relativist interpretations of religion. But if we accept a realist philosophy of science, the analogy between religious world views and scientific paradigms suggests a similarly 'realist' approach to religious belief. We have seen that it is possible to rework Kuhn's treatment of scientific paradigms in a manner that eschews relativism, and affirms the validity of treating scientific paradigms as systems that aim at objective truth. By analogy, a case can be made for rejecting the relativist interpretations of religious paradigms that are such a prominent part of postmodern thought.

Conclusion: partial postmodernism

The philosophy of science which this chapter advocates may be termed 'partially postmodern'. We have seen reasons to reject modernism's exaltation of science as the sole arbiter of what is reasonable. To reject this central doctrine of the modernist world view is to be, in part, postmodern. Yet rejecting an exalted conception of scientific rationality does not mean a recoil into a postmodern relativism, where all world views are equally valid. The arguments in favour of the rationality of scientific paradigm choice, and the viability of the concept of objective scientific truth have a wider application. They demonstrate the possibility that a religious world view, such as Christianity, may be rationally defensible, and they suggest the applicability of the concept of objective truth in the religious domain. We can thus achieve the goal of accepting the postmodern openness to religion, without lapsing into postmodern relativism. The moral of this chapter is: postmodernism, but only in moderation![21]

© John L. Taylor, 2005

---

21. This chapter was first published in *Science and Christian Belief* 10 (1998), pp. 163– 178.

5. THE POSTMODERN ATTACK ON SCIENTIFIC REALISM

John L. Taylor

Relativism

'All truth is relative' is a common claim, but what, if anything, could be meant by it?

The relativist seems committed to the following:

'X is true' = X is true for me (or perhaps, for my community)

How satisfactory is this as a claim about the meaning of truth? One of the points in my using the predicate 'is true' is to commend a proposition as one that should be believed. An assertion that 'what the President said this morning is true' carries the implication 'you ought to believe what he said'. It would be nonsense to assert, 'Everything he said is true, but you shouldn't believe a word of it.'

Yet exactly this kind of nonsense is involved in the claim that truth is relative. For if 'X is true' means 'X is true for me', then my assertion of X (or the equivalent assertion that X is true) precisely does not carry the implication 'you ought to believe X'. If truth is really 'truth for me / truth for my community', then when I assert that a proposition is true, my assertion need not be taken as a proposal for your assent, since you are a different individual and you may belong to a different community. But then, of course, I have not really made an assertion. All that has happened is that I have effectively, in a roundabout, confused manner, expressed what I believe.

Effectively, then, the relativist means by 'is true for me' something like 'is believed by me'. But if that is what the claim really amounts to, then it would seem better if it were in fact expressed this way. For once it is clear that the relativists' utterance is primarily an expression of their belief, it invites the response 'Yes, you may believe that – but should you? What reasons have you for believing that?'

The confusion of truth and belief leads us into conceptual difficulty. What is the relativist to make of the rejoinder 'Relativism may be true for you, but it is not true for me?' Are they to agree? In which case, they would seem to have given up trying to persuade us to become relativists, which will make us wonder what it is they really believe themselves. Or, are they to disagree? In which case, it would seem that some truth claims are in fact absolute.

It seems at first glance, then, that the relativist has failed to note the distinction between assertions that a proposition is true (the truth of which depends upon whether things are as the proposition says) and expressions of one's own belief or opinion. Someone who equates truth with opinion gets into a conceptual quagmire that makes genuine communication (the proposal and consideration of propositions) impossible.

Conversely, if we take it that genuine communication is possible (and of course, nobody can tell you otherwise!), it must be the case that truth is more than simply mere opinion. Truth is what we aim at in the practice of assertion – but the assertion itself may not hit the goal. This is one part of my argument, then, for the claim that the practice of making assertions presupposes an objective notion of truth.

Sociological deconstructivism

There has in recent years been a heightened awareness of the significance of the social context of theory creation. Philosophers such as Wittgenstein have argued that language use is a social activity, so that the meaning of terms in scientific theories must be explained by reference to the social context the scientists inhabit. There is much enlightenment to be gained by this renewed interest in sociology. But how exactly should we understand the relationship between theories and social contexts? One radical stance is that of the sociological deconstructivist.

The deconstructivist, as I gloss him, believes that a full explanation for the choices of scientists (or religious believers) is possible which mentions only sociological causes of belief. That is, all processes of inference considered reasonable can fully be explicated by reference to the obtaining social conditions.[1]

Sociologically reductive analyses have drawn upon Wittgenstein's rule-following argument. The idea here is that we are all members of particular linguistic communities. Our language embodies certain rules for the use of terms. These rules are not 'God given'; they are based on consensus. What makes it right to apply a term in a particular way is that the community you belong to does it that way. So it might seem that truth is reduced to human agreement.

The 'truth as consensus' model is expressed in blunt form by

------

1. This claim may seem outlandishly strong, yet it accords with the general tenor of deconstructivists such as D. Bloor and B. Barnes, of the Edinburgh 'Strong Programme'. A more qualified deconstructivist may argue that considerations of social context may not fully explicate the claims being made, but that, nevertheless, once the social context is in view, any claims to truth are undermined. This more qualified view is still vulnerable to the problems of self-reference discussed above. Early formulations of the sociological deconstructivist view can be found in B. Barnes, *Scientific Knowledge and Sociological Theory* (London: Routledge & Kegan Paul, 1974); and D. Bloor, *Knowledge and Social Imagery* (London: Routledge & Kegan Paul, 1976).

Rorty: truth is what one's peers will let one get away with.[2] If the model is right, it would follow that the epistemology of science is reduced to sociology: the explanation of what scientists believe to be true should proceed by looking at the social factors that lead to consensus.

The deconstructivist position embodies, I submit, a misconception about truth. I go about deciding whether there is cheese in the fridge by looking, not by conducting a straw poll. There is no difficulty conceiving of propositions that are universally believed, yet turn out false. There was once widespread belief in the proposition that the earth was the centre of the universe. This did not make it true. Consensus is not a sufficient condition for truth; nor, of course, is it necessary. There are many facts about the past of which we are all ignorant.

It cannot be correct, then, to adopt the 'truth as consensus' model. A further difficulty for the deconstructivist remains one of self-reference: what are we to make of the reasons offered to us for denying that there can be good reasons? That is, what is the status of the sociological theories which are supposed to supplant the 'rationalist' tales of scientific history? If they are offering us reasons, why should we not subject them to the same deconstructive analysis which they claim applies to science? And if they are not offering us reasons, why should we believe what they claim?

This latter argument really gets to the nub of the problem. The key point which should be made is that the very act of asserting propositions as things worthy of belief (an act which deconstructivists partake of every bit as much as their opponents) presupposes that there is such as thing as 'worthiness of belief' (i.e. reasonability). Participants in anything that could be called enquiry are bound, as a precondition of the meaningfulness of the activity itself, to making a distinction between what is reasonable and what is not. If any theory is as valid as any other, then there is no point in proposing any theory.

---

2. Richard Rorty, *Philosophy and the Mirror of Nature* (New York: Princeton University Press, 1979), p. 176.

Anti-rationalism

Once upon a time, everyone believed in the rationality of science. Philosophers thought they could spell out the 'scientific method' that embodied this rationality. But the history of the philosophy of science in the past century is a tale of the failure of philosophers to do this (logical positivism did not work, neither did simple empiricism, nor falsificationism etc.). Then came a generation of philosophers and historians of science (led by Kuhn and Feyerabend) who pointed out, not just that the philosophers' accounts of scientific method were problematic in their own right, but also that, when we actually look to the practice of scientists, they never seem to do what, according to the rationalistic philosophers, they should be doing. In particular, the pioneering figures during periods of scientific revolution seemed positively to contradict the established scientific procedures.[3]

All this led to the doctrine of the incommensurability of scientific theories. This is the claim that there can be no rational comparison between theories. There is a parallel claim that is made about religious belief: coming to believe is a fundamentally non-rational activity. The thesis of incommensurability has a number of sources, but two central arguments are as follows.

1. *The epistemic argument for incommensurability.* There are no neutral criteria to be used in assessing the merits of rival theories. The rules we follow in rational argument depend upon the theories we already accept. Therefore, any appeal to 'rational' considerations in assessing theories must be circular. It is this argument that figured in the famous ninth chapter of Kuhn's *Structure of Scientific Revolutions* and provides one of the motivations for his development of the idea of the incommensurability of scientific paradigms.

2. *The semantic argument for incommensurability.* Members of

---

3. See, e.g., T. S. Kuhn, *The Structure of Scientific Revolutions* (2nd ed.; Chicago: University of Chicago Press, 1970); and P. K. Feyerabend, *Against Method: Outline of an Anarchistic Theory of Knowledge* (London: Humanities Press, 1975).

different belief systems speak different languages, and there is no possibility of translating the terms of one system into the terms of another. Therefore, it is impossible even to comprehend, let alone rationally assess, what is being said by those who have a different belief system than one's own. This argument also figures, notoriously, in Kuhn's thinking, although he is equivocal about the extent of the limitation on communication.

The incommensurability thesis has led to an entirely new research programme, of a piece with the sociological deconstructivist approach described above. Instead of seeking to assess the history of science as, even in part, a progression towards an objectively true picture of the world, sociologists of science now seek to explain the choices of scientists without reference to such 'dubious' notions as rationality or truth. If the incommensurability thesis is correct, then claims by scientists to possess rational grounds for their theories must be treated as propaganda. There is then a deconstructive task to be done by the sociologist, of showing the real, non-rational determinants of belief that underly the scientist's so-called 'rational' arguments. There has been a similar move towards the sociological study of religion, with the growth of 'religious studies' departments, a focus on phenomenological studies and the decline of theology.

Now in fact we can make pretty good sense of the claims of past scientists. Even at an elementary level, it is comprehensible what Galileo was doing when he opposed the Aristotelians. There may be subtleties of argument that we miss, but it is the task of the historian to try as far as possible to uncover these. Maybe there is a sense in which our understanding will always be 'second-hand', but conceding this is far from allowing that those who operated in other paradigms belong to a different world, with no basis for mutual intelligibility with our own. Kuhn himself allowed for the possibility of partial translation, but did not perhaps concede that this undercuts the grounds for some of his more trenchantly relativist comments.[4]

Once again, considerations of self-reference arise. The case for

4. Kuhn, *Scientific Revolutions*, p. 198.

semantic incommensurability is made by describing two different paradigms, and then seeking to demonstrate that there are terms in one paradigm for which no equivalent term (with either the same sense or reference) can be found in the other. Thus, for example, Kuhn famously argued that it was mistaken to suppose Newtonian mechanics to be a special case of relativistic mechanics, since the very meaning of central terms such as 'mass' changed with the shift from Newtonian to Einsteinian physics, and no translation between these schemes is possible.

The difficulty here is that the very presentation of the case pre-supposes that we can understand the older paradigm well enough to see that the meaning of its terms differs from that of the modern one. But this means that we can in fact get a grasp of the meaning of the terms in the other paradigm. If there was real incommensurability, then we could not even be sure that the other scheme had terms different in meaning from our own. A paradigm incommensurable with our own would be a complete mystery: a string of signs and symbols of which we could make nothing.

It looks as though the semantic argument for the incommensur-ability doctrine rests upon a failure to distinguish between *difference of meaning* (which undoubtedly there may be, since what we believe may affect the meaning we give to terms) and *failure of translation* (which seems far less plausible). Newton did have a different con-ception of inertial mass than we do, following Einstein. Yet we can still make sense of what he believed and recognize the level at which he was still talking about the same property.

So much, then, for semantic incommensurability. What about the epistemic argument? Is it the case that the standards for assess-ing paradigms are internal ones? That different paradigms bring with them different concepts of what a good paradigm should be?

There is no doubt that scientific practice is informed by exem-plars. But if we step back from the particularities of individual controversies, we can perhaps discern something – a set of values, rather than rules, that is common to all scientists. Surprisingly, it was Kuhn himself who introduced the idea that there are in fact a number of 'scientific virtues'. These are values – accuracy, consist-ency, scope, simplicity and fruitfulness – that are sought by all scientists. They are to that extent 'paradigm transcendent'. Nor does Kuhn think these values are merely accidental. It is a presupposition of calling a theory 'scientific' that it is intended to exhibit these characteristics. To be scientific is to be involved in creating a theory that gives an accurate, simple, consistent and fertile account of the data.

There may, as paradigms change, be differences in the relative significance attached to individual values. For example, Aristotelian science looked for descriptive accuracy whilst post-Galilean physics sought a simple model with explanatory and predictive power. It is these differences in weighting that account for the depth and intractability of the debate during periods of scientific revolution. But the fact that there is a framework of shared values to appeal to shows that there is the possibility of a debate that is rational in an objective sense. It is simply not the case, when assessing what counts as scientific method, that 'anything goes', as Feyerabend would have it.

Conclusion and proposals

I advocate a discriminating reponse to postmodernism. We clearly live in a time of rapid, deep-seated cultural change, and it can seem in such a context as though truth and reason represent unobtainable ideals. But if the line of argument I have been pursuing is correct, then we should be wary of the deconstructivist aspirations of postmodernism. An idea of truth as a goal of rational enquiry is eminently defensible, and is indeed presupposed in the discussion to which postmodernists wish to contribute. This is why relativism, sociological deconstructivism and anti-rationalism all seem to be faced with serious conceptual difficulties and problems of self-reference.

On the other hand, there can be no doubt that the concepts of reason, truth and meaning are now subject to such intense discussion that Christians will seem naïve if they assume that it should be obvious to everyone what counts as true, reasonable or meaningful. It may well be that when we get down to the details of thinking about these concepts we shall find that aspects of the postmodern critique have validity. We aspire towards objectivity in reasoning, but, as the postmoderns stress, given human contingency, finitude, and our embeddedness in particular social traditions, in our actual transactions with others we invariably fall short of this ideal.

Perhaps – I offer this tentatively – a way ahead might be found by arguing, as I have done, that the practices of communication and enquiry presuppose that there are standards of correctness and clarity. If there were not, speech acts would simply be noises in the air, rather than genuine assertions, and there would be no sense in the activity of enquiry. But acknowledging the indispensability of the ideal of objectivity is compatible with a clear-eyed recognition of the very subjective nature of many of our actual attitudes and commitments. We may allow that 'postmodernity' is a good description of our actual cultural situation, without allowing the implication of the postmodernist rejection of objectivity as a norm for rational enquiry and truth.

This is all very much in the spirit of 'critical realism': realism, since we do not reject reason, truth or meaning as concepts with an objective basis; critical, since we keep our eyes open to the realities of our human condition which make achievement of that objectivity so hard.

The critical realist will take it that social factors do influence scientists, but that these influences do not rule out the place in an account of science of such epistemic notions as the search for truth. A critical-realist analysis will allow that a full explanation of, for example, why scientists make the decisions they do, will involve reference to the social context in which they work. However, the critical realist does not allow that the scientist's decisions are determined solely by social factors external to the practice of science. For example, a critical realist will allow that factors such as who is providing research funding do not *determine the outcome* of the research – although they will go into determining the topics chosen for research, and, to some extent, the lengths researchers go to in tackling particular difficulties. The difficulties with the deconstructivist analysis suggest that there is much to be said for exploring this way of analysing the place of social factors in science.

The exact implications of a broadly 'critical realist' position need much further exploration (particularly, once we move over to the religious sphere, as regards the vexed issues of hermeneutics and pluralism). There has been a tendency in recent Christian writings for discussions of postmodernism to be phrased in shrill polemical terms, undergirded by a sense that postmodernism constitutes a grave danger to Christianity. I prefer a cooler appraisal, in which we sift through the complex currents of contemporary thought, probing to see whether the claims being made about reason, meaning and truth stand up to the scrutiny of conceptual analysis. The outcome of this process should yield, I have been arguing, a stronger conviction of the ineliminability of notions of objective truth and reason. These are inescapable presuppositions of the very dialogue to which postmodernism contributes. If that is correct, then the Christian engagement with the postmodern agenda in both science and religion need not be trenchantly polemical, but calm, clear thinking and confident.[5]

5. This chapter was originally presented to the Christians in Science conference, London, September 2001. I am grateful to participants for their questions and comments. This chapter was first published in *Science and Christian Belief* 14 (2002), pp. 99–106.

6. MAINTAINING SCIENTIFIC AND CHRISTIAN TRUTHS IN A POSTMODERN WORLD

D. A. Carson

Introduction

I should like to begin by thanking the organizers of this conference for inviting a theologian to participate in a gathering of
eminent scientists. In one sense, of course, that mere fact is a
reflection of our times. The pressures of globalization embrace
much more than the obvious truth that highly diverse cultures
mutually influence one another today. They mean, as well, that at a
time when discrete disciplines are becoming more and more specialized, and in that sense narrower and narrower, there are many
calls for cross-disciplinary explorations, and I suppose that this
conference, in part, is a fruit of such pressures. Ideally, that is a
good thing. We must frankly admit, however, that not a few of the
strident voices that clamour for cross-discplinary study, some of
them more articulate than well advised, are crossing disciplines
with an exuberant glee that seeks to domesticate other domains of
inquiry with the hegemony of postmodern epistemology. That
sums up at least part of the contemporary clash between scientists
and many philosophers of science. 'We know how you think,' the

latter say to the former, 'and so our task is to expose your blind-spots, and teach you the proper way to think.'

Since both Christian confessionalism and science are facing a similar onslaught, it is not too surprising that we should be drawn together in a common defence. For both have something in common: we both think there is such a thing as culture-transcending truth, and that we human beings have some access to it.[1] For those who are both scientists and Christians, it is scarcely surprising that some should wonder if it might be profitable to pool our resources as we engage in this debate.

In this chapter my aims are modest. I propose to offer a summary of the challenge, a survey of responses, and a pair of suggestions.

A summary of the challenge

I had better begin with a statement about postmodernism. The expression is clumsy, the range of its reach ridiculously broad, its usage diverse. But in my view the term is still useful if we recognize that what ties its diverse usages together is the assumption of a shift in epistemology. Modernist epistemology taught us that in every discipline, and in thought itself, there are certain universal foundations on which we can build with methodological rigour;

---

1. Although this is not the place to probe the issue, I suspect that this shared belief in the existence of culture-transcending truth has something to do with the fact that on many university campuses of the Western world there is now a much higher percentage of Christians among lecturers and students who are connected with the 'hard' sciences, or sometimes with mathematics and business, than among lecturers and students who are connected with the arts and the social sciences. More commonly, I think, scientists are inclined to hold that their own disciplines, and perhaps some other hard sciences, deal with truth, but that anything outside such domains have a much looser connection to truth. In short, many scientists are modernist with regard to their own disciplines, and postmodernist elsewhere.

postmodern epistemology insists that both the foundations and the methods are culturally contrived, and therefore the resulting 'knowledge' is necessarily the function of particular cultures. Not only are there many foundations, postmodernism insists, but we should delight in the multiplicity of competing and even mutually contradictory methods. Modernist epistemology thought it could move from the individual finite thinker – the finite 'I' in Descartes's 'I think; therefore I am' – via reason to universal and objective truth. Postmodernism insists that the limitations on any finite knower are so severe that the pursuit of universal and objective truth is a mere chimera; and reason itself, though useful, is simply not up to the task. Modernist epistemology held that uncovering universal truth is both desirable and attainable; postmodern epistemology is quite certain that universal truth is not attainable, doubts that it is desirable, and suggests that pursuit of it is not only an idolatrous waste of time but leads to endless immoral manipulation of others (cf. Foucault's famous denunciation of 'totalization'). Modernism tends to emphasize the intellectual contribution of the individual or of the directed team; postmodernism lays more stress on the social determiners of ostensible 'knowledge'. For the modernist, truth (in an objective sense) is crucial, and both belief and ethics should properly be constrained by it. 'For the postmodernist, there is a rejection of truth as a coherent set of ethical precepts and standards for moral behavior. Truth must be rejected because it is coercive, normative, unambivalent, and implies universals and absolutes.'[2]

How we reached this point in Western civilization is not easily or quickly discovered. Arguably there have been key individuals who, though not properly labeled postmodern, anticipated some of its features: an Immanuel Kant, whose philosophical idealism insisted that the human mind imposes an order on to the data of sense perception not intrinsic to the things being perceived; a Friedrich Nietzsche, whose nihilism left no place for truth or morality in any objective sense, but only for the power of the gun;

---

2. Michael Jessup, 'Truth: The First Casualty of Postmodern Consumerism', *Christian Scholar's Review* 30 (2001), p. 291.

historians who recognize how easily history is turned into propaganda (Hugh Trevor-Roper, for instance, once gave a lecture to German historians in which he frightened his audience by articulating what British historians would now be saying if Hitler had conquered Britain).[3] More importantly, in the twentieth century three or four intellectual movements have coalesced. The German tradition taught us the intrinsic subjectivity of all interpretation, and bequeathed to us the hermeneutical circle; the French tradition, in one side-shoot of linguistics, gave us deconstruction, and taught us, among other things, the power of language and words over the power of science; the American tradition, with its love of anthropology and sociology, gave us the notion that each subculture constitutes an interpretative community;[4] and literary theory across the Western world has moved away from the view that meaning lies in the author of text, to the autonomous authority of the text itself, to arrive, finally, at the view that meaning resides primarily in the reader or knower in interaction with the text.

Although none of these influences can be denied, I suspect that there is a deeper and often unacknowledged commonality behind all of them, namely the intrinsic weakness of *modernist* epistemology, especially in its late form. Early modernist epistemology (i.e. from about 1600 on) was pursued by people who were mostly theists or deists.[5] Descartes himself was a devout Catholic. Despite their formal reliance on reason and the finite self, on foundations

---

3. For this last observation I am indebted to Owen Chadwick, *Acton and History* (Cambridge: Cambridge University Press, 1998), pp. 224–225.

4. In more whimsical moments, I wonder if it would not be wise to turn some of these categories on their head. Most of the American postmodern intellectuals, who hold that all human 'knowledge' is merely a social construct and therefore has no necessary connection with reality, are 1960s graduates who are deeply anti-authoritarian. So perhaps their conviction that postmodern epistemology is the truth (!) is nothing more than a function of their group anti-authoritarianism.

5. Isaac Newton, for instance, was greatly influenced by the Cambridge Platonists. Not for nothing do we find 'Reason is the candle of the Lord' in the windows of Emmanuel College.

and methods, most of them were still operating within the heritage of the Judaeo-Christian tradition. Science itself, as Roger Trigg points out in this volume, was founded on theology – in particular, on the idea that God is a law-giver who has guaranteed order and predictability in the world he created. But as more and more moderns, not least in the domain of science, abandoned the Judaeo-Christian tradition and adopted some form of philosophical naturalism, the God whose omniscience was the reservoir of all knowledge was lost to view. There was no final arbiter, no anchor, no stable reference point. Thus late modernist epistemology, by various routes, became unstable, and sired a bastard we call postmodernism. I choose the term 'bastard' advisedly: my point is that on this reading, modernist epistemology is in fact the progenitor of postmodern epistemology, even if the latter is so unlike his father that he wants to deny family likeness and commit patricide. The implication of this analogy, of course, is that thoughtful Christians should not think of themselves as either modernists or postmoderns in their epistemology. Both systems are far too unstable, far too anthropocentric – idolatrously so.

In the shift from modernism to postmodernism, the relationships between science and confessional Christianity have been undergoing some changes as well. One may usefully distinguish two opposed tendencies in late modernism: imperialism and (early) perspectivalism. Under imperialism, either science tried to control religion or religion tried to control science. One finds the former, for instance, in the hard-edged philosophical naturalism of Richard Dawkins at Oxford, or in Peter Singer at Princeton. Sometimes the stance adopted by science is an ill-defined mysticism that is nonetheless a materialistic scientism, in which nature becomes god, the corpus of empirical knowledge its sacred deposit, the scientists priests and priestesses, and the scientific method almost sacramental religious rites.[6] The same imperialism shows up when we are told that science deals with fact, while religion is about 'faith' – where 'faith' has been implicitly defined to

---

6. I am thinking, for instance, of Ursula Goodenough, *The Sacred Depths of Nature* (Oxford: Oxford University Press, 1998).

mean something like personal religious preference, with no import-ant connection and only accidental connection with reality (an understanding of faith used by no biblical writer).[7] Alternatively, some forms of religious fundamentalism, unable to read texts in line with their intrinsic genres, want all biblical passages to func-tion on the same prosaic plane. Biblical authority can then be used to quash the claimed results of science. Of course, there are devout Christians, scientists and non-scientists alike, who wrestle somewhat more creatively with perceived tensions between the Bible and science. But the tendencies of imperial control, both ways, are well known. Science and Christianity are competing cat-egories, and each is trying to control the other.

Under perspectivalism, especially in its earlier form, science and Christianity look at the same phenomena under incommensurable frameworks. 'The classic illustration of perspectivalism is the dis-tinction between the technical understanding of an end zone scoreboard of the electrical engineer who designed it and the sub-jective understanding of the die-hard football fan looking at it to see if there is hope for his or her team to make a comeback.'[8] Under perspectivalism, the two modes of talking about one thing do not succeed in engaging each other. Each talks past the other; each has little if any impact on the other. But because these are seen as mutually complementary ways of talking about reality, then, at least ideally, each makes its own contribution to *the truth*, the total description of what is.

Thus imperialism and (this older) perspectivalism have this in common: they still operate under the assumption that there is a truth to be discovered and cherished. Under the impact of post-modernism, however, the existence of objective truth began to be questioned. But how could this be so, especially for something as transparently and as eminently successful as science?

Once again, of course, there are antecedents. In the middle of

---

7. See the useful discussion by Andrew Ford, 'Believing in Science', *kategoria* 19 (2001), pp. 21–32.

8. Stanton L. Jones and Mark A. Yarhouse, *Homosexuality: The Use of Scientific Research in the Church's Moral Debate* (Downers Grove: IVP, 2000), p. 14.

the twentieth century, Michael Polanyi was demonstrating, pretty convincingly, that science has intrinsic elements that go way beyond empirical demonstration, elements that he called 'tacit truths'. By the mid-sixties, Thomas Kuhn's theories on the advance of science had called into question the now old-fashioned view that science advances by steady acquisition of knowledge, knowledge grounded in data that are rigorously tested under controlled conditions by different scientists so as to vindicate or disqualify some theory or other.[9] Even if his theory of paradigmatic advance has subsequently been qualified and circumscribed in various ways,[10] he has succeeded in calling into question the popular view (and it was never much more than the popular view) that science builds its edifice of ostensible truth on nothing but the solid foundation of a growing accumulation of indisputable facts.[11]

In this climate it is not surprising that several books detailing scientific blunders have been selling briskly. The one by Robert M.

---

9. Thomas S. Kuhn, *The Structure of Scientific Revolutions* (2nd ed.; Chicago: University of Chicago Press, 1970).

10. E.g. Frederick Suppe (ed.), *The Structure of Scientific Theories* (2nd ed.; Urbana: University of Illinois Press, 1977); Gary Gutting (ed.), *Paradigms and Revolution: Application and Appraisals of Thomas Kuhn's Philosophy of Science* (Notre Dame: University of Notre Dame Press, 1980). Kuhn, of course, is not the only non-rationalist non-realist among the philosophers of science. Others include W. V. O Quine, Paul Feyerabend, Hilary Putnam and Richard Rorty. For a useful survey, see J. P. Moreland, *Christianity and the Nature of Science: A Philosophical Investigation* (Grand Rapids: Baker Book House, 1989), especially ch. 5.

11. Some of the charges that early opponents raised against Kuhn stem from his insistence that two scientific paradigms are marked by *incompatibility*, *incommensurability* and *incomparability*. But his opponents took those words in their ordinary sense; Kuhn is in fact using them in a tighter, more technical sense, so that later discussion has largely exonerated him on this point. See especially Richard Bernstein, *Beyond Objectivism and Relativism: Science, Hermeneutics, and Praxis* (Philadelphia: University of Pennsylvania Press, 1985), pp. 80–87; D. A. Carson, *The Gagging of God: Christianity Confronts Pluralism* (Grand Rapids: Zondervan, 1996), pp. 88–89.

Youngson[12] includes something in the order of sixty major examples, and scores of minor ones. One loves the quotes. Here is Ernest Rutherford: 'Anyone who expects a source of power from the transformation of the atom is talking moonshine.'[13] Or Lord Kelvin writing in 1896: 'I have not the smallest molecule of faith in aerial navigation other than ballooning, or of the expectation of good results from any of the trials we hear of.'[14] What more must be said about phlogiston, the Piltdown man and Isaac Newton's alchemy? Youngson, the author of the book, nevertheless writes out of a framework of modernist epistemology; indeed, he seems committed to philosophical naturalism. If even such as he warn of the blunders of science, it cannot be surprising that postmoderns take the argument even farther. Thus Harry Collins and Trevor Pinch[15] not only treat us to the usual assortment of scientific blunders, but then ask how uncertainties in science are resolved. They deny that resolution comes primarily by ever clearer evidence. They insist, rather, that resolution is achieved through social consensus. For Collins and Pinch belong to a new breed of the movement sometimes labelled 'Sociology of Scientific Knowledge', or the 'Edinburgh School'. This movement holds that scientific knowledge is socially constructed and must exercise no privileged claim to objective truth about the world.

These philosophers of science are often at loggerheads with scientists. But they are catching the wave of postmodern relativism. On the streets, the trend is displayed in countless appeals to alternative medicine (very few of which have been double-blind tested), fortune-telling, astrology, the use of magnets for healing toothache, the beneficent influence of crystals, and the rest.[16]

---

12. *Scientific Blunders: A Brief History of How Wrong Scientists Can Sometimes Be* (New York: Carroll & Graf, 1998).

13. Ibid., p. 61.

14. Ibid., p. 271.

15. *The Golem: What you Should Know about Science* (2nd ed.; Cambridge: Cambridge University Press, 1998).

16. As an aside: since 1999 my wife has been battling cancer. I could not estimate the number of well-meaning people who have contacted us to

Suddenly, then, on the street, and backed up by the intellectuals of postmodernism, confessing Christianity and science find themselves in somewhat parallel positions in society. Many people now think that neither traffic in truth. They traffic in things that may be true for you, or may be true from one perspective (hence, a new perspectivalism has dawned in which multiple perspectives are not mutually complementary of some greater truth, but equally socially constructed and conveying no objective truth); but they do not tell you how things are, and so they have no binding authority on your conscience or on your belief system. You may choose another paradigm; you may opt for another science, another religion, an alternative medicine. It's really up to you or to your social group, your interpretative community. Certainly no-one has the right to say that you are mistaken, or that your religion, or science, is false. To say that is to succumb to intolerance.[17] In fact, one suspects that part of the reason for such an impassioned debunking of science among many sociologists and philosophers is allied to part of the reason for the impassioned debunking of confessional Christianity: the postmodern mood is profoundly anti-authoritarian. Confessional Christianity holds itself above the eddying waters of relativism by insisting on

---

encourage us to try this or that 'alternative medicine'. Although these suggestions have always been well meant, virtually none of them has been double-blind tested; some have been, and have failed the test. Sometimes the suggestion is prefaced by a breathless question, 'Do you believe in alternative medicine?'

17. It would take me too far afield to justify the point, but this sort of charge has become possible only by an astonishing revolution in the meaning of tolerance. It used to be that tolerance was the virtue of the person who held strong views about something or other, but who insisted that those who disagreed had an equal right to defend their views – the sort of stance picked up in the slogan 'I may detest your opinions, but I shall defend to the death your right to speak them.' Today, however, tolerance is the virtue of the person who holds no strong views, except for the strongly held view that it is wrong to hold strong views, or to indicate that someone else might be wrong.

the facts of the central revelation; science holds itself above the same waters of relativism by insisting that its methods and results transcend the relativism of social construction. Both are therefore making authority claims inimical to a generation brought up to be suspicious of 'totalization'.

One does not want to exaggerate the influence of postmodernism in our culture. There are plenty of modernists around who engage in intellectual combat with postmoderns. Some of the roots of postmodernism are withering: in France, for instance, deconstruction is increasingly viewed as passé. But that is a bit different from saying that postmodernism is passé. Critical realism may have a respected place in some intellectual circles, but postmodernism is still preceived to be the innovator, the leading edge, of cultural advancement, especially in the Anglo world. And even if it dissipates faster than I think it will, it is leaving in its wake a very large swathe of Western populations who are suspicious of all truth claims, including those of science and of confessional Christianity.

Its impact on science, science funding, the vision of desirable careers, superstition in the culture – doubtless these are things many of you who attend this conference know more about than I. The impact on confessional Christianity is something I have made an academic and professional interest for about a decade.[18] I shall restrict myself to two observations. (1) In the domain of evangelism, not least university evangelism, the hardest thing to get across these days is the notion of sin. To talk about sin is to say that certain behaviours and attitudes and beliefs are wrong, and that is the one thing postmodernism does not permit us to do. The one heresy postmodernism condemns is the belief that there is heresy; the one immoral act is the articulation of the view that there are immoral acts. But unless people adopt biblical views on sin, transgression, rebellion, trespass, guilt and shame, it is virtually impossible to articulate faithfully the good news of Jesus Christ. If we cannot agree on what the problem is, we most certainly cannot agree on what the solution is. (2) Within the church, not least in home Bible studies and discussion groups and the

---

18. See my *The Gagging of God*, referred to above in n. 11.

like, when some interpretation of screwball proportions is advanced, leaders are more and more likely to say something soothing such as, 'That's an interesting insight, Charles. Does anyone else have anything to contribute?' It has become out of vogue for the leader to ask Charles how or where he finds his so-called 'insight' in the text, or to get others in the group to criticize Charles, in the hope of bringing the entire group to a common view of what the text means. Within my own discipline, one comes across more and more books with titles such as *The Open Text, Reading Sacred Texts Through American Eyes, The Liberating Exegesis*. But the question sooner or later becomes this: How can Scripture ever reform us if by our 'liberating exegesis' we are invariably able to make it say what is comfortable to us, if we are always able to domesticate it in line with the predilections of our own interpretative community?

The challenges we face are deep and complicated.

A survey of responses

Apart from piecemeal attacks of one sort or another, responses can usefully be grouped (at the risk of oversimplification) into three camps.

1. There is a sizeable and growing literature that attacks postmodern epistemology from the standpoint of an unreconstructed, or only slightly modified, modernism. In the domain of science, one thinks, for instance, of the blistering and highly amusing book by Paul Gross and Norman Levitt, *Higher Superstition: The Academic Left and Its Quarrels with Science*.[19] One of the two authors is a physicist; the other, a mathematician. Both, apparently, are philosophical materialists. As a compendium of the worst absurdities in postmodernism, *as seen from the perspective of intelligent and informed modernism*, the book is priceless, and fun to read as well. But I doubt that it will convince anyone in the postmodern camp. Or again, the recent book edited by Noretta Koertge, *A House Built on*

---

19. Baltimore: Johns Hopkins University Press, 1994.

Sand: Exposing Postmodernist Myths about Science,[20] is a book that no-one working in the area should ignore. It will certainly make a lot of scientists feel better. But frankly, I doubt if most of the contributors have a really good grasp of what they are criticizing. Better put, they score a lot of points out of the absurdities that abound in the popular and pretentious postmodern literature, without really responding to the best of it. It is not too difficult to expose the idiocies of erroneous feminist views of the macho sperm and the bashful egg (ch. 4), the misreading of the cold fusion debacle by Collins and Pinch (ch. 8) or the false and romantic view of alchemists propounded by some feminists (ch. 16). But the fundamental division between modernists and postmoderns is a conflict of world view, where the distinction in world view is primarily epistemological. And these questions Koertge and her contributors do not address.

Similarly in the domain of literary criticism or of theology: there is a growing literature that I do not need to detail here that attacks postmodern approaches from the vantage point of an unreconstructed conservatism. Some of these publications provide reams of useful material. But few of them deal with the fundamental world-view issues, the central problems of epistemology. For even at the level of brute experience, globalization has forced us to recognize that there is at least some truth (if I may use that word) in postmodern claims. Sub-Saharan black African theologians tend to see far more corporate metaphors in the Pauline corpus than we individualists do in the West; acupuncture developed in China, not here; some cultures are more given to narrative, others to abstract analysis. In fact, at one level thoughtful Christians will want to go *farther* than postmoderns: we Christians admit not only to the subjectivity inherent in interpretation bound up with our finiteness, but subjectivity inherent in interpretation bound up with our fallenness. The rationalism and emphasis on autonomy that characterized late modernism has not, after all, always been a friend of Christians. Marxism was thought by millions to embrace a scientific approach to history, and Aryan

20. Oxford: Oxford University Press, 1998.

supremacy finds its roots in scientific discussions of race stemming from the nineteenth century.[21]

Apart from such considerations, this first set of approaches
sounds defensive, old fashioned, angry, even when it says some
true things. In other words, quite apart from the fact that (I would
argue) a thoughtful Christian epistemology should not buy into
either modernism or postmodernism holus-bolus, there is a
simple, pragmatic consideration: if all our appeals are to yesterday's epistemology, we will be perceived to be yesterday's people.
And I doubt that will strengthen our cause.

2. A second set of responses simply gives in to postmodern
epistemology. For these thinkers, modernist epistemology has been
successfully debunked; postmodernism is essentially right. And
that has a bearing on how we think of both science and religion.

Consider, for example, one of the recent books by Stan
Grenz.[22] Grenz buys deeply into postmodern epistemology, so
deeply that he has a very hard time talking about the truth of the
gospel at all, or about the truth of anything else. He thinks the way
ahead is to reshape evangelicalism to reflect postmodernism. I
have discussed that book in some detail elsewhere.[23] For my
present purposes, I will focus briefly on his chapter on science.[24] I
will not detail his entire argument.[25] Suffice it to say that about

21. See especially discussions in Jacques Barzun, *From Dawn to Decadence: 500
Years of Western Cultural Life* (San Francisco: HarperCollins, 1999).

22. Stanley J. Grenz, *Renewing the Center: Evangelical Theology in a Post-Theological
Era* (Grand Rapids: Baker Book House, 2000).

23. See my review chapter in Millard J. Erickson, Paul Kjoss Helseth and
Justin Taylor (eds.), *Modern Reformation. Reclaiming the Center: Confonting
Evangelical Accommodation in Postmodern Times* (Wheaton: Crossway, 2004),
pp. 33–55.

24. Ch. 7, 'Theology and Science after the Demise of Realism'.

25. I might mention one point. In his discussion of scientific method, Grenz
marshalls quotations from scientists who disagree as to the exact nature
of the so-called scientific method, to draw the conclusion that there is no
such thing, in order to justify the conclusion that there is *no* proper
grounding of 'truth' in scientific method since there is no such thing as a

halfway through this chapter, Grenz summarizes Thomas Kuhn, and then argues that from a paradigmatic approach to scientific revolution it is but a small step to the conclusion that 'a paradigm entails a social construction of reality'.[26] Grenz then marshalls an array of authors to justify this conclusion, starting with Michael Mulkay's book *Science and the Sociology of Knowledge*,[27] concluding that whether scientists admit it or not, they *are* theologians. Finally, Grenz returns to questions put forward by George Lindbeck: Does the move to nonfoundationalism (i.e. to postmodernism) entail a final and total break with metaphysical realism?[28] That comes right to the point. But what is Grenz's answer? Here it is: 'Formulated in this manner, the question is both improper and ultimately unhelpful. It might be better stated, How can a post-foundationalist theological method lead to statements about a world beyond our formulations?'[29]

But why is the question either improper or 'ultimately unhelpful'? It is improper only if postmodernism in its strongest sense is true, and we cannot know anything 'true' about the real world. But in that case, the question is not unhelpful; it should merely be answered, 'Yes, there is a final and total break with metaphysical realism.' When Grenz goes on to say that the question might be better stated another way, he is indulging in sleight of hand. For the alternative he offers is not the same question, phrased another

---

stable scientific method. The most reflective of scientists have always recognized the limitations of 'scientific method' and the adaptations that are made to particular 'methods' to accommodate each discipline, not to mention the interplay between controlled experiment, scientific theory and tests of theory (see, e.g., David Lindley, *The End of Physics: The Myth of a Unified Theory* (New York: Basic Books, 1993). But Grenz, like all post-modernists, takes any admission of weakness or incompleteness to be a confession that there really is no such thing as objective truth in scientific discipline.

26. Grenz, *Renewing the Center*, p. 238.

27. London: George Allen & Unwin, 1979.

28. Grenz, *Renewing the Center*, p. 245.

29. Ibid.

way; he has simply refused to answer the first question and has asked an alternative question, namely, 'How can a postfoundationalist theological method lead to statements about a world beyond our formulations?' And his answer to that question, influenced by Pannenberg, says, in effect, that the only kind of realism of which we can speak is 'eschatological realism', with reference to the universe as it will be. There are several muddled confusions here, too, but for the moment I shall have to pass them by.[30]

So confessional Christianity and science, in Grenz's view, are both in the same hopper, precisely because postmodern epistemology governs both. Yet so far as the academic world is concerned, in some ways they have been forced into this hopper from different sides. Before widespread appeal to postmodern epistemology, science was widely thought to be dealing with facts and truth (and most scientists still think that today), while religion was widely thought to be dealing with subjective experiences of the numinous, with minimal truth content. That's not how confessional Christians saw things, of course, but it was how science and Christianity were widely perceived in the university world. But now

---

30. In fairness, Grenz then goes on to say that Christian theologians have some similarities to the so-called critical realists, in that we maintain 'a certain undeniable givenness to the universe' (p. 245). But what the right hand gives, the left hand takes away, for Grenz argues that this givenness is 'not that of a static actuality existing outside of, and co-temporally with, our socially and linguistically constructed reality. It is not the objectivity of what some might call "the world as it is." Rather, seen through the lenses of the gospel, the objectivity set forth in the biblical narrative is the objectivity of the world as God wills it, as is suggested in the petition of the Lord's Prayer, "Your will be done on earth as it is in heaven" (Matt. 6:10)' (p. 246). And thus Grenz segues into eschatology. But the confusion of categories is palpable. How does Grenz *now* know what the *eschatological* reality will be? If he replies, 'By revelation,' then what stops us from knowing, in measure, what the world *now* is, by revelation? In any case, the Bible does not encourage us to think that the eschatological world is more real than the present one, but that it is sinless.

that both science and Christianity have been unceremoniously plopped into the hopper of postmodernism, both have been relativized. Nevertheless, because they have approached the hopper from opposite sides, science and Christianity sometimes evaluate the impact of postmodernism a little differently.

Science tends to view the hopper with deep misgivings because it demands that science give up its claim to objective truth, to meaningful realism. Conservative Christians, who hold that the claims of Christianity are no less true, perceive the same danger, but some are tempted to think that postmodernism offers to Christianity more opportunity than threat. When the university was controlled by modernist epistemology, and the so-called truth claims of Christianity were summarily dismissed as the product of 'faith' (abysmally defined), Christianity as a system of thought could be marginalized. Now, it is argued, precisely because *every* perspective has the right to be heard, and *every* stance reflects a world view and an interpretative community, Christianity has a place at the table after all, and may be welcomed back into the cultural discussion. The best brief response to this perception came from Os Guinness in 1994:

> Christians who have prematurely declared victory over modernity are in for a cruel disillusionment . . . It is true that modernism was openly hostile to religion and that postmodernism is much more sympathetic on the surface. But it is naive to ignore the price tag. Postmodern openness allows all religions and beliefs to present and practise their claims. But it demands the relinquishing of any claims to unique, absolute, and transcendent truth. For the Christian the cost is too high.[31]

3. The third set of responses belongs to the category of critical realism. Stanton Jones and Mark Yarhouse write:

> We are *critical realists*, which means that we believe that there is a real world out there where it is possible to know and know truly (hence,

---

31. Os Guinness, *Fit Bodies, Fat Minds: Why Evangelicals Don't Think and What To Do About It* (Grand Rapids: Baker Book House, 1994), pp. 61, 108.

'realism'), but we also believe that our theories and hypotheses about that world, and our religious presuppositions and beliefs about reality, color and shape our capacity to know the world (hence, 'critical realism').[32]

But this critical realism has many faces. It is an expression that covers a wide range of approaches. They have this in common: they all claim that we can know something about the real world, but that our claims are modest, owing not least to our finiteness, our capacity for distortion. Some philosophical materialists are abandoning the rawest form of modernism for this more nuanced stance.[33] Other self-defined critical realists use the expression to allow for miracles and acts of divine self-disclosure, for ways of knowing in a God-centred universe. And I confess that this is the stance with which I resonate.

And that brings me to my concrete suggestions.

A pair of suggestions

The topic assigned me requires that we consider how to maintain scientific and Christian truths in a postmodern world. In this last section it might have been useful to launch into a survey of all the helpful suggestions that have been put forward, for in fact there have been many. They include, for instance, learning how to demonstrate the inadequacies of both modernist and postmodern epistemology, which demonstration opens up a space for something more mature and more plausible; considering how the existence of an omniscient, self-revealing God necessarily changes one's approach to epistemology; focusing on world-view formation; working through what can be known *of God* in a finite and fallen world; demonstrating with myriads of examples how much

---

32. Jones and Yarhouse, *Homosexuality*, p. 15.

33. E.g. Michael Shermer, 'Colorful Pebbles and Darwin's Dicturm', *Scientific American* 284.4 (2001), p. 38, who argues that science is 'an exquisite blend of data and theory'.

can be communicated from one person to another, or from one culture to another, even though the task is not always easy; and much more. But here I want to focus on two points.

1. It is a great help to acknowledge that no truth which human beings may articulate can ever be articulated in a culture-transcending way – but that does not mean that the truth thus articulated does not transcend culture. This point is extraordinarily important, and often overlooked. If we articulate a truth in English, since all language is a cultural artefact our articulation of the truth is culturally constrained. But that does not mean that the same truth cannot be articulated in another culture, often in another way.

The point is perhaps most easily explained by appealing to an example. In 1980 Charles Kraft published a book with the title *Christianity in Culture: A Study in Dynamic Biblical Theologizing in Cross-Cultural Perspective.*[34] In that book Kraft argues for an approach to the Bible that would shift how we use it in missionary work. The Bible, he says, is really a book of case studies. It is therefore imperative that we apply the appropriate case study to a particular culture. If a missionary is called to a culture that practises polygamy, for instance,[35] surely it is better to begin with David or some other Old Testament figure who enjoyed more than one wife and who was blessed by God, rather than to turn to the monogamy of the New Testament. Each culture should have the 'case study' applied to it that seems to fit best. If then we ask if there are certain things in the Bible that transcend all cultures, that are demanded of people in any culture if they are to become Christians, things that are certainly not endemic to that culture apart from the coming of Christianity, Kraft replies that there are not many, but there are a few. He thinks that they include a handful of crucial confessional statements such as 'Jesus is Lord' and 'Jesus died and rose again the third day.' These are truly transcultural and non-negotiable elements to Christianity.

---

34. Maryknoll: Orbis, 1980.
35. Kraft himself spent a couple of years in Liberia.

Quite apart from Kraft's doubtful understanding of the Bible as a book of case studies, and quite apart from the tricky question of how he knows that certain statements in the Bible are transcultural and not others, his conclusions are both too open and too closed, too liberal and too conservative. They are too open, too liberal, in the way that his approach will allow most cultures to get 'off the hook' in too many areas. Wherever the Bible seems to say something a bit constraining or rebuking, we smartly turn to another part of the Bible and thus escape the sanctions. It is a very comforting method. Such an approach, however, will have little or no power in reformation. But his conclusions are also too closed, too conservative. He holds that certain statements, such as 'Jesus is Lord' or 'Jesus died and rose again the third day', manage to transcend culture. But strictly speaking, of course, they do not; no statement uttered by a human being can. For a start, such statements are inevitably spoken in one language or another – and if in this language, it is not in that language, and thus the statement is culturally constrained.

The significance of this point is clearly seen if we imagine an ill-informed missionary from the West somehow learning to speak fluent Thai, and flying to Bangkok and boldly declaring, in Thai, to those leaving a Buddhist temple, 'Jesus is Lord.' What will these people think he is saying? Apart from the strangeness of the scene, they will hear him to be affirming, among other things, that Jesus is inferior to Gautama the Buddha. That, of course, is not what he thinks he has been saying. But within their world view, when a person reaches the highest level of exaltation, as Gautama did, nothing can be predicated of him: he is neither good nor bad, hot nor cold, lord nor unlord and so on. So if someone says, 'Jesus is Lord,' he has predicated something of Jesus, and clearly Jesus has not advanced as far as the Buddha.

If that is all there is to be said, postmodernists might well rub their hands in glee and smirk, 'Carson is finally catching on. Human beings cannot escape the constraints of culture. Even the utterances we most highly cherish cannot escape being culture-bound.' True. But something more must be said. That same missionary, if he or she takes the time to learn the culture as well as the language, and to communicate the Bible's storyline and unpack its theological assumptions and asseverations instead of mere clauses, can in time make clear to Thais, in their own language, what we mean when we confess 'Jesus is Lord' in English – indeed, in substantial measure what Paul meant when he wrote 'Jesus is Lord' in Greek (Romans 10:9).

In short, no truth that human beings may articulate can ever be articulated in a culture-transcending way – but that does not mean that the truth thus articulated does not transcend culture. Kraft's attempt to secure a handful of transcultural Christian confessions fails, not because there are no transcultural truths, but because whatever transcultural truth there is cannot be communicated in a culture-transcending way. To put the matter this way means that simply because all utterances are conveyed within some cultural matrix or other does not mean that knowledge of culture-transcending truth is impossible.[36] And that is so for both science and religion – or for any other domain, for that matter.

2. The overwhelming majority of postmodern writers have assumed the truth of an indefensible but usually unacknowledged antithesis. If you allow that antithesis to stand unchallenged, a competent postmodern will almost always win the debate. If you destroy that antithesis, the postmodern does not have much left on which to stand.

What is that controlling but often unacknowledged antithesis? It is this: *Either we can know something absolutely and omnisciently, or we must give up claims to knowledge of objective truth.* The reason why that antithesis is so dangerous, of course, is that you can always show that finite human beings know nothing absolutely and omnisciently: there is always more to know, either in the thing itself or in its relations with everything else. So if the antithesis is left to stand, and the first of the two alternatives is ruled out owing to

---

36. The point is implicitly recognized in many discussions of revelation and accommodation. Calvin, for example, who holds that the Bible is the Word of God, insists nevertheless that it was an act of accommodation for God to reveal truth in human language, embedded as any language is in the limitations of finitude that necessarily characterize all human cultures.

human finiteness, only one alternative remains: we are left to wallow in the mire of relativism.

It is far better, I think, to argue that finite and fallen human beings may know some true things partially, even if nothing exhaustively. Then the antithesis is destroyed.

Certainly that is much closer to common experience of know-ledge acquisition. Students begin to study some new discipline, whether quantum mechanics or *koinē* Greek, and initially their progress is very slow. Every new idea takes a while to absorb. Paradigms or equations must be memorized and understood; then they must be utilized in examples and problems. But after years of study, all those elementary steps are just that, elementary. Far more complex structures or arguments may be absorbed or evaluated at much greater speeds. None of this assumes an absolute mastery of the discipline, an omniscient grasp of the discipline. In fact, higher levels of learning within the discipline will disclose how many things are still disputed. But the progress in knowledge acquisition does suggest that some things may be known truly even if nothing is known exhaustively.

Various models have been deployed to make this point clear.[37] Imagine a common graph. On the positive x-axis are measured years, in a strictly linear fashion. On the positive y-axis is measured the distance of some human's understanding of something or other from a perfect and exhaustive understanding of that thing – or, otherwise put, from the reality itself. Suppose, then, that we asked a 5-year-old lad, from a Christian home, why he believed that God loved him. Assuming he is bright and well taught by his parents, he may well reply by quoting the words of John 3:16. Of course, he would have no knowledge of the Greek text; he would know nothing of debates over the meaning of 'world' or of the relative claims of 'only begotten' or 'one and only'; he would know nothing of debates over the various Greek verbs for 'to love'; he would not have thought through how this text is to be linked to another text in the same chapter, a bare twenty verses on, that

---

37. I have discussed some of them in *The Gagging of God* – including the one described in the following lines.

speaks of God's wrath; and so on. Still, his appeal to John 3:16 does answer the question; he has in some measure answered the question correctly. He does not think that John 3:16 describes the virgin birth, or reflects on the sex life of sea turtles. His choice of John 3:16 shows that he understands it well enough as an appropriate answer to the question that was put to him. We might say, then, that the lad's answer is positioned fairly high up in the top right-hand quadrant of the graph, and only five units removed from the y-axis. Doubtless his knowledge of John 3:16 still leaves a great deal to be desired.

By the time he has graduated with a degree in the classics and another in theology, however, his position on the graph is perhaps twenty-five units from the y-axis (he is 25 years of age), and much closer to the x-axis. After completing a doctoral dissertation on the Fourth Gospel's understanding of the love of God against the Jewish background, the graph of his increase in knowledge is still heading in the same general direction. In fact, the graph is tracing out an asymptotic approach to the x-axis. Even fifty billion years into eternity (if we may speak of eternity in the categories of time), the graph that represents the proximity of his knowledge to the actual reality never touches the x-axis, because omniscience is an incommunicable attribute of God. It is simply not available to finite beings. But to argue that finite beings therefore cannot truly know *anything* is decidedly unhelpful. That conclusion is true *only if one initially assumes that the only meaningful way of speaking of 'knowledge' and 'objective truth' occurs when the knowledge belongs to Omniscience, when the truth is what God alone knows it to be.* Certainly in some discussions that is a useful point to make. But to run from that truism to the commonly assumed antithesis adopted by postmodernists is a leap too far: *either we can know something absolutely and omnisciently, or we must give up claims to knowledge of objective truth.* For finite human beings (the 'we' in the antithesis) can know some things truly, even if partially. To appeal to the standards of omniscience to eliminate the possibility of true but partial knowledge among finite and fallen beings made in his image is to erect a false standard. To argue that either we can know something absolutely and omnisciently, or we must accept the status of all human knowledge as lost in a sea of relativism, is a counsel of despair grounded in an indefensible antithesis.[38]

I have not discussed all the wrong turns that our biblical scholar might take in the pursuit of his understanding of John 3:16, any more than I have discussed the wide variety of missteps and accidents that sometimes go into scientific advance.[39] Such phenomena will embarrass us only if we pretend that all advance in knowledge must be in a straight line of improvement – and that is precisely what no-one should claim who wants to discuss the acquisition of (true) knowledge by finite and fallen beings. My point in this section is simpler: finite beings usefully speak of knowing some things truly, even if they are the first to acknowledge that we cannot know anything exhaustively. To deny this on the ground that we do not enjoy omniscience is to turn the merest truism (namely, we are not omniscient) into a tautology (finite beings cannot enjoy omniscient knowledge). But it does not reliably address the question as to how human beings may know some things truly.

Concluding reflections

We need to be modest, I think, in our expectations about how well our arguments will succeed with the public at large. So much is

---

38. This is not meant to be the beginning of a responsible Christian epistemology. It is merely an attempt to debunk an assumption that has corrupted too much of the debate. Of course, if metaphysics deals with questions of truth, and epistemology deals with questions of knowledge and certainty, then the graph I have drawn suggests that the question being addressed concerns the relation between metaphysics and epistemology – and that presupposes, rightly, that to deal at length with how much 'knowledge' finite human beings can have of the 'truth' involves fundamental assumptions in the domain of metaphysics. Arguably the progressive turns, in the wake of the Enlightenment, toward progressively more autonomous reason, have generated a fair bit of the problem. But such matters cannot be explored here.

39. See ch. 7, by Colin Russell, in this volume.

shaped by our mass media, most of whose spokespersons are as abysmally ill-read in science as in theology. Moreover, one of the effects of globalization and rapid communication is what the sociologists call instant reflexivity. Fickle moods can be changed almost instantly as some reflexive response to a new stimulus is called forth in a torrent of trendiness. It is very difficult for either good science or good theology to prosper and act wisely under such conditions.[40]

But we must try. We must try with confidence in the God whose Word holds sway, and who demands an accounting of all of us, measured much more in terms of faithfulness and poverty of spirit than in terms of success and triumphalism.[41]

© D. A. Carson, 2005

---

40. One wonders if the events of 9/11 will do more to overturn the pretensions of postmodern arrogance than all the books that have been written since the 1980s. For suddenly people are willing to talk about 'evil' again (even if some of the talk is not very probing or realistic).

41. This chapter was first published in *Science and Christian Belief* 14 (2002), pp. 107–122.

7. HAS SCIENCE ANYTHING TO DO WITH HUMAN VALUES?

Colin A. Russell

Introduction

The notion that science might depend on values external to itself obviously assumes recognized boundaries between what might be properly termed 'science' and what might not. Its dependence on theological belief has been frequently discussed, but what of other values that might be understood as generally 'human'? Where – if at all – do the boundaries lie?

This first became a major and visible issue in the furnace of scientific controversy after about 1600 when one's opponents could be accused of transgressing beyond the boundaries and allowing themselves to import foreign values into chemistry, physics or whatever was being presented as science or natural knowledge. Times without number scientific rivals have been accused of prejudice, of confusing fact with hypothesis and of belonging to the 'wrong' school of thought. Being of a different nationality might be bad enough, as when a complaint was made of the French that they rejected Dalton's atomic theory 'for the same reason that vaccination was so ill received in that country, –

because it was discovered by an Englishman'.[1] The speculative system of romanticism known as *Naturphilosophie* was blamed by the Swedish chemist Berzelius[2] and the German chemist Liebig[3] for scientific errors at about the same time.

Yet all this assumed that, ideally, science should be independent of human values. Only in our own time has a serious effort been made to present a radically alternative view, and to promote a revisionist view of the nature and history of science. This 'strong programme' sees science as simply a social construct and therefore no longer a custodian of any special kind of 'truth' about nature. It was one of the most distinctive precursors of contemporary postmodernism, for implicit in the postmodernists' agenda is the denigration of special 'truth claims' in general, and particularly by science. Their denial of a 'metanarrative' or 'big story' is as damaging to science as it is to history.

To people hostile to science this has been welcome news: a further taming of the monster. As one young historian of science rather rashly said to me during an inspection of his department, his great aim was to use history as a tool for 'cutting science down to size'. To those whose life is spent in science, such views are not merely offensive; they are virtually incomprehensible, but that does not prevent their wide circulation.

At issue is the nature – and future – of science. To appreciate where we are now, we must recall that in connection with our understanding of natural phenomena there are two polarized views.

At one extreme stands the positivist, scientistic notion that we *can* know the truth about Nature, but only by rigorous testing in the laboratory, observatory, field-station and so on. Here can be found true objectivity. Science is thus *nothing but a body of knowledge*

---

1. Anon., 'Account of Progress in Foreign Science', *Quarterly Journal of Science* 12 (1822), p. 322.

2. S. Lindroth, 'Berzelius and his Time', in E. M. Melhado and T. Frangsmyr (eds.), *Enlightenment Science in the Romantic Era* (Cambridge: Cambridge University Press, 1992), pp. 9–34.

3. W. H. Brock, *Justus von Liebig, the Chemical Gatekeeper* (Cambridge: Cambridge University Press, 1997).

about the natural world, built up by painstaking observation and experiment.
All other knowledge depends, more or less, on emotion, hunches,
superstition, myth or whatever, and as such is inferior in quality to
scientific knowledge. This is an old idea, owing much to the
French philosopher Auguste Comte and to the scientific naturalists who gathered round T. H. Huxley and sought to exalt the
social status of science at the expense of other groups, notably
religious ones. It is also reflected in the Victorian emphasis on
'facts' (as advocated by Mr Gradgrind in Dickens's novel *Hard
Times*). The scientist, therefore, if not a superior person, is certainly engaged in a superior kind of activity. He should receive
special admiration and respect in society.

There was an almost inevitable reaction. After the Second
World War some sociologists began to argue (the 'strong programme') that not only are all scientific theories socially
determined, but also that there is little other basis for them. For
example, Latour believes we must abolish the distinction between
science and fiction because nothing extraordinary and nothing
'scientific' ever happens in laboratories.[4] Collins makes the even
more remarkable assertion that 'the natural world has a small or
non-existent role in the construction of scientific knowledge'.[5] In
knocking the scientists from their privileged pedestal, they found
themselves making claims more extreme than those of their most
voluble opponents. For these sociologists, *science is nothing but a
social epiphenomenon.*

A coalition emerged of historians, sociologists, feminists and
others who wished to rewrite the history of science in a postmodern way, often in the guise of Science and Technology Studies (STS).
All agreed that the past should not be viewed through the lenses of
the present, and that 'Whiggish' historiography was to be abhorred.
Instead of being Whigs, they have earned for themselves the

---

4. See B. Latour and S. Woolgar, *Laboratory Life: The Social Construction of
Scientific Facts* (London: Sage, 1979); B. Latour, *Science in Action* (Milton
Keynes: Open University Press, 1987).

5. H. Collins, 'Stages in the Empirical Programme of Relativism', *Social
Studies of Science* 11 (1981), p. 3.

unendearing term 'Prigs', implying a 'narrow-minded superiority' in making a virtue of their ignorance of modern science.[6] Part of the problem lies in the fact that such views are usually, but not always, taught by sociologists or historians with little or no experience of scientific research, a situation that has been deplored by, among many others, the American historian of physics Stephen Brush.[7]

The situation in the 1980s has been caustically described by my former colleague Arthur Marwick. He states that postmodernists

> overran much of English Literature and established the puppet state of Cultural Studies. They walked, without even token resistance, into History and Philosophy of Science, being embraced by weeping Sociologists; flamboyant hopes of conquering the high peaks and cantons of Natural Sciences were, however, exposed as ill-conceived. Parts of the marcher lands of History fell easily, though it was here that some of the nastier fighting took place.[8]

Since then many historians have discovered the inability of postmodernism to cope with the chains of cause and effect that they observe, or to permit large-scale analyses of great events. The disillusion has been reinforced by the strange affair known as the Sokal hoax. In 1996 the physicist Alan Sokal published a paper in the journal *Social Text* (a periodical favoured by the cultural studies community). Using the language of the social constructionist and the jargon of postmodernism he set out a series of absurd propositions (including one that π was neither universal nor a constant).[9] The editors failed to recognize that here was a hoax, and one with a considerable sting in its tail. By publishing it, they revealed something of the credulity and gullibility of those

6. E. Harrison, 'Whigs, Prigs and Historians of Science', *Nature* 329 (1987), pp. 213–224.

7. S. G. Brush, 'Scientists as Historians', *Osiris* 10 (1995), pp. 215–231.

8. A. Marwick, 'All Quiet on the Post-Modern Front', *Times Literary Supplement* 23, February 2001.

9. A. D. Sokal, 'Transgressing the Boundaries: Towards a Transformative Hermeneutics of Quantum Gravity', *Social Text* 46.7 (1996), pp. 217–252.

who saw science just as a social construct, and so fell for Sokal's ruse. Very soon Sokal disclosed elsewhere that his purpose was serious. He wanted to draw the academic Left from an irrational, relativistic anti-science stance.[10] His hoax created enormous ripples and people are still writing about it.

Both views described above are extremist, both are unattractive for their portraits of scientists either as cultural imperialists or as deluded fools, and both suffer from the fallacy of reductionism ('nothing-buttery'). Life is simply not like that, with every phenomenon explicable in only one set of terms. We require a far more sophisticated and mature analysis that does not ignore vast areas of human experience simply because they do not fit into a preordained scheme.

We shall therefore look at two aspects of science and human values.

Where human values do impinge on science

By 'human values' are meant values held by human beings either as members of a particular culture or society, or just as individuals. Many papers and books address the question as to whether such values impinge on science in general.[11] It may be helpful to examine some specifics.

First, there is the *initial choice of science as a sphere of activity*. The basic question at the start of a scientific career is 'Why choose to do science in the first place?' Among the answers are many that are rooted in ideals outside science itself. They include:

- *Social kudos*: in the nineteenth century many chose chemistry because of its manifest power over nature, giving to its adherents a rise in social status. Later, biology became

---

10. A. D. Sokal, 'A Physicist Experiments with Cultural Studies', *Lingua Franca* 6.4 (1996), pp. 62–64.

11. E.g. R. E. Vander Vennen, 'Is Scientific Research Value-Free?', *Journal of American Scientific Affiliation* 27.3 (1975), pp. 107–111.

prestigious because of its supposed power to offer explanations that had hitherto been provided by the church. Desperate attempts to acquire social status through science were evident in the invention and promotion of the 'conflict' myth.[12]

• *Self-fulfilment*: many modern scientists, from Faraday onwards, have pursued science at least in part because of the sheer satisfaction afforded.

• *Power of example*: countless young people have been influenced toward science by the example of good science teachers or by seeing scientists at work.

• *Theology*: Bacon articulated the view that science was to be pursued for the greater glory of God and the good of man's estate, and many Christians have echoed those values in the centuries following.

Then, secondly, there is *selection of research topic*. Here one finds a bewildering variety of determinants, from the intentions of one's supervisor and the availability of grant money, to high matters of ethics and even theology. The subject is discussed in detail elsewhere.[13] A third way in which science and human values interact is in one's *behaviour in the laboratory*, a topic addressed in chapter 8 of this volume.

When we come to a fourth interaction, we approach a far more sensitive issue. This is the question of *how scientists construct theories*. Here indeed comes the crunch, for a scientific theory is often taken (wrongly) as a description of how the world really is. At the very least it should be taken as a tentative statement of the truth about nature. But it seems that human values may intrude rather more than is sometimes expected.

• Theories may emerge from individual convictions or experiences unrelated to science. The proposal by Copernicus of a

---

12. C. A. Russell, 'The Conflict Metaphor and its Social Origins', *Science and Christian Belief* 1 (1989), pp. 3–26.

13. C. A. Russell, 'What Lessons from the Past Aid our Choice?', *Perspectives in Science and Christian Faith* 53.4 (2001), pp. 241–247.

heliocentric cosmos (1543) reflected his Neoplatonic background and a certain disenchantment with Aristotle; he made very few astronomical observations and all the empirical evidence came centuries later. In chemistry Kekulé is famous for having first perceived his hexagonal structure for the benzene molecule in a dream (1861–62, published 1865), hardly a conventional route to scientific data. It has even been said that Heisenberg's Uncertainty Principle arose from the need for physicists to distance themselves from the much-criticized scientific arrogance in Germany after 1918. And so on.

- Theories may emerge from a consensus, 'atmosphere' and the like. Hence the large number of priority disputes when different people independently come to something like the same conclusions. These may arise from inventions, as with the constant battery of Daniell and Becquerel; or from great theoretical schemes, as in the cases of Darwin versus Wallace over evolution, or Frankland versus Kekulé over valency. In the last case, H. E. Armstrong observed in a statement of wider generality, 'The problem was in the air . . . chemists everywhere had it in mind.'[14]

- Theory construction can be inhibited by a 'negative' atmosphere of thought. Such was the fate of the atomic theory in France, which was frowned upon by the chemist Marcellin Berthelot because it smacked too much of faith and even religion. A highly influential politician who became Minister of Public Instruction in 1886 and later Foreign Secretary, Berthelot virtually forbade the use of the word 'atom', even in discussions of organic chemistry, where it is almost indispensable. Since the disciples of Berthelot succeeded him in key government positions, chemical theory fared badly in certain French institutions until the Second World War.[15]

- Theories may well be shaped by the current paradigm (Kuhn).

---

14. H. E. Armstrong, 'Oration at the Lancastrian Frankland Society', *Lancaster Guardian*, 26 January 1934.

15. Georges Bram and Nguyên Trong Anh, 'The Difficult Marriage of Theory and French Organic Chemistry in the 20th Century', *Journal of Molecular Structure (Theochem)* 424 (1998), pp. 201–206.

This is much more than a mere 'climate of opinion'; it is an intellectual framework that survives until it collapses under the weight of its own inadequacies and then gives place to another (a scientific 'revolution'). This was the case for Newtonianism until the coming of relativity, and there are many other instances. Since these paradigms are agreed by the scientific community it can be said that here society, in the shape of the scientific establishment, is profoundly affecting the way in which theories in science are generated. The problem is that, since the paradigms usually work so well, many scientists are unaware that alternative paradigms might well lead to different interpretations and theories. However, the more history they know the less probable this mistake will be!

Thus it seems that human values do enter into even the actual formation of scientific theories. But that is not all. Such theories have to be published, and here again it is sadly untrue that objectivity reigns unchallenged. So we come to a fifth interaction, the *publication of scientific results*. Again, several generalizations are possible:

- Scientific publication may be withheld or promoted for quite non-scientific reasons. Two classic cases of the former may be cited. One was the reluctance of Copernicus to publish his *De revolutionibus* for fear of persecution by the Roman Catholic Church. Only at the instigation of close friends, and on his deathbed, did he allow publication to proceed. The other was the circumstances surrounding the appearance in print of Darwin's *Origin of Species* (1859). He had long hesitated to publish, again for fear of religious objections, but particularly in deference to his wife, Emma. Eventually he was goaded into 'going public' by realization that an alternative theory of evolution had been developed by A. R. Wallace, and his friends urged him not be 'pipped at the post' by his rival. Today the often frantic proliferation of research papers of varying quality is promoted by the demands of the UK University Research Assessment Exercise – a social inducement if ever there was one!
- Scientific publication depends much on the process of refereeing. One always hopes that 'peer review' is fair, but even if it is, it

still reflects the scientific consensus of the time. And that, as we
have seen, may involve values that cannot strictly be called
'scientific'. However, even by those standards, refereeing can be
sometimes blatantly one-sided. Studies of the Royal Society in
the nineteenth century have shown that the refereeing process
was generally confined to a small number of 'safe' individuals
who could thus, by approval or the opposite, secure or destroy
an aspiring candidate's claims to be seriously considered by the
Royal Society. Sometimes justice was manifestly not done. Thus
an unfavourable report by Tyndall on a paper by James Joule
clearly reflects the former's attempt to thwart an established scientist more powerful than himself (he was blemished in
Tyndall's eyes by his association with William Thomson and
with Christianity). Similarly, T. H. Huxley and G. Busk 'con-
signed to the archives' an apparently worthy paper by P. H.
Gosse, a member of the Plymouth Brethren and opponent of
evolution.[16] Examples like this can unfortunately be multiplied
but do make clear that the descriptions of the universe promulgated in the name of science are far from the value-free
statements they may pretend to be.[17]

All this would seem to be grist to the mill for those postmodernists who delight to debunk the scientific enterprise.
Unfortunately for them there are other matters to consider in relation to the truth claims of science. These crucially revolve round
the question of verification.

Where nature answers back

By this I do not intend to personalize – still less deify – 'Nature',
merely to indicate that all our scientific theories have to be brought

16. A. J. Harrison, 'Scientific Naturalists and the Government of the Royal
    Society 1850–1900', PhD thesis, Open University, Milton Keynes, 1988.
17. H.-D. Daniel, *Guardians of Science: Fairness and Reliability of Peer Review*, tr.
    W. E. Russey (Weinheim: VCH, 1993).

to the bar of reason to see whether they have any kind of correspondence in nature itself. As Kekulé once famously asserted, 'Let
us learn to dream, gentlemen, but let our dreams be put to the test
of the waking understanding.'[18] And that involves an interrogation
of nature. How then do we test our theories?

Most obviously, we do so by *crucial experiments/observations*. These
include the test for stellar parallax that eventually vindicated
Copernicus (Bessel, 1838), the experiments of Joule establishing
the mechanical equivalence of heat (1849), the Michelson–Morley
experiment (1887) to see if the speed of light indicated the earth
to be ploughing through a stationary ether and so on.

We also test theories *on the basis of their predictive power*. If predictions are consistently fulfilled it becomes increasingly credible that,
in some sense at least, our theories are correct. Thus when
Mendeléef discovered the periodic law and wrote down his
Periodic Table (1869), he recognized several 'gaps' and predicted
that these would one day be filled by elements as yet undiscovered.
For years these boxes remained empty until in 1875 the first,
gallium, was discovered in a zinc ore. Shortly afterwards scandium
and germanium were identified and the periodic law was trium-
phantly vindicated. What Mendeléef did not predict was the
existence of a complete new 'group' of elements, the inert gases
(Group 0). But when the first, helium, made its unexpected
appearance, the theory was not abandoned: its predictions were
simply extended and soon four or five others of the helium family
were discovered. Countless similar examples can be quoted from
all branches of science.

Theories may also be verified or refuted *by their effect on problem
solving*. Many theories have proved fruitful in solving multitudes of
problems, suggesting they may be true descriptions of nature. An
example is the atomic theory from about 1808 to 1860. It was
widely used at first just as a problem-solving tool, but only later
did some sceptical chemists accept that atoms were 'real'. Similarly
the structural formulae in organic chemistry progressed from

---

18. F. A. Kekulé, 'Speech to the German Chemical Society', *Berichte* 23 (1890),
   p. 1306.

being elegant but symbolic representations of how a molecule might sometimes behave to acceptance as literal two-dimensional representations of a three-dimensional reality.

Finally, *by their superiority to alternatives* some theories have gained high degrees of credibility. Such was the case when Kepler's ellipses replaced the circles of Copernicus, when a wave theory of light edged out the old corpuscular theory, when relativity took over from Newtonianism, when oxygen displaced phlogiston, when uniformitarian geology supplanted a catastrophist view of earth history and so on.

Thus in numerous ways the theories of science gain increasing credibility, and there comes a time when most people working in the same field will accept that something very like truth has been established. If so, there is an objective reality within nature, which the scientist must strain every nerve to ascertain.

Conclusion

In all these ways of verifying scientific views of nature it is clear that human values continually apply. This is true in the choice and evaluation of competing theories, in the reliance placed on one experiment as compared to another, and in many other ways. Polanyi was right to stress scientific understanding as a form of personal knowledge.

We have to conclude that science, like every other human activity, is fallible. Errors, usually accidental, are everywhere in the long struggle with nature. This is no surprise to the Christian who has long known our sinfulness denies perfection to all we do. And because it is fallible and prone to error, science proceeds along a path that is strewn with debris of abandoned theories; yet it is determined to correct mistakes and get things as right as humanly possible. Thus theories accepted at one time are modified later, such as in Kepler's revisionist treatment of Copernicus's circles. Others once regarded as mistaken may be reinstated in a new form, as when Rutherford rescued transmutation from the fantasies of the alchemists. Yet other schemes formerly deemed mutually exclusive are seen to have a strange compatibility, as is the case with waves and particles.

Also, we cannot deny that science pursued for ignoble ends, or subject to an alien ideology, is bound to give a fundamentally flawed appreciation of the Creator's handiwork. Such may have been the case with the declarations of pure water by the analysts employed by London water companies in the mid-1800s; they were paid to affirm excellence, even though they had no adequate criterion for doing so. In the Lysenko affair in Soviet Russia the discredited notion of inheritance of acquired characteristics was promoted for reasons connected with Marxist ideology. When science is part of a power struggle like that of the Victorian naturalists, with a 'conflict' thesis as a principal weapon, their reporting of present and past pictures of nature is so easily distorted. The struggles of a clique to establish control over any part of science are little different from the power struggles within Old and New Testaments.

Yet despite all the inadequacies of our questions, the errors and blunders, the stumbling attempts to grasp something infinitely wonderful outside ourselves, most scientists share a profound conviction that deep within nature there is something answering back. Our knowledge is inevitably partial and incomplete. We see through a glass darkly. Yet that incompleteness does not mean that no objective reality is there, nor that scientific 'truth' is a myth.

In the light of this conviction there are very practical reasons for science to resist the claims of postmodernism. In the year 2000 Stephen Brush showed the poverty of attempts to see science simply as a social construction. He writes:

> To the extent that the construction thesis . . . is taken seriously by those politicians and administrators who control the funding of research, it undermines the prospects of mainstream science for financial support. (Why do you need expensive equipment if you are just making up the results of your experiments?)[19]

More recently, it has been pointed out that in Latin America

---

19. S. G. Brush, 'Postmodernism versus Science versus Fundamentalism: An Essay Review', *Science Education* 84.1 (2000), p. 115.

science is persistently underrated and 'history of science has slipped into, at best, a dilettante activity lacking in creativeness'.[20] For this the author blames 'the nonsense of post-modernist ideas'. Clearly there is much more to this than just intellectual debate in academia.

Finally, the crucial question arises as to how Christianity relates to the struggles of science against postmodernist relativism. The answer may be far from obvious. Elements of postmodernist thought have much to teach us, especially in its relentless war against scientism, its critique of positivist philosophy, and its denial of the scientist's claim to absolute truth. However, in its inability to distinguish between sense and nonsense postmodernism has to be challenged, and not least from a theological standpoint. As John Polkinghorne wisely observed, 'If science does not attain absolute truth, surely it can lay claim to verisimilitude.' As he also remarked, 'science is socially influenced but it is not socially constructed'.[21] It seems to many who take both science and the Bible seriously that a form of critical realism is the nearest we can get to a position that does full justice to both science and Christian theology.

Brush has argued that it is too simple to envisage a battle between science ('the Right') and postmodernist relativism ('the Left'). He believes the real 'right wing' is not science but religious fundamentalism and that the latter poses a much more powerful threat to science, which is thus left somewhere in the middle. That may well be true in the USA where 'Creationists' have considerable political muscle and can force schools to change their syllabus, to abandon the teaching of evolution, for example. However, for those Christians who take the Bible seriously without drawing Creationist conclusions the issue is very different.

20. C. E. Sierra, 'Post-modernism as an Epistemological Obstacle in the Teaching of the History of Science: The Latin-American Case', *Education Forum (Newsletter of the Education Section of the British Society for the History of Science)* 39 (2003), pp. 39 (5–6).

21. J. Polkinghorne, *Beyond Science* (Cambridge: Cambridge University Press, 1996), p. 11.

It seems that, in opposing postmodernist nihilistic relativism, science and the Christian faith are on the same side.[22] This is hardly surprising if the roots of Western science lie in Christian theology.[23] Each has a stake in truth and objectivity, for different though related reasons. The scientist believes that out there, in the world of nature, there is truth to be discovered and shown to be demonstrable again and again, independently of the immediate social context, because it is God's truth embedded in nature. Equally, the Christian holds the gospel to be true for all people at all times, and Christ to be the Truth of God incarnate. Was Pontius Pilate the first postmodernist (John 18:38)?

Today Christianity may not need science to bolster its claims, but it can surely recognize an ally. Although science no longer proceeds from consciously held theological axioms, it would do well to realize that especially today it needs to re-examine its ideological roots and to reaffirm the nature of its quest. If not, the 'age of science' may be nearer its termination than anyone might imagine.

© Colin A. Russell, 2005

---

22. R. Trigg, 'Does Science Deal with the Real World?' *Interdisciplinary Science Reviews* 27.2 (2002), pp. 94–99.

23. E.g. C. A. Russell, *Cross-Currents: Interactions between Science and Faith* (Leicester: IVP, 1985), revised and reprinted (London: Christian Impact, 1996); R. Hooykaas, *Fact, Faith and Fiction in the Development of Science* (Dordrecht: Kluwer Academic, 1999).

8. THE SCIENTIFIC COMMUNITY AND THE PRACTICE OF SCIENCE

Denis R. Alexander

One of the positive side effects of postmodernism, as chapter 7 makes clear, is the highlighting of the very human and fallible qualities of the scientific community. Scientists are a somewhat motley crew, with a tendency to scruffiness. A winner of the Nobel Prize in Cambridge cycles to work every morning in a T-shirt, irrespective of rain or shine, summer or winter. The average laboratory contains voters for all the major political parties; introverts; computer geeks; socialites; depressives, the exuberant, the shy and the merely placid. In other words the scientific community represents a typical cross-section of the society in which it is embedded. Apart from the incessant background noise of the radio, my laboratory is characterized by incessant chat, laughter, serious discussions of techniques or of data, frequent grunts, cursing when something goes wrong and occasional moments of great pleasure when an experiment works really well and generates interesting data. Those who have just received news that their recent manuscript has been turned down by a top journal may retire to the toilet to grieve in solitude for a while, later returning glumly to face up to the boring task of preparing it for submission elsewhere.

Every year my institute holds an open day for local school pupils who are hosted by the different laboratories to carry out hands-on experiments as part of our contribution to the under-standing of science. These are generally supervised by PhD students and younger postdocs. At the end of the day the pupils fill in a questionnaire to provide some feedback. Apart from com-ments on the food they had for lunch (inevitably), it is striking how many make comments like 'I was amazed to find that scien-tists are normal people who crack jokes.' Raised on films in which the evil scientist in a white coat tries to destroy the world, they suddenly face social dissonance as the media images in their heads clash with the reality before them. And perhaps that is one of the most valuable lessons of their visit – that scientists are ordinary flesh-and-blood humans like themselves, with all the same fancies and foibles.

Given the obvious fact that the scientific community is a very human community, comprising individuals who are only too fal-lible, how do scientists in practice try to ensure that their data and their theories represent a reliable body of constructed knowledge? And are their efforts in this direction successful?

Telling the truth in science and in faith

Central to the scientific enterprise is the practice of truth telling. This might seem so obvious that it barely requires mentioning. Yet it has often been highlighted by historians of science as an impor-tant element of the scientific revolution. The seventeenth-century natural philosophers (as scientists were then called) were very aware that in their espousal of the importance of the empirical method they were overthrowing centuries of dependence upon the authority of the ancient Greek philosophers.[1] Before then the role of medieval scholars was to demonstrate their prowess in expounding the writings of the ancients. As the historian Peter

---

1. D. R. Alexander, *Rebuilding the Matrix: Science and Faith in the Twenty-first Century* (Oxford: Lion, 2001), ch. 4 and pp. 244–245.

Harrison has remarked, 'It was not the observation of animals and plants which counted, but whether all the relevant written sources had been consulted . . . Only gradually did it dawn on scholars that the empirical world might serve as a standard by which textual accounts of living things should be judged.'[2] Steven Shapin has drawn attention to the way in which the early Royal Society, with its motto *Nullius in verba* (take no one's word for it), came to equate trustworthiness with gentlemanly origins. Since a gentleman was held to tell the truth at all times, someone as gentlemanly as Robert Boyle (one of the founders of modern chemistry), for example, had a head start in his ability to persuade others of the veracity of his experimental results. When Boyle wrote his *Sceptical Chymist* (1661) he was careful to invoke witnesses of unimpeachable reputation to testify to what they had seen. His experiments on mercury, published in 1675, were witnessed by Henry Oldenburg and by 'the noble and judicious' Lord Brouncker. The sceptic in the *Sceptical Chymist* plays the role of the examining magistrate to determine whether the scientific claims made are true or false.[3]

Today the role of 'gentlemen' in establishing scientific facts may not be quite so prominent, but the centrality of truth and of trustworthy witness to the truth lives on. In the context of contemporary scientific practice, John Ziman comments that 'The acceptance of consistent, coherent and plausible testimony from knowledgeable, disinterested witnesses is an essential feature of all practical reasoning. Knowing how to evaluate testimony is a basic requirement for membership of any culture,' and 'In effect, academic science is a culture where a reputation for reliability – that is, *credibility* – is the prime personal asset.'[4] This is reflected in the way that scientists tend to read the scientific literature. They will

2. P. Harrison, *The Bible, Protestantism and the Rise of Natural Science* (Cambridge: Cambridge University Press, 1998), pp. 74, 77.

3. S. Shapin, *A Social History of Truth: Civility and Science in Seventeenth-Century England* (Chicago: University of Chicago Press, 1994).

4. J. Ziman, *Real Science: What it Is and What it Means* (Cambridge: Cambridge University Press, 2000), pp. 97, 160 (italics original).

take much more notice of a publication from a lab that they respect for its long-term credibility rating, and will tend to ignore publications stemming from scientists who have a track record for getting things wrong.

The scientific community has some well-established practices for establishing and preserving the integrity of their data. Although these practices vary somewhat depending on the type of science, the principles are the same and may be illustrated by those practised within my own research community of UK research council funded biological bench-scientists:

- Laboratory notebooks are dated and experiments should be written up as soon after collecting the data as possible. All important experimental details should be described, including technical errors made during the experiment that might impinge on later interpretations. Primary data, wherever possible, should be attached or incorporated within the lab book in some way to provide a record that should be kept for at least ten years in a secure location. Each page of the lab book should be signed off by the scientist's line-manager to confirm that the results have been properly recorded (not least to secure against later patent disputes concerning priority of discovery). Lab books are kept in fireproof cabinets overnight and for longer-term storage. They represent the historical records of witnesses to what was seen and measured. They are the modern equivalent of 'the noble and judicious' Lord Brouncker.
- The first critic of the scientist's results is their own supervisor. At regular intervals they will pore over the recorded results together, discussing, debating and often disagreeing over their interpretations. The scientist who thought early in her career that she had obtained an interesting result will be deflated as her supervisor points out that the fascinating extra band on the gel (or whatever it is) is merely an artefact arising from some obvious quirk of the technique. The scientist will be dismayed as his supervisor insists on repetition of the experiment umpteen times until a consistent pattern of results emerges. In the biological sciences changes in parameters often have to be really big before people take them seriously. Yet this is not

always the case, and sometimes quite small differences can be important. Many years of research experience are necessary to make the judgment between overscepticism and overconfidence in the reliability and significance of any given body of data. Even then we can still get it wrong, being dismissive of a result that later turns out to be really important or, conversely, naïvely overinterpreting data that in fact could equally well receive a more trivial interpretation. Quantification and statistical analysis are really important in assessing certain kinds of experiment.

• The next 'layer' of criticism that the scientists face occurs as they present their results, not yet published, to their peers in lab meetings, departmental seminars and, with time, the wider scientific community at international meetings. Often the initial bubble of enthusiasm at the excitement of some new results is quickly popped by a colleague pointing out more mundane explanations for the same data. But equally colleagues can make valuable suggestions about other techniques and approaches that would be worth trying. Scientists are a community who help each other, criticize each other and sometimes fight like cats and dogs to establish their control of resources or priority over some discovery – a bit like a family really.

• Finally the day comes when the scientist submits a paper that summarizes, not unusually, three or more years of work. The paper represents the tip of the iceberg: most of the work accomplished represents repeated experiments, or experiments that never worked, or blind alleyways that came to nothing. Normally a paper goes out to two or three referees who act anonymously, and again the data and interpretations are subject to critical analysis. Referees can be ruthless and dismissive, the more so if the paper has been submitted to one of the more prestigious journals. In any research field everyone knows which are the best journals and which are not worth reading, and it is certainly more difficult to publish in the former than the latter. The refereeing process is by no means perfect, but no-one has yet managed to think up a better system. Scientists' papers may be refereed by their direct rivals, although many journals (not all) will exclude rivals as referees at the authors' request.

Referees' reports, again anonymously, will eventually be returned to the scientist with a list of criticisms and suggestions for further experiments, sometimes involving more laborious months of work, or take even longer (news received with great groans). But when the revised manuscript is sent in and accepted, all the effort will seem worthwhile in retrospect. More importantly, if the system has worked as it should, this long process of criticism and revision will have refined the experimental results and their presentation to the point at which only the best and most reliable data will see the light of day on the pages of a scientific journal.

There is a sense in which the role of referees is to assess the credibility and authenticity of scientific authors as the witnesses of their results. As an example of how the process works, a few days prior to writing this I was refereeing a paper for a well-known biological journal and recommended in my report to the editor that it be returned for significant revision. One of the main problems of the paper was that it showed results without giving any idea as to how representative they were and how many times the experiments had been repeated. Whereas the text talked about 'striking differences' in the control and test samples illustrated in the figure, when one looked at the figure in question the differences looked pretty minor to my eyes and there was no quantification or statistical analysis to support the claims that were being made.

• Even when the paper has finally been published, there is always the possibility that some significant error of fact might later be found in the results that has an impact on the conclusions drawn. It is then the author's duty to publish a retraction in the same journal describing the error, and all journals occasionally publish such retractions. Whilst the errors may be for perfectly valid reasons, sometimes beyond the control of the scientists involved, publishing a retraction is deeply embarrassing for those involved, but is nevertheless essential in maintaining science as a body of trustworthy knowledge.

So 'truth telling' in science is not some impractical ethereal ideal, but the daily goal of all working scientists, without which the scientific enterprise would collapse. No scientists begin their research project from 'ground zero' – all are building on the labours of others stretching back over many centuries. It is this accumulation of reliable knowledge provided by faithful witnesses that enables science to keep proceeding at its current breathless pace.

Any Christian reading the preceding paragraphs will have been struck by the resonances between biblical faith and scientific practice. The importance of truth telling is deeply woven within the warp and woof of Scripture. The God we worship is the God of truth (Psalm 31:5) who speaks truth (Isaiah 45:19) and we are called to reflect his character in our lives (Psalm 51:6). Avoiding lies is a central biblical command (Leviticus 19:11). 'The LORD detests lying lips, / but he delights in men who are truthful' (Proverbs 12:22).[5] God delights in truthful accuracy: 'The LORD abhors dishonest scales, / but accurate weights are his delight' (Proverbs 11:1). The phrase 'I tell you the truth' is recorded 78 times by the Gospel writers as they cite the words of Jesus, who pointed to himself as the Truth (John 14:6). Closely integrated with the practice of truth in biblical thought is the idea of being a faithful witness. Whereas a false witness will not go unpunished (Proverbs 19:5), Christians are called to be faithful witnesses of all that God has said and done through Christ (Acts 1:8), who is himself the ultimate exemplar of the 'faithful witness' (Revelation 1:5). The disciples were witnesses of the resurrection and of the other historical events described in the Gospels (Acts 1:22; 3:15; 5:32; 10:39). When Luke wrote his Gospel he was careful to point out that his record was based on eyewitness accounts so that Theophilus might 'know the certainty of the things you have been taught' (Luke 1:1–4). The apostle Paul constantly emphasized his role as a witness of what he had seen with his own eyes, and the way in which his faith would collapse if that witness was false (1 Corinthians 15:15–17). The New Testament emphasizes the reliability of the evidence for the resurrection by the fact that there were multiple witnesses (1 Corinthians 15:6), reflecting the

---

5. All quotes in this chapter are from the NIV.

insistence of the Old Testament law that matters of fact must be established by several witnesses at least (Deuteronomy 19:15).

So telling the truth about God's creation is a profoundly important task that, as a goal at least, is practised by all scientists, irrespective of whether they believe in God or not. In this respect, at least, scientists share much with historians, at least with those historians who espouse a realist view of the value of historical research. Richard Evans, Professor of Modern History at the University of Cambridge, has put it well in his robust critique of postmodernism entitled *In Defence of History*:

> It is not true to say that historians are 'not too concerned about discrete facts'. On the contrary, whatever the criteria for the facts' selection, the vast majority of the historian's efforts are devoted to ascertaining them and establishing them as firmly as possible in the light of historical evidence . . . interpretations really can be tested and confirmed or falsified by an appeal to the evidence; and some of the time at least, it really is possible to prove that one side is right and the other is wrong.[6]

There is a sense in which scientists play multiple roles as the creators, recorders and interpreters of history, only in their case they act as their own recorders in writing down what happened at a certain time and place in a particular set of circumstances. The lab book in this sense is like a historical document that gives an account of what happened. It is of course the account of one (or a group) of particular individuals, interpreting data within a particular interpretative framework, as I shall discuss further below. But if the dates in the lab book are false, or in other ways the records do not appear to match the accounts provided by other eyewitness accounts, then doubt may be cast upon the historical record.

Fraud in science

As with any human community, occasionally there are those within

---

6. R. J. Evans, *In Defence of History* (London: Granta, 1997), pp. 127, 128.

the scientific community who practise fraud. The impact, however, of fraud within science is particularly devastating for reasons that will be apparent from our discussion so far. Since scientists build on the foundations provided by others, if those foundations are made of sand, then, at the least, an enormous amount of time can be wasted in following blind alleys, in trying to repeat results unsuccessfully and in writing grant submissions based on what (unknowingly) are false presuppositions. In the biomedical research area, in particular, the implications of fraud can be dangerous for human health. Not surprisingly, therefore, accusations of fraud are met within the scientific community by a great deal of hand-wringing, and such cases are widely publicized, for example in the News and Views sections of high profile journals such as *Nature* and *Science*.

The temptation to generate fraudulent data in science is particularly strong because there is such pressure on younger investigators to 'publish or perish'. In contrast to many professions, scientists face a very uncertain future as they embark on their PhD. Once this is completed they typically continue with one or more short-term contract postdoctoral positions, but there is still no guarantee that they will eventually obtain a permanent research position, and every transition to a new position depends to a large degree on their publication record. The old adage of 'publish or perish' has never been more true than in the cut-throat world of competitive science. Most cases of fraud in science stem from these kinds of pressures.

A dramatic case of fraud was recently uncovered involving the work of Jan Hendrik Schon of Bell Laboratories in the USA. Schon's research on molecular scale electronic devices and induced superconductivity in carbon 'buckyballs' led to a steady stream of papers in the world's leading journals, including *Nature* and *Science*. But it is now known that Schon perpetrated one of the biggest frauds that the physical sciences have ever seen, fabricating and misrepresenting data on a massive scale.[7] After the fraud was

---

7. G. Brumfiel, 'Misconduct Finding at Bell Labs Shakes Physics
Community', *Nature* 419 (2002), pp. 419–421.

uncovered *The Wall Street Journal* alleged that *Nature* and *Science* 'are locked in such fierce competition for prestige and publicity that they may be cutting corners to get "hot" papers'. Possibly. But the issues are more complicated than that.[8] Since referees' reports are anonymous, it is difficult to assess their depth and accuracy. Refereeing standards do vary, and referees can be too busy or too careless to do their job properly. If that happens it is the responsibility of the editor of the journal (normally a very senior scientist) to send the paper out again to new referee(s). Most referees that I know are fair and thorough, often spending many hours poring over a single paper to assess its worth. There are particular dangers involved when the results described are very exciting or unexpected, not fitting within the current paradigm of a particular research field. Editors of journals are naturally eager to be the first to publish such material, but equally any referee worth his or her salt must exert a higher degree of scepticism about unexpected findings. In other words, the bar on the high jump is likely to rise considerably for the dramatic results. So if the scientist manages to jump over not once but many times (as in the Schon case), then the crash is all the greater when it eventually happens. When fraud is revealed, referees sometimes break their anonymity to state publicly that they always believed the results were defective, and had stated so in their report to the editor of the journal, but that their comments had been ignored.

Many journals require that all authors (there can be many) of the paper sign the submission form accompanying their manuscript to confirm that they are all in agreement with the results described. But even that does not completely guard against fraud. In one bizarre incident several cardiology researchers from London's Imperial College found that they were co-authors of a paper published in the *New England Journal of Medicine* in 2002 that they knew little or nothing about.[9] It eventually emerged that of

8. D. Adam and J. Knight, 'Publish, and Be Damned', *Nature* 419 (2002), pp. 772–778.

9. D. Adam, 'Paper Retracted as Co-Author Admits Forgery', *Nature* 421 (2003), p. 775.

the eight signatures that appeared on the submission, several had been forged by a co-author, who then wrote to the journal to confess what he had done. Such a case, thankfully rare, normally leads to the end of a scientific career; no cheat is likely to get another decent job in science.

Sometimes fraud cases can drag on for years, even leading to book-length descriptions of their intricacies. One of the most famous recent cases in the biological sciences involved the laboratories of the Nobel Prize winner David Baltimore and his associate Thereza Imanishi-Kari, both at MIT in Cambridge, USA, at the time of the episode. The case arose from a paper in immunology submitted to the journal *Cell* in 1985 reporting that expression of a rearranged immunoglobulin-heavy chain gene caused alterations in the repertoire of expressed endogenous immunoglobulin genes. The paper was eventually published in April 1986. The data were produced in Imanishi-Kari's lab but it was Baltimore who became the spokesman for the authors, and in due course the lightning rod for their critics. Doubts arose because another scientist in Imanishi-Kari's own lab had difficulty in reproducing the results using the same reagent. This by itself is not that unusual (some reagents no longer work properly if, for example, they have been stored at the wrong temperature). But other anomalies came to light, leading to a long and tortuous investigation that was not finally laid to rest until 1996, ten years later, when the Appeals Board finally exonerated the authors of all charges raised by the Office of Research Integrity.[10] Fortunately not all fraud accusations take so long to resolve, but the case at least highlights the enormous importance attached to the integrity of scientific data and the great lengths to which scientists and government investigators will go in order to establish the veracity, or otherwise, of claimed findings. Truth really does matter in science.

I myself once had the unhappy experience of chairing a committee set up to assess an accusation of scientific fraud. One major lesson that came out of that affair was the importance of dating,

10. D. J. Kevles, *The Baltimore Case: A Trial of Politics, Science, and Character* (New York: Norton, 1998).

recording and storing primary data accurately. Without those essential historical records being in place, and safely stored, investigators lay themselves open potentially to the charge of fraud. This is one good reason why a failure to record results properly can in itself lead to disciplinary procedures in many research institutes.

Should the fact of fraud within the scientific community make us trust scientific knowledge less in general? Funnily enough, probably not. For a start, fraud thankfully remains relatively rare. Of course it is very likely that not every fraudster is exposed. But even if we doubled the number of fraudsters, and doubled the number of fraudulent papers published, these would still remain a tiny proportion of scientific publications as a whole. The penalties for being caught are very high: almost certainly loss of job and of any future research role within the scientific community; a court case with fines or imprisonment in the worst cases. And the extent of angst within the scientific community about cases of fraud highlights the importance that scientists place on truth telling. People who police their own communities are often the most zealous law-keepers, and whistle-blowers are generally other workers within the same lab whose suspicions have been aroused by various forms of malpractice. We are fortunate to have inherited a strong culture of integrity within science, which it is the responsibility of every scientist to maintain. As Edmund Burke said, 'It is necessary only for the good man to do nothing for evil to flourish.'

It is also a great strength of science that it is a self-correcting process. Fraudulent papers, as well as papers that may be wrong for quite innocent reasons, are gradually winnowed out by normal scientific practice. One point that might surprise the public at large is that science at the cutting edge may seem contradictory or confused, with observations that do not seem consistent with each other. But that is the nature of scientific research; indeed one of its great satisfactions is seeing the inconsistencies resolved as experiments proceed and new theories are formulated. Science is like an ocean liner cutting through the waves at high speed. Look behind you and you will see the steady wake of the ship left imprinted on the ocean surface: in the analogy this is the well-established results that end up in textbooks and are taught to the next generation of undergraduates. But at the bows of the ship is froth, foam and confusion: this is the cutting edge of science where it is not uncommon for several contradictory papers to appear simultaneously. With time (sometimes years, or even generations, depending on the type of science) the issues will be resolved one way or the other, and the bow-wave will pass on to new questions and challenges. For a time the structure of DNA and the question of the genetic code were controversial questions with rival theories competing with each other in the scientific literature, but those particular questions have long been resolved and the answers belong to the long biological wake stretching back behind us as the good ship *Biology* steams ahead into new uncharted waters.

The self-correcting process of science is somewhat analogous to natural selection. Scientists tend to depend on the best published work for their future research programmes. But if they try building on that work as a presupposition for their next grant application, and then eventually their experiments fail to turn out as expected, they might eventually find (albeit painfully in some cases) that the other lab's results are wrong. So there is a continuous 'natural selection' process going on in science whereby the best theories and the best data are constantly being tested by the scientific programmes of other sections of the scientific community, and only the best eventually survive. Meanwhile the dross is left to lie in the scientific literature, eventually to be neglected and forgotten. Just as the precise process whereby genetic variation is generated is irrelevant to the process of the natural selection of genotypes, involving the testing criterion of reproductive success, so by analogy downright fraudulent papers, as well as papers that are wrong for other non-fraudulent reasons, will equally be eventually weeded out by the winnowing work of many scientists, although this process may well take some time. To complete the analogy: the papers that survive with flying colours will prove to be the most fruitfully 'reproductive' for the future of a particular research field, spawning in turn a plethora of new discoveries.

Christians above all should be setting high standards in integrity and in truth telling in science. Their commitment to truth should reflect their worship of the God of truth. In a tragic incident from the history of science a committed Christian, with the best of intentions, propounded a theory that made it appear that God was deceiving the scientific investigator. Philip Henry Gosse FRS was one of the great Victorian naturalists whom Stephen Jay Gould described as the 'David Attenborough of his day'. Gosse wrote dozens of scholarly and popular books on natural history and his election to the Royal Society was supported by, amongst others, Darwin's great defender Thomas Henry Huxley. But Gosse attempted a reconciliation between science and geology in a book called *Omphalos* (the Greek word for 'navel') in which he proposed that the whole of creation, complete with its biological diversity, exists in the mind of God who, by divine fiat, wills that his creation is actualized at a particular moment in history. At the dramatic moment of creation, wrote Gosse, 'the world presented, instantly, the structural appearance of a planet on which life had long existed'.[11] The merry-go-round of creation is invisible until the whistle blows, when it appears complete with tree-rings, tortoises with laminae on their plates and human navels. Gosse's Christian friends at the time were dismayed: Charles Kingsley made the rather obvious point that the whole fantastic theory made God into a deceiver on a grand scale ('You make God tell a lie' wrote Kingsley). Gosse provides a striking example of the damage that can be caused when Christians within the scientific community, however well meaning, fail in their God-given task of telling the truth about his world.[12]

11. D. R. Alexander, cited in *Science and Christian Belief* 16.2 (2003), pp. 181–183.
12. A. Thwaite, *Glimpses of the Wonderful: The Life of Philip Henry Gosse 1810–1888* (London: Faber & Faber, 2003). Those whose knowledge of Gosse is derived only from his son Edmund's bittersweet biography *Father and Son* should redress the balance by reading Anne Thwaite's excellent biography. Philip Henry Gosse was a gifted and successful naturalist, and the fact that he wrote one seriously misguided book should not detract from his many achievements in the sciences, nor, for that matter, from his faithful Christian witness both within and without the scientific community.

Can we be sure about scientific knowledge?

Truth telling, by itself, is clearly not sufficient to construct a body of reliable scientific knowledge: there is much more to it than that. In addition, there is a broad range of practices that contribute to the reliability of scientific knowledge that is worth publishing in well-refereed journals.[13] Some of these practices are as follows.

Refutation

The twentieth-century philosopher of science Karl Popper famously made the ability to obtain falsifying counter-evidence in principle as the key demarcation line that separates science from non-science. In normal everyday science, refuting evidence does indeed play a key role in many research fields. In biomedical research, if the band on the gel is not there when your hypothesis predicted it should be, well, tough, so much the worse for your hypothesis. But in the big theories of science, life becomes more complicated. There are plenty of examples from the history of science when scientists did not give up their pet theories when refuting evidence was found. Darwin was worried when Lord Kelvin, during the latter half of the nineteenth century, kept revising downward the age of the earth, as eventually its reduced age did not seem to be long enough to accommodate a process of evolution by natural selection. But Darwin didn't give up on evolution; instead making later editions of the *Origin of Species* more Lamarckian. The inheritance of acquired characteristics is a useful mechanism for speeding up evolution. As it turned out, Kelvin was wrong and Darwin was right (about evolution, not about Lamarckianism), but whether to give up a theory due to evidence that counts against it is much easier to assess with the advantage of hindsight. In general, big theories in science tend to be remarkably resilient to counter-evidence – they explain so much so well that anomalies are often put on the back-burner to address sometime later. A fairly hefty accumulation of refuting data, or at least one

---

13. Several of these practices are discussed at greater length in Alexander, *Rebuilding the Matrix*, ch. 8.

major item, is needed before a really big theory crashes to the ground. But in everyday science, certainly the kind of biomedical research in which I am involved, most scientists are faithful Popperians even if they have never heard of Popper. In much biomedical research it is perfectly possible for someone to have an idea on Monday morning (or, perhaps, more likely in the bath on Sunday when the mind is nice and relaxed), test the idea in the lab during the week, and show by Friday that it is definitely wrong. Refutation contributes significantly to the reliability of scientific knowledge.

Can religious claims, or other types of metaphysical belief such as atheism, be refuted? Of course there are no universally accepted criteria for refutation in religion or in philosophy analogous to the refutations of daily 'mundane science'. It is precisely the possession of such criteria that gives power to scientific methods as tools for constructing a body of reliable knowledge about the physical world. The price paid for such reliability is, of course, the restriction of science to questions about the properties of the physical world. However, a strong case can, I think, be made for an analogy between the function of refutation in the 'grand theories' of science and the refutation of metaphysical belief systems. Are there common criteria that could universally be accepted by anyone as a refutation of Christian theism? The early Christians clearly thought so in their defence of the historical claims of Christianity. For example, it might be somewhat anachronistic to label the apostle Paul a 'Popperian', but he did write to the early church in Corinth that 'If Christ has not been raised, our preaching is useless and so is your faith' (1 Corinthians 15:14). In other words he perceived both his faith and that of the early church as resting on a historical claim that, if untrue, would clearly refute his belief system. Since Paul was writing his letter to Corinth within a few decades of the purported event, he was clearly putting his message at risk by raising the possibility of refutation, since it might still have been possible for someone to produce the dead body of Jesus, recognizable due to embalmment, and so demonstrate that the resurrection had never happened. We are not in the same position as the apostle Paul, but at least such reflections draw attention to the way in which the mode of argumentation used within the scientific community to justify truth claims in this context is not as distant from the realm of religious discourse as is sometimes assumed.

Reproducibility

Those who have tended to criticize Popper have pointed out that in practice, as mentioned above, scientists do not always drop their theories once counter-evidence begins to accumulate, but instead depend more on the affirmation of theories by their repeated testing in different laboratories. But refutation and reproducibility should be taken as different sides of the same coin. One or the other may be of more relevance depending on the scientific question being addressed, but generally both are critically important in the establishing, or otherwise, of scientific theories. It is especially powerful when a theory makes a prediction of what ought to be the case, sometimes on quite theoretical grounds, and this is then confirmed by later experimental findings.

Scientists have the special privilege of coming to belief in something that no-one else in the world (to the best of their knowledge) yet knows or yet believes, for the simple reason that only they have discovered it and know it. As well as being a privilege, this is also a serious responsibility. The literature must be eagerly scanned in case someone else has the same result. Conferences are attended with a feeling of some foreboding in case someone stands up and announces 'your' discovery. But once the scientist's discovery has been published, the results are worrying for a different reason. Since they are novel, what happens if no-one else can repeat them? What happens if your facts are right, but your interpretation is wrong? It is therefore enormously reassuring when the results are repeated and indeed extended by many other laboratories around the world. For nothing reflects the gracious faithfulness of God in his created order so much as the reproducibility of the world we observe. If the same experiment is repeated under exactly the same conditions in any part of the world, then the same results really will be obtained, irrespective of language, culture, race or religion. Not only does this fact help to underpin the reliability of scientific knowledge, but it also helps to explain why scientists tend not to take seriously the postmodernist suspicion of metanarratives, with their attempt to replace them with fragmented realities constructed by different communities, or even individuals, with each community immersed in its own 'language-game'. That is not the experience of scientists who travel to international conferences and find that the universe itself appears to have its own 'metanarrative', one written in the language of mathematics, giving rise to properties that are reproducibly accessible to all people, irrespective of their background or culture. DNA really is best described as a double helix and not a triple helix – in South America as much as in India, Japan or Cambridge. There are facts that have to be reckoned with (not least in the genetic constitution of our own bodies) and no amount of denial of 'metanarratives' will make these facts go away.

Coherence

Coherence is often looked to as one of the hallmarks of reliability in science, just as it is in faith. In science, Darwin's theory of evolution has often been taken as an example of the way in which a novel theory can bring coherence to a wide range of facts that otherwise remain incoherent. As the biologist Ernst Mayr has written:

> The theory of evolution is quite rightly called the greatest unifying theory in biology. The diversity of organisms, similarities and differences between kinds of organisms, patterns of distribution and behaviour, adaptation and interaction, all this was merely a bewildering chaos of facts until given meaning by the evolutionary theory.[14]

Darwin's goal in the *Origin of Species*, which he referred to as 'one long argument', was to marshal an immense array of varied evidence that only made sense if the theory of natural selection was correct. Much of this evidence was already known previously. It was Darwin's brilliance to see the same evidence in a new light in support of a novel theory.

---

14. Ibid., p. 245.

The challenge for a big scientific theory is not only to explain a wide array of disparate observations at the beginning when the theory is first launched, but also to continue to absorb new data successfully at later dates. In this respect Darwinian theory has waxed and waned over the years. For example by 1900 the theory of natural selection had become marginalized in the biological community, partly because the 'units of inheritance' remained abstract concepts and additionally because, as already mentioned, Lord Kelvin had reduced the age of the earth so much that to many it seemed impossible – surely correctly – that so much biological diversity could emerge by such a mechanism in such a short time (ironically even Darwin's bulldog, Thomas Henry Huxley, never believed in natural selection). But then genes were rediscovered by several groups simultaneously in the early years of the twentieth century and the fusion of genetics with maths in the 1920s and 1930s led to the so-called neo-Darwinian synthesis in which the twin theories of genetic variation and natural selection were combined into what we currently understand as Darwinian evolutionary theory. More recently stunning confirmations of the theory have emerged, and continue to emerge, from molecular genetics, not least from the sequencing of the human genome. Every day our own bodies synthesize thousands of miles of DNA, encoding the 'fossil genes' of our ancestors that we ourselves no longer utilize.[15] We are all walking fossil museums – a fact that should at least help to keep us humble!

Scientists who have gained new insights into the properties of matter have often remarked how they were attracted to the new theory by its elegance and ability to explain a broader array of phenomena than previous theories. Dirac and Schrödinger, two of the founders of quantum theory, remarked that 'It was a sort of act of faith with us that any equations which describe fundamental laws of Nature must have great mathematical beauty in them. It was a

---

15. E.g., see G. Finlay, 'The Ape that Bears God's Image', *Science and Christian Belief* 15 (2003), pp. 17–40. The article is available for free download from www.cis.org.uk.

very profitable religion to hold and can be considered as the basis of much of our success.'[16]

Of course theories, especially the big theories of science, are never *completely* coherent. There are always rough edges and unsolved mysteries in any theory, otherwise scientists would be out of a job, but it is certainly the case that a high degree of coherence correlates with increased certitude that something is in fact the case. The reliability of scientific knowledge is tightly correlated with the ability of its theories to absorb new data and help them to make sense within a larger story.

Technology – science works

Technology is far older than science and science only started making a significant impact on technology in the nineteenth century, an impact that has been greatly extended up to the present day. If we accept technology as representing the practical application of science to human needs, then in a sense scientific theories are continually being tested and confirmed all the time around us in our daily lives. For, at the end of the day, good science works well. If you apply techniques based on good science for practical ends, then the technology has a good chance of working just as well. Conversely faulty science will lead to faulty technology. You really do have a better chance of getting better by going to a doctor who practices Western medicine than by going to the witch doctor. HIV really is the cause of AIDS and if you don't know that, then your life could be at risk. And every time you fly at 30,000 feet surrounded by hundreds of tons of metal, it is good to know that the laws of physics and aerodynamics are unlikely to change in mid-flight.

Because God is faithful in sustaining the properties of matter ('sustaining all things by his powerful word', Hebrews 1:3) we can trust in his upholding power and be thankful that he has created a universe with coherent properties that we can utilize to serve human needs in a rational and reproducible way. So technology

---

16. Cited in M. Longair, *Theoretical Concepts in Physics* (Cambridge: Cambridge University Press, 1984), p. 7.

increases our conviction that we can really be sure about at least some of the properties of God's world: if it were not so, then our technologies would not work. Indeed Christians can and should worship God with their technologies.[17]

Facts and theories

It will be apparent from our discussion so far that facts never exist in isolation from theories and there is an intimate relationship between them. Sociologists of science normally highlight this point by saying that facts are 'theory-laden'. By that they wish to point out that all facts are collected within a particular context, and that their meaning is shaped by particular interpretative frameworks even as they are being collected. Data within science are often obtained using specialized instruments and machines that impose their own kind of meanings upon the results that emerge. For example, my research involves genetically manipulating the immune systems of mice in order to see what happens to lymphocyte development and function. The instruments and techniques that we have at our disposal to investigate these parameters are sophisticated and accurate, but they can only give us one 'slice' of the reality that is going on – other 'slices' may be ignored simply because they cannot readily be measured. Our instruments are like nets with meshes of a certain size that will only catch certain types of fish. A thorough scientific investigation will use many different nets to get at the problem from as many different angles as possible.

Theories are the interpretative frameworks that render data coherent that are collected using all the various techniques and approaches available. Providing the scientists' instruments are operating correctly and the scientists are not hallucinating, it seems reasonable to label the data that they collect as 'facts'. These facts may of course be immensely varied, depending on the type

17. D. R. Alexander, *Worshipping God with Technology*, Cambridge Papers 12.4, 2003. Available for free download from http://www.jubilee-centre.org/cambridge_papers/

of science involved. But providing you carry out the experiment under precisely the same conditions and keep getting comparable results each time, then it seems appropriate to label the data as 'facts'; indeed facts that have to be reckoned with in the assessment of rival theories. Theories in turn are like maps that integrate the facts and show how they can be connected to render a scientific landscape meaningful. This is why grants committees often like to see phrases like 'hypothesis-driven research' in grant applications because it demonstrates that the applicant has (hopefully) clear ideas about what might be the case and now wants funding to find out if the hypothesis is supported. A scientific hypothesis is not a full-blown theory; it is a suggested theory – to begin with it is 'epistemically fragile', to coin Ziman's phrase. Conversely, no torpedo can sink a grant application quicker than the dismissive comment 'This project looks like a piece of stamp-collecting,' meaning that the application is written as if the scientist wants to gather a great array of data without any clear idea of what ideas are being tested in the process.

Like everything else in the philosophy and practice of science, what I have just claimed is somewhat contentious, because there are branches of science in which either there is great emphasis placed on theory generation, sometimes with little hope of obtaining data that will decide between rival theories, at least in the near future; or at the other extreme there are sciences where the collection of data is primary and theory building plays a less important role. Mathematical physics and cosmology provide plenty of examples of the former. It took the best part of half a century before Einstein's theory of relativity was adequately tested and confirmed. Einstein himself was not at all impressed by the experimental confirmations of his theory, once remarking that 'I do not by any means find the chief significance of the general theory of relativity in the fact that it predicted a few minute observable facts, but rather in the simplicity of its foundation and in its logical consistency.'[18] Theories in mathematical physics are

---

18. Quoted in L. Wolpert, *The Unnatural Nature of Science* (London: Faber & Faber, 1992), p. 99.

favoured for their elegance, internal consistency and fit with the equations. As Lev Landau has remarked, cosmologists 'are often in error but never in doubt!'[19] But even Einstein's theoretical insights eventually had to pass empirical tests, which they did with flying colours; and if string theory in physics currently seems untestable, this is not to say that ways may not be found of comparing rival theories in the future.

Non-scientists sometimes draw a greater demarcation line between 'facts' and 'theories' than is warranted, suggesting that 'facts' are those things that we can be certain about, whereas the use of the term 'theory' implies necessary uncertainty. 'It is only a theory' can be a phrase thrown at something that one disbelieves. But this fails to take account of the frustratingly sloppy ways in which scientists use language. Imagine a list of facts on the left side of the page and a list of theories on the right. If a theory has been tested so thoroughly and for so long and in so many different contexts that no-one is in the slightest doubt that it is correct, then scientists tend to move the theory from the right side and place it on the left, particularly if it is not a big theory of science (like the big bang in cosmology, evolution in biology, or plate tectonics in geophysics) but refers to a smaller domain of investigation. For example, there were rival theories about how information was encoded in the genes in the 1950s, but now we know which theory is correct, the 'triplet codon' is an accepted fact and has moved from the right to the left column. In the late eighteenth century there were various rival theories concerning the age of the earth, namely whether it was only a few thousand years old or millions of years old, but that issue was resolved during the nineteenth century and the long age of the earth moved into the 'facts column' as a result.

The conversion of 'theories' into 'facts' as the level of certitude increases might seem to support the idea that scientists are not, or indeed cannot be, really sure about their theories. But this is far from the case. When successful theories persistently stay in the right hand column, then it generally means that their role is to

---

19. Cited in Ziman, *Real Science*, p. 225.

provide coherence for a great array of disparate data. And if over the years, decades, or even centuries, essentially the same theory goes on providing coherence and absorbing new data with effortless ease, providing an ongoing paradigm within which scientists successfully continue to pursue their research programmes, then there seems to be no good reason to doubt it. This explains why scientists can be just as passionately committed to the Big Theories of science as they are to the reliability of their data. Indeed more so, for it is the theories that make the data interesting – facts by themselves without connections can be pretty boring. On the other hand, even big successful theories can eventually be brought crashing down by an accumulation of counter-evidence. In reality, however, big theories are often swallowed up by even bigger theories rather than being contradicted outright, like a big circle enclosing a smaller circle. For example, Newtonian physics remains valid for many applications (like flying to the moon), but Einstein's theory is more powerful because it not only explains the phenomena encompassed by Newtonian physics, but also other things that Newton's theory cannot explain successfully.

God and critical realism

Scientists would never sweat long hours in the lab, spend days on writing grant applications and papers, or continue to pursue such a difficult career path, unless they actually believed that there was a reality in the external world to describe, and that in some way their research results were providing increasingly accurate maps of that reality. But, equally, few scientists are naïve enough to think that their descriptions of the reality around them are in any sense complete or exhaustive. Whether they have ever heard of the phrase or not, in practice the vast majority of working scientists are 'critical realists': they believe that their theories model a world 'out there' that has a real objective existence, and they are therefore realists in the philosophical sense of this word. But equally they acknowledge that all their facts and theories represent a very partial account of all that potentially can be known, and that their scientific maps, whilst in many ways accurate representations of reality, are nevertheless invariably only partial accounts of the truth.

As Roger Trigg points out in chapter 2, Christians in particular have a good basis for holding to a realist view of the world. As scientists who are Christians within the scientific community we believe that God has brought into being a created order that only goes on existing because of his continued say-so. Without the active ongoing will of God there would be nothing for scientists to describe. And what we describe has objective reality in that it goes on existing irrespective of whether there are humans present who can describe it, because the eternal God has always been there from the beginning to observe the universe. But in creating humanity to subdue the earth, God has given us rational minds that can be used to generate reliable knowledge about the universe around us, knowledge that can be used wisely (or not) in subduing and stewarding the earth for God's glory. All that scientists describe are the works of God in creation because there is nothing else to describe. The faithfulness of God in his creation means that its properties are consistent and reproducible, thereby making science possible. Part of that faithfulness is reflected in the workings of our own minds so that we can use our minds to generate accurate and reliable information about God's creation, information that is never infallible, always open to revision as new data emerge, but which, with time, provides facts about our world that we can be sure about.

So can we be sure about anything? You bet we can, providing that the scientific community practices consistent truth telling, self-criticism, accurate reporting and recording, rigorous refereeing and the other social practices that generate good science that I have outlined in this chapter. Christians who are scientists rejoice in this privilege of telling the truth about God's amazing creation.

© Denis R. Alexander, 2005

9. QUANTUM PHYSICS: A CHALLENGE TO SCIENTIFIC OBJECTIVITY?

Peter J. Bussey

The quantum revolution

In the year 1900 the German physicist Max Planck announced a hypothesis that was to turn the world of science upside down. Using existing theories of physics, he had been attempting to account for the spectrum of heat and light that comes from hot objects such as furnaces, or the sun. These theories had not worked; the attempt had been a complete failure. The only way to get the mathematics right appeared to be to assign a totally new property to the heat and light radiation.

It seemed unavoidable to suppose that the radiation, instead of being emitted in a continuous manner from a hot object, was emitted or absorbed only in small lumps, which Planck called 'quanta'. The energy in one lump of radiation needed to be proportional to its wave frequency. If that were the case, the experimental observations could be explained.

This was the birth of what came to be known as 'quantum theory'. In this account I shall attempt to explain the essentials of this modern branch of physics, and show why it has had far-reaching and indeed controversial implications for our view of the physical world.

As the twentieth century progressed, and radical ideas found their way into almost every other area of human culture, so it was also in physics. Albert Einstein is best known for his theory of relativity, which transformed the way we think about space and time. In another remarkable development, he took Planck's quantum ideas and showed that they would make sense of a newly discovered phenomenon known as the photoelectric effect. When light is shone on a metal surface, electrons can be ejected to give an electric current. The properties of this current, Einstein showed, are also explained if light comes in quantized lumps. One quantum of light ejects one electron from the metal surface, and gives its energy to the electron. The 'lumps of light' are in fact behaving like small particles, and they were later given the name 'photons'.

Many experiments have confirmed that light behaves this way. It is not an obvious fact of nature, because an ordinary light beam contains so many photons that their individual presence is not easily detected. Just as the individual molecules in a jet of water are not normally evident to us, so neither are the individual photons in a beam of light. They are so small, and there are so many of them.

At this point, all that was implied was a need for a new theory of light, but far more revolutionary developments were on the horizon. For over a century light had been known to propagate through space as waves, with properties such as frequency and wavelength. It was established that light waves consist of oscillating electric and magnetic fields. Two light waves, like all waves, can add up or cancel each other out at any point in space – a phenomenon known as 'interference'. The bright colours we see when the surface of a CD is viewed at certain angles are an example of interference: if the angle is right, light waves of a given colour will add up, and the result is a particularly bright beam of that colour at that angle.

During the 1920s it was discovered that electrons, the small particles that are constituents of atoms, also show interference properties. When passed through crystalline materials, they were found to come off with unexpectedly high intensities at some angles, and low intensities at others. It became clear that just as light waves have certain properties of particles, so atomic particles can have properties of waves. This applies not only to electrons, but also to protons and neutrons and other elementary particles.

This was a mind-shattering development, which completely transformed the way in which physicists had to think about matter. Earlier, everyone had taken atomic particles to be tiny material objects. They would have the kinds of properties expected of small pieces of matter: shape, mass, position in space, velocity, energy and so on. Now physicists were telling the world to believe that these entities have, in addition, a second set of properties – wave properties – that are totally incompatible with the first set! The problem is that an object cannot have the property of a unique position in space while possessing a wave structure: the latter requires that an extended range of positions be occupied. The situation is paradoxical.

Things went on from bad to worse! Not just atomic particles, but atoms themselves – even molecules and footballs – were deemed to have both traditional properties and also wave properties, according to the new quantum theory. The smaller and lighter the object, the more easily observable are its wave properties. Thus the wave properties of electrons can be demonstrated relatively easily by modern techniques, whereas those of footballs are in practice not discernible at all. In principle, though, they are there.

Particles as waves

Imagine a beam of light approaching a barrier in which there are two narrow parallel slits. Those light waves that manage to pass through the two slits go on to strike a light-sensitive detector – for example, a photographic film – at some point beyond. What will happen there? At the places on the detector where the light waves arrive in phase and reinforce each other, a bright intensity will be recorded, but a low intensity will be recorded where the waves arrive out of phase and tend to cancel each other. The detector, in fact, records a series of bright and dark bands, known as 'interference bands'.

Exactly the same experiment, we now realize, can also be performed with a beam of electrons! Again there will be a pattern of alternating bright and dark interference bands in an electron detector (another photographic film, say) placed at a point beyond the barrier with the slits. Classical physics would absolutely not have predicted that particles such as electrons could produce interference patterns. More recently, experiments using atoms and even sizeable molecules have shown this wave-implying behaviour.[1]

Physicists had long been familiar with the idea that light waves can go through two slits and then combine to form an interference pattern. Now electrons are doing the same thing! Yet surely an electron is a particle? How can a particle go through both slits at the same time – surely it must go through one slit or the other? The quantum physicist replies that things have changed now. The electron is *fundamentally different* from any crude picture of it as a kind of tiny spherical object. It can indeed have the property of being spread out in space, in its guise as a wave – and as such it can perfectly well pass through two slits at the same time.

Within an atom, electrons are often imagined as tiny things orbiting round the atomic nucleus, like planets round the sun. This again will not do. The electrons in an atom in fact exist in spread-out wave patterns, each occupying a volume of space around the nucleus. The best visualization of them would be like fuzzy clouds having a certain shape and density. Once more, the situation differs markedly from our normal ideas of solid, material objects.

Randomness in quantum physics

An electron, then, can have particle properties such as position and velocity, and also wave properties such as wavelength and frequency. But can one electron possess both sets of properties *in a*

---

1. At present the largest objects for which quantum properties have been demonstrated include the football-like molecules comprising a network of sixty carbon atoms known as 'buckminsterfullerene', or more colloquially as 'buckyballs'. Quite a large molecule, and this is not the largest example.

well-defined way at the same time? No – that indeed would be a logical impossibility! The properties that are displayed in a well-defined way depend on the circumstances, and on what has been done to the electron. We could ensure that it has a definite position, for example, by having it interact with something whose position is precisely defined. There are ways of setting up a beam of electrons with a well-defined wavelength. The type of property exhibited arises out of the physical situation.

If an electron is in a wavelike state, its position is not well defined. What will happen if it is put into an apparatus that measures position? This might be a set of small electron detectors. Whichever of these fires would tell us that the electron is located at the position of that detector. Now even if the electron position is not well defined, one of the detectors will still fire – but which of them does so *will now be largely random*! At any given location in space, the electron simply has a certain probability that it will be found there. This probability is proportional to the intensity of the original electron wave at that point.

Scientists in earlier periods saw the universe, at least in regard to its physical behaviour, as a kind of gigantic mechanical system. If you have a complete physical description of such a system, and if you know what natural laws are operating, then in principle you can calculate everything about its future behaviour. In practice this is unattainable; we have neither the knowledge nor the computer power to work out the future of the universe other than approximately. A precise calculation would nevertheless be possible in theory, if the laws of nature are taken as rigid determining principles that oblige everything to operate in a completely exact way. The traditional analogy was to liken the universe, viewed thus, to a colossal piece of clockwork.

The abandonment of this principle, perhaps more than any other feature of the new theory, has proved a stumbling block to many in their attempts to come to terms with quantum physics. The author C. S. Lewis, who certainly believed that human beings possess qualities that go beyond the laws of physics, wrote in the 1940s:

The older scientists believed that the smallest particles of matter moved according to strict laws . . . Some modern scientists seem to think – if I

understand them – that this is not so. They seem to think that the
individual unit of matter . . . moves in an indeterminate or random
fashion . . . Those who like myself have had a philosophical rather than
a scientific education find it almost impossible to believe that the
scientists really mean what they seem to be saying.[2]

Einstein himself could not accept this development, and protested
repeatedly that 'God does not play dice.'

Nevertheless, 'controlled randomness' seems here to stay. To
take another example, atoms of a radioactive element decay at
times that are constrained by the element's having a certain half-
life, which is determined by physical laws. Subject to this
constraint, the time when a given atom decays is random. All
this is seriously contrary to the idea of a mechanical universe,
and it seems that many people might have preferred a mechanical universe.

The new view of matter

Quantum physics has a quality of strangeness compared with our
everyday notions of how things work. The conceptual difficulties
stem from two main features: that definite values of certain physical quantities are incompatible with each other, and that
occurrences of certain processes have an unpredictable, random
element. These affect our view of physical nature quite radically.
The partial 'breakdown of law and order' represented by randomness is perhaps the easier concept to understand. Let us now
consider the accompanying 'breakdown of definiteness'.

Overall, it has been said that modern physics is 'non-
Aristotelian'. This means that we can no longer say of a thing that
it has a fixed set of physical properties or attributes, each possessing a definite value.

For example, an object in our everyday[3] environment might be

---

2. C. S. Lewis, *Miracles* (London: Fontana, 1960), p. 25.

3. For easier comprehension I use the word 'everyday' instead of the usual

described as having a colour, namely red, a mass, namely two tons, a temperature, namely 40 degrees, a velocity, namely 50 kilometres per hour and so on. Now, it is certainly possible to make a list of properties that a quantum object such as an electron might have: position, energy, wavelength and the like. However as we have seen, precise, definite values of all of these properties are not mutually compatible. Some or all of the listed properties, at any given time, must have values that are to some degree ill defined or 'fuzzy'. Which properties are definite and which are indefinite depends on the state the quantum object is in. That in turn depends on what has previously happened to it.

What, you might ask, does nature gain from all this subtlety? Well, it does mean a considerably increased flexibility in the repertoire of properties that a particle can possess and make use of, so to speak. Its ordinary set of properties can now be combined with wave properties too. It would take many pages to outline the range and richness of the physical phenomena that quantum ideas make possible.

The idea of complementarity

The so-called 'uncertainty principle', associated with the physicist Werner Heisenberg, describes the situation by saying that there are pairs of properties that are 'complementary', meaning that the more certain or definite one of the properties is, the more uncertain and indefinite the other must be. Position and wavelength are complementary quantities. The more well defined the position is, the less well defined is the wavelength, and vice versa.[4]

We have to be quite strict about this point! It is not that a particle in a wavelike state still possesses a precise position, but we do not

---

technical terms 'macroscopic' and 'large-scale'. 'Quantum physics' and 'quantum theory' are used in place of 'quantum mechanics'.

4. It is more normal to express this in terms of momentum rather than wavelength, but for non-physicists the argument is easier to follow in terms of wavelength. The logic of the argument is the same.

know the value of that position. Having a well-defined wavelength *precludes* it from having a well-defined position. But in any case, if we measure an electron's position and get a particular value, the electron really does at this point have that definite position. Wavelength now becomes indefinite; any definite wavelength value the electron might have had is lost. The electron's subsequent behaviour will develop out of its newly acquired precise position.

These ideas apply to any kind of quantum measurement, or 'observation'. Whenever a particle interacts with a measurement apparatus, it jumps randomly into a new state with a definite value of the measured property. This is the so-called 'quantum event' or 'quantum jump'.

What can we know about a particle?

From all the above, we might very well wonder how much objective knowledge is possible about an electron or other atomic particle. Part of the answer consists of a new way to describe a particle's physical condition, instead of the previous 'Aristotelian' language. The relevant concept now is of the particle's *quantum state*. This can be expressed mathematically, and whatever measurement we choose to make on the particle, the mathematics will give us the probability of getting any specified result; that is, we can calculate the probability of obtaining a given position value if position is measured, a given wavelength value if wavelength is measured and so on. What is not possible is to measure all these things simultaneously.

The 'quantum state' carries all the physical information about the particle, and is considered as something quite objective and well defined. If a particle's quantum state and physical circumstances are known, then it is perfectly possible to calculate what its state will be at any future time – provided that no kind of experimental observation is made on it meanwhile, since this would produce a random change in the state. There is a well-established mathematical equation, known as 'Schrödinger's equation', which enables us to do this calculation. To this extent, quantum physics is still definite.

How can we know a particle's quantum state? It may be possible to work it out from the previous history of the particle, but otherwise an experimental investigation may be needed. In a quantum situation a single measurement is not generally sufficient, though: we would most likely need to prepare large samples of particles with this same quantum state. Then we would arrange to perform a variety of measurements, repeating them many times to estimate the probabilities of all the possible outcomes. From this we should be able to establish the state of the particle. Some experimental uncertainty will always remain, but this is the case with any scientific measurement.

So objective knowledge can indeed be obtained about a quantum particle. The difference between quantum physics and the earlier physics – referred to as 'classical physics' – is that formerly one could think of measuring everything at once on the same object. In the quantum situation, many different measurements may be needed to build up knowledge of a particle state. But it is in principle knowable as accurately as we wish.

Waves and wave-functions

The quantum state of a particle such as an electron, we have just said, can be described by a mathematical expression. Reflecting the particle's wavelike nature, this expression is often known as the 'wave-function',[5] and it tells us about the form of the wave, anywhere in space. If a measurement takes place, the particle state randomly changes – so, therefore, does the wave-function. This random quantum event is often called the 'collapse of the wave-function'.

How is the wave-function to be understood? For light waves, the corresponding quantity denotes oscillating electric and

---

5. The word 'function' is a technical mathematical term, used to denote an expression whose value depends on one or more quantities occurring in it, such as position and time in the case of a quantum wave-function.

magnetic fields, but the electron wave-function is so far just a mathematical tool. Within the limits of quantum randomness, it can predict the future behaviour of the electron, just as a weather-forecasting formula may be able to predict the future weather. But of course, the weather formula is certainly not the weather itself! How closely, then, can the electron wave-function be identified with the actual electron?

The wave-function, or any other formulation of the quantum state, can presumably be designated as an *attribute* of the electron, in place of its traditional set of physical properties. It can first be thought of in predictive and future-oriented terms. Interpreted in the narrowest way – which we will later question – it does not tell us anything at all about 'what the particle is', but only about 'what the particle might do'; that is, about the probabilities of future quantum events such as occur in experimental measurements.

The quantum events amount to 'observations' of the electron, and give us experiential knowledge about it. They are our sole source of such knowledge. How about the electron's existence in between the events? Does a particle have any existence at all, then, or is 'reality' confined to the quantum events themselves? By definition, whatever occurs between observations is not observationally known, and there are those who would deny the electron's real existence at these intermediate times, on the grounds that it is 'metaphysical'.

Such a viewpoint, however, reduces the whole of physical reality to what can be known by ourselves, and that sounds dangerous. Are we so important in the universe? And is 'knowledge' the real crux of existence?

Of atoms and cats

Possibly the most intractable problem in quantum physics is illustrated by the famous 'cat' paradox, proposed by the quantum pioneer Erwin Schrödinger. The question concerns when a wave-function actually 'collapses'. What happens, when a particle enters a detector and interacts with it? The supposition is that an extremely complicated wave-function will develop, encompassing the states of the particle and all the atoms in the detector. If there are several detectors, there arises an even more complicated wave-function, which includes the original particle together with all the atoms in *all* of the detectors – their states all linked together in one enormous mathematical expression.

But this is still a mathematical formula and still a wave-function. Not yet having 'collapsed', it still tells us about the full set of probabilities for each of the detectors to count the particle. As far as this gargantuan wave-function is concerned, the particle still exists in each of the detectors.

At some stage a 'choice' occurs, and just one detector gets to count the particle. The wave-function 'collapses'. But standard quantum theory fails to give any clue as to when or how this random quantum event actually takes place. Is it when the electron first enters a detector? Or is it when the numbers of atoms involved in the wave-function become sufficiently large? The theorist Eugene Wigner proposed that 'it is the entering of an impression into our consciousness which alters the wave function'.[6] At present we have no answer to this question.

Schrödinger imagined an 'infernal' experimental device containing a radioactive atom and a cat. It is arranged that the cat will stay alive if the radioactive atom remains undecayed in a given period of time, but will be put to death if the atom decays. The wave-function for this situation combines both possibilities. Now if such a wave-function genuinely denotes the physical state of the system, which of course includes the cat, then the condition of the cat is uncertain in a rather serious way. Just as an electron can pass simultaneously through both of two slits, or be simultaneously in several detectors, so the cat can likewise be in a state in which it is at the same time both alive and dead! This seems hardly plausible, but present quantum theory has no way to exclude it.

The suggestion was made by Wigner that 'quantum [theory], in its present form, is not applicable to living systems, whose

---

6. E. P. Wigner, in I. J. Good (ed.), *The Scientist Speculates* (London: Heinemann, 1961), p. 284.

consciousness is a decisive characteristic'.[7] But will this really solve the problem? Schrödinger's paradox is surely just as perplexing if the cat is asleep, or anaesthetized.

On the other hand, if wave-functions are considered *merely* as mathematical predictors, we are left with no picture or concept whatever of the real nature of a quantum particle – or indeed of any difference between the quantum behaviour of electrons and of cats.

The Copenhagen interpretation of quantum physics

In all of the above, the reader *ought* to feel puzzled. It has been remarked that whoever is not disturbed by quantum physics has not understood it! The strangeness of the situation has provoked a number of suggestions to interpret what is going on.

The best-known viewpoint is known as the 'Copenhagen' interpretation, since some of its early advocates were from that city.[8] There are variant versions, but basically they say the following. The language used in quantum physics has to be derived from the world of everyday physics, because this is the only suitable language available to us. The Danish quantum theorist Niels Bohr stressed, '*however far the phenomena transcend the scope of classical physical explanation, the account of all evidence must be expressed in classical terms*'.[9] The wave-function is to be regarded purely as a predictive instrument. The quantum events are intrinsically random; there is no 'invisible clockwork' underlying them. And

---

7. E. P. Wigner, in B. d'Espagnat (ed.), *Proceedings of the International School of Physics 'Enrico Fermi', Course 49* (New York: Academic, 1971), p. 17.

8. However, the Copenhagen physicists did not like this ascription, since they themselves rejected all other viewpoints! See L. Rosenfeld, in H. P. Stapp, 'The Copenhagen Interpretation', *American Journal of Physics* 40 (1972), p. 1115.

9. N. Bohr, in P. A. Schilpp (ed.), *Albert Einstein, Philosopher-Scientist*, Library of Living Philosophers (New York: MJF, 1970), p. 209 (italics original).

little or nothing can be said about the 'real nature' of an electron or other atomic particle.

Some members of the Copenhagen school went so far as to *deny* the real existence of the atomic particles. According to Heisenberg, we are able to talk objectively only about measurement processes and the like. 'The conception of the objective reality of the elementary particles has thus evaporated . . .'[10] But it hardly needs saying that this viewpoint leads to severe problems. What about the reality of atoms; or of molecules? What about that of assemblies of molecules, such as pieces of apparatus? At what stage does reality begin?

Bohr argued for the existence of a 'fundamental distinction between the measuring apparatus and the objects under investigation', namely the atomic particles.[11] This 'fundamental distinction' is associated with the need for one set of concepts in quantum physics, and another in everyday, classical physics. A different mode of reality for the two realms is implied. But it is hard to reconcile such a strong statement with the fact that the everyday world is built up out of quantum objects. Large-scale systems are even quantum systems themselves, though their quantum nature is too fine-scaled for us to observe in practice. A distinction at the conceptual and behavioural levels between the two physical realms is evident, but surely not at the 'fundamental' level? For the sake of philosophical tidiness, Bohr and his school were here constructing an artificial dividing-line that seems unsustainable and that just introduces another set of problems. In particular, we have the 'reality' question.

A possible escape route might be to take up a late remark by Heisenberg that 'the Copenhagen interpretation is not in itself a complete overall world-view. It was never intended to be such a

---

10. W. Heisenberg, 'The Representation of Nature in Contemporary Physics', *Daedalus* 87 (1958), p. 95. An expanded discussion of Heisenberg's views is given by P. Davies in his introduction to W. Heisenberg, *Physics and Philosophy* (Harmondsworth: Penguin, 1989).

11. N. Bohr, *Essays 1958–62 on Atomic Physics and Human Knowledge* (New York: Wiley, 1963), p. 3.

view.'[12] But it was certainly intended as a complete interpretation of quantum physics! If no objective reality exists in the quantum realm or, by extrapolation, even in the everyday realm, then we are in a serious dilemma. There might then indeed be a logic towards saying that human consciousness is what defines reality.

Einstein was very much affected by these issues. He voiced a strong objection to the attitude that only what is observable is 'real', saying 'What I dislike in this kind of argumentation is the basic positivistic attitude, which from my view is untenable, and which seems to me to come to the same thing as Berkeley's principle, *esse est percipi*.'[13] That is, 'to be is to be perceived' – or in the quantum case, to be observed.

Now if in fact we are able to observe an entity *whenever we choose to do so* – as is taken to be the case for a quantum particle – then its objective existence surely has to be accepted.[14] The hypothesis 'the particle exists' is confirmed whenever it is tested. A clear recourse is therefore to bite the bullet, accept 'metaphysics' and allow the particle to exist whether it is observed or not. It has numerical attributes that are the parameters of its quantum state.[15] Even with this rather minimal account of the particle, it would seem perverse to deny that it really is there.

Quantum theory, it must be appreciated, enables some very general statements to be made about physics, for example about

---

12. Heisenberg, 'Representation of Nature', p. 1114.

13. A. Einstein, in Schilpp, *Albert Einstein, Philosopher-Scientist*, p. 669.

14. Of course, classical physics observations could be made *continuously*, which gives this type of positivism no foothold. One is reminded of the positivism of Mach, who rejected the existence of atoms for many years as a metaphysical abstraction, because they had not been experimentally observed. But in due course, as we know, they were observed. Experiment thereby confirmed a theory and disproved a philosophy.

15. Space is lacking to discuss another celebrated quantum issue, namely the 'Einstein–Podolsky–Rosen' paradox. This involves states containing two 'entangled' particles, and the solution is to regard these as intrinsic two-particle states up until an observation is made. Non-specialists may disregard this footnote!

the nature and characteristics of atoms and about the different chemical elements. These accounts provide a great deal of physical insight and have a strong flavour of 'reality' about them, and all this is quite independent of the nature of quantum observations. Since Bohr and Heisenberg, the theory of elementary particles has developed in many diverse ways, as has experiment. We even study the inner structure of particles whose reality the Copenhagenist might deny. All of this, while retaining the essential quantum principles, seems based on a sense of underlying physical reality, apart perhaps from some of the more abstract theories. The Copenhagen interpretation is surely too restrictive.

Some less orthodox viewpoints

I have mentioned the suggestion that consciousness is what makes quantum events happen. The converse is also imaginable, although among both physicists and consciousness researchers this appears to be a minority view.[16] But if consciousness is the cause of quantum events, what processes were happening on earth during the millions of years before the development of higher animal life? They were surely a precondition for the appearance of consciousness, and so there is a chicken-and-egg situation. A version of the Schrödinger's cat paradox might even arise in which after many millions of years of total cosmic indeterminacy, the consciousness that resolves the issue is *itself* both present and absent at the same time! Would this logically oblige consciousness to appear, since the opposite choice by definition cannot happen? Most physicists would find this entire scenario unconvincing.

There are other unorthodox interpretations of quantum theory, of which I shall mention two. A number of physicists, unhappy with the Copenhagen position and with randomness and indeterminacy, have argued that an invisible, hidden physical mechanism does exist after all. Theories constructed on this basis are known as

---

16. See, e.g., S. R. Hameroff, A. W. Kaszniak and A. E. Scott (eds.), *Towards a Science of Consciousness*, vol. 2 (Cambridge, MA: MIT Press, 1998), p. 3.

'hidden variables' theories. However, in so far as these theories make predictions that differ from standard quantum theory, experiments have to date shown them to be incorrect. Usually, though, they are contrived to give results identical to the normal theory.

Another alternative to randomness is to suppose that nature does not really make choices at all. Everything that can happen does happen. Whenever an electron could give a count in one of several detectors, it is proposed that the universe multiplies into several versions of itself, each corresponding to one of the possibilities! We too multiply, and each version of ourselves, in its own version of the universe, is aware of that particular outcome of the experimental measurement. By now, there are untold myriads of universes, and so this is known as the 'many worlds' interpretation. But it is all so extravagant (and no-one has actually detected these universes experimentally) that its followers are in a somewhat small minority. It simply shows the remarkable extremes to which some will go to avoid randomness in physics.

Although obviously no *mechanism* may be demanded for a process that is random, we still might seek a 'rationale'. Why should quantum events happen? All we know at present is that they do. At the end of the day, the large majority of physicists do not worry too much about these quantum puzzles. The mathematical formalism works, correct predictions are made, and at this level the entire theory succeeds fantastically well. In this practical sense, everything is 'understood'. The Copenhagen position has itself been interpreted as denoting such a pragmatic attitude.[17] This is fine as far as it goes, we may happily grant, but it should at the same time be realized that pragmatism is a philosophical name for avoiding asking deeper questions.

Quantum physics as a 'scientific revolution'

Without doubt, the move from classical physics to quantum physics represents a dramatic example of a 'scientific revolution',

---

17. Stapp, 'Copenhagen Interpretation', p. 1098.

exactly the kind of thing Thomas Kuhn had in mind in his well-known thesis that that is precisely how science makes its most important progress.[18] The move from classical to quantum ideas demanded – as we have seen – a radically new set of concepts about how the universe operates. Certainly, we may term this a 'paradigm shift'.

Kuhn's proposal was not received uncritically.[19] The reader of his book can easily be confused by the shifting usages of the word 'paradigm',[20] and there is often a lack of clear distinction between 'paradigm' and 'theory'. For our present purposes a paradigm may be understood as 'the set of concepts and assumptions within which a scientific theory is stated and makes sense'. We have seen very clearly that quantum physics uses a significantly different set of concepts and assumptions from the earlier 'classical' physics.

So, we ask, is classical physics 'wrong'? It will be helpful to refer briefly to another area. Newton in the seventeenth century produced a theory of forces that gave a spectacularly successful account of what was observed in physics and astronomy at that time, and for more than two centuries afterwards. Einstein's relativity theory then replaced certain of Newton's background assumptions, and accounted for even more physical phenomena. Therefore, says Kuhn, Newton's theory was 'wrong'.[21] But Newton's *theory* is still extremely accurate as a special case of Einstein's theory, provided that all velocities concerned are small compared with that of light. It was Newton's *paradigm* that was not right.

---

18. T. S. Kuhn, *The Structure of Scientific Revolutions* (3rd ed.; University of Chicago Press, 1996).

19. See the discussion by John Taylor, ch. 4 in this volume.

20. One reader claimed the word was employed in twenty-two different ways in the book! See the later postscript in Kuhn, *Structure of Scientific Revolutions*, p. 181.

21. Ibid., p. 98. Kuhn argued that Einstein's and Newton's basic physical concepts are not simultaneously understandable. He was mistaken; physicists go to a lot of trouble to ensure that a new theory can communicate with the old one.

In fact the same *theory* – understood as a set of specific laws and structures applying to given physical systems – can sometimes be understandable and truthful within significantly different paradigms, though maybe with varying degrees of precision. The equations of classical physics, thus, constitute a perfectly good theory of physics even within a quantum paradigm, provided that the circumstances in which they are used are appropriate. That is to say, we must be dealing with large systems of many particles, and working to a precision that is much less fine than the quantum uncertainties. These conditions are amply fulfilled in nearly all normal human-scale activities. A classical paradigm can then be used as a practical convenience, since its concepts are applicable and accurate enough in this context. The quantum revolution left the 'classical level', in effect, largely undisturbed – unlike the chemical revolution that replaced phlogiston by oxygen to explain combustion. Here the older viewpoint had to be completely abandoned.

The Copenhagen interpretation, in a like manner, aims to use a quantum paradigm at the atomic level, and at the same time a classical paradigm at the everyday level. The latter is used to define the physical terminology, and is also taken to define the ontology, namely 'reality'. But this hybrid paradigm is problematic since it leaves the quantum-level ontology quite unclear.

Quantum physics and postmodernism

Postmodernism has introduced a strong element of subjectivism and philosophical relativism into our culture. This would naturally lead to a number of questions for the quantum physicist.

- What is the role of the 'observer' in quantum physics? Much is said about 'observations'. Do two different human observers of a quantum situation observe the same thing?
- Treated entirely pragmatically, do the prescriptions of the theory – that is, the results of the definitions, equations and quantum 'laws' – accurately correspond to the physical world? If so:

- Could different paradigms encompass the same basic 'quantum theory'? In that case, could we say that any one alternative viewpoint is 'better' or 'truer' than another?

The answer to the first point is that only a minority of physicists would insist that a *human* observer is needed. A computerized robot could be programmed to perform a set of quantum measurements, and the results would be just the same (apart from the random element) as if done by a human being. What we call a quantum 'observation' is really just a certain kind of physical process that may be able to tell us something. Two human beings watching the apparatus will both see the same thing: the actual 'quantum observation' has already occurred by the time a signal is presented to human cognisance. It occurred, in an obscure way, in the process of amplification by which a quantum-level interaction generates a large-scale effect in the apparatus.

The basic phenomenology of quantum processes is therefore perfectly objective. Two human observers cannot do different measurements on the same electron at the same time, and the observation that does take place is an unambiguous occurrence whose outcome will be agreed by both of them.

And, of course, if the theory did *not* give an accurate account of the physical world, it would long ago have been amended or discarded. Quantum theory has in fact enabled us to understand not only atomic physics but also the whole of chemistry, in so far as the necessary elaborate calculations can be achieved. It is a remarkably successful branch of science.

In quantum physics, we note next, a certain type of 'alternative viewpoint' exists in association with different mathematical formulations of the equations. However, one formulation can always be transformed mathematically into another. They are logically equivalent, and the physical content is the same. We use what is most convenient in a given context. These are not different paradigms in Kuhn's sense.

But the different interpretations of quantum physics that were set out earlier are very far from logically equivalent. They should be seen as different possible paradigms, within any of which the theory can be expressed. Is there scope for the postmodernist here?

A postmodernist addressing a conference of quantum physicists might give an interestingly provocative talk. '*All* these interpretations are valid,' he might say, 'given that the equations fit the experimental data. If you are rather subjectively inclined, then for you the consciousness paradigm is true! But if you are a radical pragmatist with no belief in anything beneath the surface, then why not adopt the Copenhagen position? For those who feel an urge to believe in real things, the Copenhagen position can be beefed up a little by attributing reality to the particles as described by their wave-functions. The born-again Cosmic Mystic should go for a many-worlds approach. And as for you classical traditionalists – salt of the earth – well, you have the absolute right to hold to a hidden variables theory! Please don't let's talk about *objective* truth, though. It's so much more socially acceptable to have a pluralism of quantum interpretational paradigms.'

Now the audience of such a talk would not at all be happy. Each adherent of each viewpoint would maintain that their own particular viewpoint was true, and the others defective or even nonsensical. The history of real-life quantum debates gives ample evidence of this. If it were possible, most would want to find a crucial experiment that would vindicate their own position. The Copenhagenist would invoke Occam's razor, rejecting all the other positions as unnecessarily complicated. Nearly everyone would reject the extravagance of the many-worlds position. There would be philosophical argumentation. The postmodernist would think that they were all out of their minds, but they would think the same about the postmodernist. Within the world of science, the philosophical relativism of the postmodernist appears as simply incoherent.

The point here is that on the basis of the historical development of science, scientists have formed common impressions, not always very well defined, about what the universe is like, what general principles operate, and what makes a good scientific theory. A quantum revolution strains this situation, but while there may be some room for different perspectives to be held, the quantum interpretations discussed above appear too disparate for peaceful coexistence. They seem to go towards the heart of issues that are actually worth arguing about. They are not just different kinds of 'private conceptual wallpaper', but seem to be about how the real building is constructed beneath the wallpaper layers. And at any time – as Einstein had been hoping – a superior paradigm might perhaps appear that will clarify everything better.

There is a further comment to make. It might turn out that at some point the paradigms get out of control because our rational understanding has reached the limit of what it can achieve. This could amount to a kind of 'frontier of mystery', which we cannot attempt to discuss here. Another possibility could be that the situation is rational but outside *human* rationality. The correct paradigm is beyond us. Both these situations are compatible with a religious point of view and could even invite it. They imply a further reality that is actually *there* – as it were, a deeper type of objectivity.

Conclusions

Quantum physics has presented its practitioners with some remarkably subtle problems in natural philosophy. Its aims, clearly, are to extend our rational understanding and our accurate knowledge of the physical world. Both these things are important, for if either broke down, the subject would no longer be science. However, many of its aspects are extremely counter-intuitive.

Paul Dirac, one of the founders of quantum theory, famously remarked that to make progress in such an area it is necessary to get the mathematics right first, and leave the philosophy until later.[22] This is more or less what the early developers of the subject did – they adopted a 'minimal paradigm' encompassing the ideas outlined in the opening sections of this chapter. This enabled the theory to be rigorously formulated so as to give clear, objective predictions for experiment.

But there are difficulties with the minimalist 'Copenhagen' viewpoint. A satisfactory conceptual framework is in the end essential for a convincing scientific theory, and so there have been a variety

---

22. P. A. M. Dirac, in A. R. Marlow (ed.), *Mathematical Foundations of Quantum Theory* (New York: Academic, 1978), pp. 1–8.

of further proposed paradigmatic developments, normally referred to as interpretations: in other words, attempts to understand 'what the theory means'. The reader will have gathered that I tend to favour some kind of realist approach. But in any case, the meaning must be seen as something objective, because it is after all a *scientific* paradigm, and it is the business of science to be objective. The debates are about which of the various proposals may be *true*. Postmodernist subjectivism is contrary to the spirit of science.

Truth in this context might refer to further experimental consequences implied by an interpretation. Or it can be philosophical – along the lines of what kind of interpretation is actually acceptable as a good scientific paradigm. Questions like these relate to deep judgments about the nature of science and of the universe, and we can hardly avoid calling them metaphysical.

Yes indeed, there is no running away from the matter. Metaphysics is alive and well in physics. Its presence cannot be denied – even though it may not always be allowed to announce its name at the party!

© Peter J. Bussey, 2005

10. TRUTH IN THE GEOLOGICAL SCIENCES

Robert S. White

Can we have reliable knowledge of things that happened in the distant past, long before humans existed to give eyewitness accounts, perhaps even before any life existed on earth, maybe even before the earth itself was formed?

I shall argue that we can give a strongly affirmative answer to this question. Furthermore, there are extremely valuable lessons to be learnt from studying the way the earth has responded in the distant past to climatic changes, to global environmental perturbations and to high risk but rare events such as earthquakes, volcanic eruptions, floods and extreme weather conditions. The geological record contains a history of such events that is highly relevant to humankind at the present and which is of great importance simply because the most extreme and, therefore, the most dangerous events are also the rarest: so rare, indeed, that there may be no similar events in recorded human history to prepare us for such occurrences. Paradoxically, the number of people likely to be killed or injured by such natural catastrophes is far higher now than at any time in the past, despite our relative scientific and technological sophistication, because urban concentrations and world population densities are higher than they have ever been before.

The scientific method

The scientific enterprise endeavours to understand the natural world through observation, experimentation and extrapolation from known conditions to wider circumstances. Typically, results from experiments in a laboratory are extrapolated to the wider world, or indeed to the universe at large. New scientific theories are reckoned to be useful and become widely accepted if they successfully predict the behaviour of the natural world better than existing theories, and if they fit in with currently known data.

Although the scientific enterprise has been remarkably fruitful, and has led to huge technological advances that, on the whole, have greatly improved the lot of humankind, there are several important caveats to the nature of science that are not always recognized. First, all scientific theories are only provisional and are likely to be revised as more information becomes available, or as new or more accurate measurements are made. In this sense, the scientific theories are only a model of an underlying reality, which they approximate to a greater or lesser degree. Truth ultimately does not lie in the particular mathematical theory that describes some aspect of the behaviour of the natural world, however elegant that theory may be: truth lies in the underlying reality.

A good example of the provisional nature of scientific theories is provided by the theories that describe the mechanical motion of bodies. Newton's Laws of Motion, first propounded in 1686,[1] are

---

1. Newton published these ideas on 5 July 1687 in his *Philosophiae naturalis principia mathematica* (often called *Principia* or *Principia mathematica* for short). It is interesting that Newton wrote in his *Principia* (1713) the phrase *Hypotheses non fingo*, by which he meant that 'I do not assert that any hypotheses are true'. Newton wrote that 'whatever is not deduced from the phænomena must be called an hypothesis; and hypotheses, whether metaphysical or physical, or based on occult qualities, or mechanical, have

an extremely powerful description of the motion of everything from billiard balls to planets. They are sufficiently good to send a man to the moon, or to describe the motion of the planets round the sun. But Newton developed them on what are now known to be conceptually incorrect ideas. Einstein's theories of relativity provide a much better description of the motions of bodies, particularly at velocities approaching the speed of light or near massive bodies. You certainly need the theory of general relativity to explain black holes. Nevertheless, Newtonian mechanics remains a simple, fruitful and useful model for many purposes because it reproduces the behaviour of the real world sufficiently accurately for many practical purposes. It is highly unlikely that Einsteinian mechanics is the last word in describing the real world. So it is important both to remember the provisional nature of all scientific theories, however good they may seem to be, and also to remind ourselves not to invest more meaning in the equations than is warranted. Professor Hawking, although one of the best physicists of his generation, is simply not correct in asserting that if we could write down the equations of everything – the so-called Grand Theory – we would 'know the mind of God'.[2] All we would have is a rather good description of how matter behaves, and even then it would still remain provisional, because a still better description almost certainly would lie round the corner.

The second common misconception about science is that

---

no place in experimental philosophy. In this philosophy particular propositions are inferred from the phænomena, and afterwards rendered general by induction' (tr. Andrew Motte, 1729, available online at http://members.tripod.com/~gravitee/). Newton was firmly grounded in the importance of scientific theories explaining observable phenomena without recourse to outside agencies.

2. S. W. Hawking, *A Brief History of Time* (London: Bantam, 1988), p. 193. See also D. Wilkinson, *God, the Big Bang and Stephen Hawking* (Tunbridge Wells: Monarch, 1993), for a helpful account of the contributions made by Stephen Hawking to understanding the early origins of the universe, and for discussion of how to relate science and religion, particularly in the area of astronomy.

accepted scientific theories explain everything in their purview. Almost always this is untrue. What the most successful theories do achieve is to provide powerful overarching paradigms which have a richness of explanatory and predictive capability that makes them both widely accepted and useful in understanding the material world. The theory of evolution is a good example of this. For many decades it has stood the test of time and the addition of huge amounts of new data, including the vast array of data obtained from the sequencing of the human genome. But with almost all successful theories there are still observations or results that do not fit. Scientists are well aware of this, but the populace at large often is not. The few things that do not fit do not invalidate a successful grand theory.[3] Sometimes these misfits are due to wrong observations, or to perturbations by some other small effect that is not accounted for in the grand theory. Often the misfits provide valuable incentives for future research work, which may lead to refinement of the grand theory. Occasionally the number of misfits accumulates to be so large that the theory is overturned and replaced by a new paradigm. But the notion that any given scientific theory is absolutely correct in all situations is generally false, however powerful or important the theory may be. This again underlines the fact that scientific theories are approximations to reality, useful working models of how the material world behaves. The material world does not display particular properties in order to obey a 'law of nature' or a mathematical equation: rather, our theories and 'laws' are simply descriptions, to a greater or lesser degree of approximation, of how the real world behaves.

The third point that is often not recognized by non-scientists is the extent to which the corpus of scientific understanding and observations is deeply interlocking and interdependent. Any new theory has to explain the body of knowledge at least as well as the theory it replaces. For example, as is well known, some Christians

---

3. For a discussion of how scientists often accommodate observations that apparently do not fit any existing theories, without breaking their faith in the correctness or usefulness of the main theories themselves, see Del Ratzsch, *Science and its Limits* (Leicester: Apollos, 2000).

hold a young date of around 10,000 years for the age of the earth, based on their reading of Scripture. This age is a factor of half a million times smaller than the accepted scientific age of the earth of 4,560 million years, not exactly a minor difference! The 'young earth creationists' who espouse such views maintain that they can be supported scientifically if, for example, radiometric decay rates were grossly different in the past. Although it is difficult formally to exclude this possibility as a point taken in isolation, the fact is that if the rates of radiometric decay were that much different, then a whole structure of other well-attested scientific results would also collapse across a wide range of interlocking disciplines, including chemistry, physics and biology, with nothing to replace them. It is simply not possible to change one property of the world in isolation from our scientific understanding of its other physical properties viewed as a whole.

Geological sciences

The scientific methodology used in investigating geological phenomena is the same as that outlined in the preceding section for studying the material world around us at the present day. This approach is enshrined in the basic geological principle that 'the present is the key to the past'. Just because something happened either a long time ago (temporally different), or a long way away (spatially removed), it does not mean that we should drop our normal expectation that the way that the material world behaves is consistent. After all, we make the same assumption every day of our lives. If we see a cricket ball fly over the wall and out of sight, we expect it to fall to the ground in just the same way as if we had seen it fall.[4] If we come home from work and find a cricket ball lying amidst shards of broken glass in our greenhouse we assume that it landed there at an earlier time, breaking the glass as it fell,

---

4. I am leaving aside the philosophical question that arises at a very small quantum-mechanical level as to whether the presence of an observer affects the outcome of a physical process.

even though we did not see it happen. We would not dream of saying that the laws of physics might be different just because we did not see something happen on the other side of the house, or even on the other side of the world. The consistency of 'nature' is what makes science both possible and fruitful. Indeed, from a Christian perspective, the consistency of the way the world behaves is a sign of God's own gracious nature, in that he creates a world in which we can live, which we can understand and in which we can therefore fulfil the creation edict that we should care for and be stewards of the earth.

It is striking that by using the laws of physics as we understand them today, it is possible to explain the behaviour of the universe back to within a fraction of a second of its formation some 13,700 million years ago. That this works so well, and fits all the relevant observations we can make, is a strong indication that our understanding is indeed correct. It is philosophically possible, of course, that the past is an illusion and that it only looks that way because an omniscient God has shielded the truth from us. We might all have been created yesterday, complete with false memories of the past. However, this is not compatible with all that we know of God's consistent, truth-telling character both from Scripture and from the experience of God's dealings with men and women through the ages. Neither Christian nor atheist would accept the view that we are deceived about what we can see, measure and record about the behaviour of the natural world.

But having stressed that we can come to a good understanding of the past using our current knowledge of how the world works, we should not fall into the trap of thinking therefore that nothing in the past was different. It was certainly very different one microsecond after the big bang, when the temperature was around 10 million million degrees kelvin. Yet it is possible to have a good understanding of the physics of that state. If we come down to earth, as it were, the geological record shows that there were times in the past when the whole earth was in an ice age, much colder than the present, and other times when it was much hotter on average than today. Although some geological environments, such as those found beneath the remote, deep oceans or those that gave rise to the deposition of chalk, reflect the slow but steady accumulation of sediments, there are many other geological records that are dominated by sudden catastrophes. For example, overbank floods from rivers crossing flood plains, such as the Mississippi or the Nile, happen in a matter of hours, yet may leave a thick layer of sediment across a broad region. The biggest floods may happen only once every few decades, or even once every few centuries, yet the sediment deposits they generate dominate the geological record preserved from that area, with little sediment from the intervening years. Other catastrophic events such as volcanic eruptions, tsunami, landslides, meteor impacts and the like, similarly and even less surprisingly, leave abrupt and unique geological records over large areas that nevertheless account for only a tiny fraction of the time elapsed in the geological record of the region. The consistency we seek, and make use of in interpreting the past is consistency of the physical laws, which does not necessarily lead to uniformity of sediment or rock production. The interaction of normal physical processes may produce a wide variety of outcomes, which is why the geological record provides a rich source of knowledge about the natural environment, and about some scenarios that humankind may face in the future.

Some aspects of using science to investigate the geological past are identical to what we may do in a scientific study of present-day objects. For example, it sometimes happens that ripples are preserved in sands and muds deposited in ancient rivers. By studying ripple formation in a laboratory flume tank, it may be possible to deduce the current direction and rate of flow that formed the ancient ripples now preserved in rock: by this means the current flows hundreds of millions of years ago in a particular place may be understood.

But there are also some marked differences between geological studies and laboratory studies of phenomena. The main difference is that the geological record is all that we have. Often the rocks are eroded away before they can be studied. In this respect geological science has a lot in common with the forensic science used at crime scenes to work out what happened. The criminologist may be able to work out the date or time of death by comparing the state of decay of a murder victim with decay under controlled experiments studied in the laboratory. Similarly it may be possible to deduce the conditions under which rocks were laid down or subsequently buried and altered by pressure and temperature changes, by careful analogy with studies performed under known conditions.

To continue for a moment the analogy with forensic science, in a court of law the witnesses are asked to swear to tell 'the truth, the whole truth and nothing but the truth', and the jury members to 'give a true verdict according to the evidence'. But when they are deciding a verdict, having considered all the evidence, the jury is usually directed to decide whether or not the defendant is guilty 'beyond reasonable doubt'.[5] This is the case even for issues that are, literally, a matter of life and death. Decisions don't get much more important than that!

There is a subtle difference between finding the absolute truth of something that happened in the past, and deciding in the light of all the evidence what the most likely scenario was 'beyond reasonable doubt'. In many ways, this is an excellent analogy for the way scientists, including geological scientists, do their work. They find the best explanation for the phenomena they are studying, taking account of all the other information that is available. Of course, sometimes new data or techniques that only subsequently become available may show that the original inference or interpretation was flawed or even plain wrong. To return to the example of

5. It is interesting to note that the Anglo-American legal requirement for a jury verdict based solely on the evidence presented in court, rather than a decision of guilt based on personal knowledge of the defendant, or on the outcomes of ordeals inflicted on those suspected of witchcraft, had its roots in the late seventeenth-century Baconian philosophical thinking that arose from strict consideration of the evidence. Bacon was one of the founders of the scientific method that insisted on putting primacy on the evidence. This is also reflected in the motto of The Royal Society, *nullius in verba* (broadly, 'take no one's word for it' – but rather test it yourself). See also Barbara J. Shapiro, *Beyond Reasonable Doubt and Probable Cause: Historical Perspectives on the Anglo-American Law of Evidence* (Berkeley: University of California Press, 1991), http://ark.cdlib.org/ark:/13030/ft409nb30v/

forensic science, in several high-profile law cases in the UK defendants have been acquitted, sometimes after many years, when new forensic techniques have shown that the previous interpretations of the evidence were unsafe, or even wrong. On the other hand, new techniques, such as DNA profiling, have sometimes led to convictions many years after the crime because they raised the likelihood of guilt to 'beyond reasonable doubt'.

The way that geological science progresses has a lot in common with the consideration of evidence in a court of law. For both there exists a body of observations that has to be honoured in all interpretations. Any interpretation of the evidence is subject to testing, either by cross-examination in a law court, or in the case of geological science by making new observations. New understanding in geological science is often achieved through one of two main routes: new rock outcrops that have never before been seen are studied (exposed perhaps in cutting a new road, or discovered somewhere remote that has never before been visited), thus leading to new information; or new techniques or measurements are devised that put additional constraints on the object of study (analogous to the development of DNA profiling in criminal forensic study, which provides a new type of information). We shall look at some specific examples of this in the following sections.

It is also worth noting that there are important differences between criminal forensic science and geological science: the crime scene is usually a 'one-off' special case, whereas most geological phenomena are part of a continuum resulting from natural processes that recur repeatedly in the course of earth history. Furthermore, scientists often have the option of going back to the rock record in the same or in an adjacent place to make more measurements. So in that respect geological scientists have perhaps an easier job, even though their evidence may be many millions of years old.

How does scientific knowledge compare with Christian knowledge? There is one large difference between them, namely that scientific knowledge in general, including geological knowledge, deals only with material aspects, causes and explanations of observable phenomena, whereas Christian knowledge deals not only with those, but also with the reasons why things are the way they are – the most important being that God created and sustains the universe and enters into a loving, personal relationship with every Christian believer. Since Christian knowledge derives ultimately from revelation by God and from a personal relationship with the living God, the depth of understanding and growth of that knowledge increases as the relationship deepens, in an analogous manner to the way that human relationships grow when nurtured. However, there are also some similarities between scientific and religious knowledge in the realm of truth about the material world, so I outline these here.

One clear fact is that this side of heaven, we shall know and understand the truth only partially. We can at present only 'know in part'.[6] This applies both at the philosophical level of what can be known by us, the creatures of a creator God, and also at the practical level of what finite humans can deduce from the created order around them. Only the creator God can know the full truth. Nevertheless, the Christian would affirm that God has not left us in the dark. He has revealed himself to us, through the Bible,[7] through the incarnation of himself in Jesus,[8] and through nature (Paul writes that God's invisible attributes, namely, his eternal power and divine nature, 'have been clearly perceived, ever since the creation of the world, in the things that have been made'[9]). God has made us in such a way, and he has made himself known to us, that we can understand sufficient of the truth to be able to respond to the creator God. As a passage in Deuteronomy puts it, 'The secret things belong to the LORD our God, but the things that are revealed belong to us and to our children for ever, *that we may do all the words of this law*' (my italics).[10] Similarly, in the realm of the natural order, we can understand how it works sufficiently well to be able to make decisions as to how to use the created order for

---

6. 1 Corinthians 13:12, ESV.

7. 'All Scripture is breathed out by God', 2 Timothy 3:16, ESV.

8. John 14:8–11.

9. Romans 1:20, ESV.

10. Deuteronomy 29:29, ESV.

the welfare of others, and to be able to behave responsibly in its care and stewardship. This provides the imperative to keep doing science to the best of our ability, and to keep studying the world around us, because by doing so we honour our creator God and it is part of the worship we offer him.

Plate tectonics: an example of a step change in understanding the world

The theory of plate tectonics, the idea that the outer skin of the earth is made up of a few large chunks, or rigid 'plates', that move across the surface of the globe, carrying the continents with them, has had a major impact on our understanding of how the earth behaves and has provided us with a powerful integrative and predictive framework that now underpins the study of geology. Yet plate tectonics is a relatively recent idea, dating only from the mid-1960s.[11] Prior to that, the continents of the earth were thought to be fixed in place, and geologists spent considerable time trying to fit their observations into that fixed framework, resorting to ever more complicated schemes to explain such observations as why underwater sediments containing corals that were deposited at the bottom of the sea are now found at the summit of Everest, the highest mountain in the world,[12] why coal which was undoubtedly formed in a subtropical climate is now found in Antarctica, close to the South Pole, and

---

11. The main idea of plate tectonics was proposed in a short paper by the geophysicist Tuzo Wilson in J. T. Wilson, 'A New Class of Faults and their Bearing on Continental Drift', *Nature* 207 (1963), pp. 343–347.

12. Rock samples collected from the summit of Everest at 8,848 metres (29,029 feet) above sea level are made of limestone containing fragments of corals and conodonts (fossil teeth) originally deposited underwater during the Ordovician age (450–500 million years ago). For details see M. P. Searle et al., 'The Structural Geometry, Metamorphic and Magmatic Evolution of the Everest Massif, High Himalaya of Nepal – South Tibet', *Journal of the Geological Society, London* 160 (2003), pp. 345–366.

conversely, why in the past, glaciers existed close to sea level in what is now equatorial Africa.

The change from a view of the world where the continents and oceans are essentially fixed in their positions to a mobile, plate tectonic view is an interesting case study in how a major paradigm shift occurred in the way observations were understood, without in any way changing the nature of those observations. The observations remained the same, yet suddenly they were placed in a powerful explanatory framework by the new paradigm. The reality of the geological record in no way changed: but our understanding of what could be inferred from it improved by leaps and bounds.

The seeds of the idea that continents could move around on the globe – which rapidly became known as 'continental drift' – were sown in 1910 by an American geographer, F. B. Taylor,[13] and more famously by the German meteorologist Alfred Wegener (1880–1930), the son of an evangelical minister. He was struck, as have been so many others, by the remarkable congruence of the coastlines of Africa and South America on either side of the Atlantic Ocean. When he also discovered a report of palaeontological evidence for a land bridge between Brazil and Africa, this confirmed in his mind the idea that the continents had once been joined, but had subsequently drifted apart. He first published his ideas in 1912, and more fully in a book that was revised several times over the next twenty years, including a widely circulated translation into English in 1924.[14] Yet his ideas were not welcomed uniformly, and indeed there was much hostile comment: Philip Lake was to write in a contemporary review of the book that Wegener 'is not seeking truth; he is advocating a cause, and is blind to every fact and argument that tells against it'.[15]

---

13. F. B. Taylor, 'Bearing of the Tertiary Mountain Belt on the Origin of the Earth's Plan', *Geological Society of America Bulletin* 21 (1910), pp. 179–226.

14. See A. Wegener, *The Origin of Continents and Oceans* (London: Methuen, 1966), for an English translation from the 4th revised German edition by J. Biram.

15. P. Lake, *Geological Magazine* 59 (1922), p. 338, quoted by A. Hallam, in *Great Geological Controversies* (Oxford: Oxford University Press, 1989), p. 147.

So why were Wegener's ideas widely discounted at the time, although in retrospect we know that he was right about the fact that continents could and did move relative to one another, and indeed practically every schoolchild in Britain knows that he was right, because plate tectonics is on the national curriculum? One reason may be that he introduced his ideas of continental drift by discussing the forces required to move the plates. However, it is clear that those forces were unrealistic, and the mechanism proposed by Wegener for moving the plates is not viable: furthermore, that was also clear to most people at the time. Since no-one could explain how such forces could arise, or be sustained, the compelling observational evidence for the reality of continental drift was ignored. Interestingly, even when the occurrence of continental drift was overwhelmingly accepted by the geological community half a century later, there still was no known explanation of why the plates moved. But although the mechanisms were not understood, the observational evidence was so strong that plate tectonics was nonetheless accepted universally as an explanatory framework for geological interpretation.

What caused the shift to acceptance of the reality of continental drift were new observations of the seafloor made by geophysicists in the early 1960s. Prior to that time, the deep ocean floor was barely explored, even though it comprises almost 70% of the area of the earth. Yet the key to confirming that continents had broken apart lay in the new crust formed beneath the intervening oceans. There was a rapid expansion of seafloor exploration using geophysical techniques in the period following the Second World War. These new observations led to the

----

This book also contains fascinating accounts of several other renowned geological controversies. Philip Lake was indeed correct that Wegener uncritically advertised anything that apparently supported his views, including several ideas that were widely thought to be incorrect at the time, and subsequently were shown definitely to be wrong. This certainly undermined acceptance of his view that the continents moved with respect to one another, even though that was in fact correct and became widely accepted four decades later.

proposal by two Cambridge geophysicists in 1963 that new seafloor was being formed under the oceans by a process that came to be called seafloor spreading.[16] This was a bold hypothesis, based on a tiny amount of data recorded from the Indian Ocean, but extrapolated worldwide. Even the senior author of that seminal paper recalls commenting to a colleague shortly before it was published in the scientific journal *Nature* that 'if they publish that they'll publish anything'. However, the proposal was testable elsewhere, and those tests were made rapidly. Soon, it became obvious that the new theory explained a widely diverse range of existing geological and geophysical data extremely well, and as new areas were studied they were found to fit well too.

Plate tectonics has remained a powerful integrative and explanatory overarching theory that is used in all arms of the geological sciences. It can explain such diverse things as the occurrence of speciation when continents break apart, the production of mountain belts with formerly underwater sediments high on their summits, and the reasons for the locations of belts of earthquakes and volcanoes. The development of new techniques and measurements has done nothing but strengthen the theory. For example, by the end of the twentieth century it was possible to measure the slow rates of movement of the plates (typically of the order of a few inches, or a few tens of millimetres per year), using new high-precision satellite positioning techniques, and these were found to match extremely well the rates predicted decades earlier from much longer-term geological data.

For the Christian, there are two striking conclusions to be drawn from the plate tectonic revolution, one a warning and the other an encouragement. The warning is that all scientific understanding can only be provisional, and that we should always be conscious that our understanding is limited, although likely to improve in the future. We should never imagine that we hold the final truth. The encouragement is that God in his graciousness has given humans creative minds so that they are able to see consistency and patterns

---

16. F. J. Vine and D. H. Matthews, 'Magnetic Anomalies over Oceanic
    Ridges', *Nature* 199 (1963), pp. 947–949.

in sparse data, to make abstract and inventive leaps of imagination, and so ultimately to gain an understanding of the world he created and in which we live. The very comprehensibility of the world is a mark of God's consistency and loving-kindness to us.

The age of the earth: an example of gradual improvement in understanding

If the advent of plate tectonics demonstrates the way insights from creative individuals can revolutionize understanding of the world around us and of how observations fit together, the way in which the age of the earth has become better constrained demonstrates the more gradual improvements that come from the continual development of new measurement techniques. I also address the issue of dating here because the age of the earth is one on which some Christians disagree. Some hold that Scripture will not allow the earth to be more than about 10,000 years old, based on the genealogies in the Old Testament. So it is useful to outline our understanding of how the much greater age of the earth is derived from scientific observations of the world and the universe in which we live. I shall then address how we should treat the scriptural and scientific evidence.

Charles Lyell (1797–1875), one of the founders of geology as a science, was strong in his assertion of the importance of assuming the constancy of physical laws if we were to make sense of the past. Indeed, the very title page of his magnus opus *The Principles of Geology* contains the crux of his beliefs in the subtitle: *An attempt to explain the former changes of the earth's surface by reference to causes now in operation.*[17] He wrote of the laws of nature that 'Their immutable constancy alone can enable us to reason from analogy, by the strict rules of induction, respecting the events of former ages, or, by a comparison of the state of things at two distinct geological epochs, to arrive at the knowledge of general principles in the

___

17. C. Lyell, *Principles of Geology, being an attempt to explain the former changes of the earth's surface by reference to causes now in operation*, vol. 1 (London: Murray, 1830).

economy of our terrestrial system.'[18] Lyell's views were often taken
as suggesting that almost unlimited time was available for the geological strata to be laid down. So, right from the beginning of
geology as a science, it is clear that extremely long time periods on
the earth were envisaged by the new practitioners of the science,
far longer than those recorded by human history.

The earliest attempts at estimating the age of the earth came
from measurements of the thickness of layers of rock, combined
with estimates of the rate at which they were accumulated. For
example, in the first edition in 1859 of his book *On the Origin of
Species*, which laid out the case for evolution by natural selection,
Darwin calculated the age of the earth as approximately 300
million years.[19] Shortly after this, John Phillips, the Professor of
Geology at Oxford University, made a similar calculation using data
from the Ganges Basin to estimate the rate of sedimentation, and
came up with an age for the earth's crust of 96 million years.[20] The
next main player in calculating the age of the earth was Lord
Kelvin (1824–1907), the leading physicist of his day and, incidentally, firm in his belief in the existence of design or divine order.
From arguments about the heat production by the sun he first
deduced that the sun was probably less than 100 million years old,[21]
and subsequently from arguments about the heat loss from the
earth derived a best estimate for the earth's age of 98 million years,
with a range from 20 million to 400 million years.[22] Towards the
end of his life he preferred the lower end of these estimates.[23] His
arguments were mathematically sound, and seemingly superior to
the geological estimates by Darwin, Phillips and others. They

---

18. From Lyell's *Principles of Geology*, quoted by Hallam, *Great Geological
    Controversies*, p. 49.
19. C. Darwin, *On the Origin of Species* (London: Murray, 1859), p. 282.
20. J. Phillips, *Life on Earth: Its Origin and Succession* (London: Macmillan, 1860).
21. Lord Kelvin, *Macmillans Magazine* 5 (1862), p. 288.
22. William Thomson (Lord Kelvin), 'On the Secular Cooling of the Earth',
    Philosophical Magazine (series 4) 25.165 (1863), pp. 1–14.
23. Lord Kelvin, 'The Age of the Earth as an Abode Fitted for Life', *Annual
    Report of the Smithsonian Institution* (1897), pp. 337–357.

shook Darwin sufficiently for him to reduce his estimate of the age of the earth by a factor of 2 or 3 in his second edition of the *Origin of Species*, and he removed his calculation entirely from the third edition. Ironically this made Darwin present a more 'Lamarckian' view of evolution in later editions of the *Origin* because Darwin could not see how his suggested process of natural selection could produce such a vast array of biological diversity in so short a time.[24] But other geologists still felt certain that Kelvin's calculations, however clever, simply did not provide sufficient time to produce the geological strata they walked over and hammered.

The resolution of this impasse was provided at a stroke by the discovery of radioactivity, first reported in 1896 by Henri Becquerel, and its recognition in 1903 by Pierre Curie as a source of heat in radium. Radioactive fission provides a massive heat source in the earth, while nuclear fusion (and to a lesser extent fission), is the main heat source in the sun. Kelvin had known nothing of radioactive processes, which is why his estimates based on cooling of the earth and the sun were more than an order of magnitude too small. Once the heating caused by the decay of radioactive elements was included in the calculations, the age of the earth required to explain its present temperature increased immensely. Rutherford quickly became a leader in the new field of radioactivity, and it is striking that very early in the game, in 1904, he suggested that the decay of helium trapped in minerals might provide a way of calculating geological ages. By 1917 the first timescale was published for the fossil-bearing rocks (called the Phanerozoic, which covers the period from 550 million years ago to the present), using radioactive decay. There is surprisingly little difference between the 1917 estimates of age and the best modern-day timescales. By 1931 Arthur Holmes, one of the leaders in the field of dating the age of the earth, reported that the earth was 'probably not less than 1,600 million years, and is probably much less than 3,000 million years old'.[25] From then on it was just a matter of improving the estimates as better rock

---

24. D. R. Alexander, *Rebuilding the Matrix* (Oxford: Lion, 2001), pp. 188–189.

25. Quoted by Hallam, *Great Geological Controversies*, p. 128.

samples were examined and as the rates of decay were refined and new isotopic decay systems were investigated.[26] The best current

Table 1: Significant Dates in the History of the Universe[27]

	Years before present
Origin of the universe (from microwave background radiation)	13,700 ± 200 million
Formation of first stars	c. 13,500 million
Formation of first galaxies	c. 12,700 million
Origin of the solar system (= origin of Earth)	4,566 ± 2 million
Completion of formation of Earth by accretion	4,510–4,450 million
Oldest known minerals on Earth (zircon grains from Yilgarn craton, western Australia)	4,404 ± 8 million
Oldest known rock on Earth (Acasta gneiss, north-west Canada)	4,000 million
Earliest evidence of life on Earth (carbon isotope fractionation, from Akilia, south-west Greenland)	3,850 million
Earliest microbial fossils on Earth (microbial biofilms, stromatolites)	3,500 million
Oldest multicellular animal (Ediacaran faunas)	575 million
First eutherian mammal	c. 135 million
Earliest hominid (*Australopithecus*)	c. 5 million
Early modern *Homo sapiens* (from Herto, middle Awash, Ethiopia)	160,000–154,000
Adam and Eve (Garden of Eden)	c. 10,000–9,000 BC
Birth of Christ (comet, historical records, Bethlehem)	April 5 BC
Crucifixion of Christ (lunar eclipse, historical records, Jerusalem)	Friday, 3 April AD 33

---

26. For further details on dating the age of the earth see G. B. Dalrymple, *The Age of the Earth* (Stanford: Stanford University Press, 1991).

27. For original references to dates shown in table 1, see Alexander and White, *Beyond Belief.*

estimates of selected significant events are listed in table 1, with the origin of the earth now dated as 4,566 million years ago.

Since the 1950s many new isotopic decay systems have been developed for dating rocks, as instruments have been built with better resolution and precision. There are well over forty different radiometric dating techniques in current use, each based on different radioactive isotopes. Differing isotopic systems all have different half-lives, so decay at different rates. This provides opportunities for cross-checking dates from the same rock, by using different decay systems and is a critical test of the methodology. Half-lives of commonly used isotopic systems cover a wide span: examples are 106,000 million years for samarium-147 to neodymium-143; 18,800 million years for rubidium-87 to strontium-87; 1,260 million years for potassium-40 to argon-40; and 700 million years for uranium-235 to lead-207. Shorter time periods are best investigated using the decay of isotopes generated in the atmosphere by cosmogenic processes, and include 1.52 million years for beryllium-10; 300,000 years for chlorine-36; and 5715 years for the well-known carbon-14. In most cases decay rates are known to within 2%, so uncertainties in the dates derived from radiometric decay are of a similar magnitude of a few per cent. The span of half-lives makes it possible to date rocks of differing ages by choosing the appropriate isotopic decay systems.

Radiometric dating is by no means, however, the only way of dating the earth's strata. The most basic method of geological dating, and historically the first used, is to put a sequence of rocks into chronological order. This is conceptually straightforward: younger rocks usually lie above older rocks unless they have been subsequently disturbed. An important extension to this ordering is that it is possible to correlate rock units of the same age around the world, provided they carry some unique identifier that changes through time. Fossils are an excellent example of this: throughout geologic history numerous species have developed and then become extinct, so if identifiable fossils are present, they can be used to 'tag' the age of that rock to be the same as all others around the world which carry the same fossils. This dating is improved if assemblages of different fossils can be used rather than just single species. However, it is important to note that this only tells us the *relative* age of a rock layer in the global sequence.

Other than radiometric dating, the other main method of calculating the absolute age of a rock is to use known cyclic changes, such as annual tree ring growth or predictable variations in the earth's orbit. The simplest method of dating is to count annual cycles, such as tree growth rings, back in time. Individual tree ring widths vary according to local climate changes. If all the trees in one region exhibit the same climate-controlled patterns, tree rings can be counted back beyond the lifespan of individual living trees by finding older timber with sufficient overlap in years to correlate the distinctive tree-ring pattern from the younger to the older. By this means, a unique tree-ring chronology has been built from trees in central Germany extending back beyond 8400 BC, and similar chronologies have been developed elsewhere.

Annual layers are also found in coral growth rings, in lake sediments (called 'varves') and in snow layers accumulated in continental interiors, such as the Greenland icecap. In the latter case, cores have sampled ice formed more than 200,000 years ago. Counting of annual layers in the uppermost ice is unambiguous, but at greater depths, as layers become compacted, it is possible that some annual layers may be overlooked. Conservative estimates of the errors in counting annual layers increase from about 2% at 11,000 years to 10% at 150,000 years.

Perhaps more surprisingly, changes in the earth's orbit cause long-term cyclicity in climate patterns, known as Milankovitch cycles. Eccentricity of the earth's orbit round the sun produces 100,000 and 413,000 year cycles, while the tilt and precession of the earth's axis of rotation creates cycles at 21,000 and 41,000 years respectively. Identification of these cycles by their effect on ancient sediments allows precision dating back to 30 million years. Prior to that we cannot predict the earth's orbital parameters sufficiently well to use them for dating, although cyclicity can still be detected.

So far I have discussed only dating material we can sample, such as rocks found on earth. How do we date astronomical events during the first two-thirds of the history of the universe, before the earth was formed? The answer is to use the normal scientific technique of investigating physical processes and extrapolating them to the wider sphere of the universe. For example, by assuming that the speed of light is constant, a conclusion supported by a myriad different investigations by theoretical and experimental physicists, we can use the doppler shift of an identified spectral line of light coming from distant parts of the universe (the 'red shift') to work out how far it has travelled, and therefore how old it is. This assumes the veracity of the Hubble law, which states that the further away an object is, the faster it is moving away from us.

The best currently determined age of 13,700 million years for the origin of the universe comes from observing the intensity of the microwave background radiation that permeates space. In this case, assuming a model of the expansion of the universe that fits known physical laws and observations, the amount of energy present as microwave radiation can be used to constrain the time since the radiation was first created.

Three striking things stand out from the list of significant dates in table 1. First, the earth has only existed for the last one-third of the age of the universe. Secondly, life existed on earth almost as soon as the environmental conditions made it possible to do so: almost the oldest rocks that have been discovered show evidence of carbon-based life. And ever since that time, through thousands of millions of years, the conditions on earth have remained favourable for such life to continue. This is quite remarkable, because life as we know it requires a relatively narrow band of environmental conditions to survive. If the temperature of the earth's surface were to increase to above 100°C, as indeed has happened on other planets, all the water would boil off and that would be the end of life on earth as we know it. We can take this either as an amazing coincidence or, from a Christian standpoint, as an example of God's providence in continually upholding and sustaining the world as a place fit for life. The third striking point is that, despite living organisms having existed on earth since soon after its formation, humans have only been present for a tiny portion of the most recent history. To put this into perspective, if the history of the universe were to be compressed into one year, humans would have been present for only the last five minutes before midnight on New Year's Eve. The perspective this places on our position in the time frame of the universe is humbling and provides striking significance to the assertion of the Bible that God made humans as the pinnacle of his creation.[28]

To finish this section, I return to the question of how we can hold with integrity both scientific and scriptural evidence for the nature of the universe in which we live. If the Bible is read as meaning that the age of the earth is only around 10,000 years, then one possibility might be that the earth only *appears* to be much older. This was argued as long ago as 1857 by P. H. Gosse, with his famous suggestion that God created Adam with a navel.[29] Although science cannot address such a suggestion, it raises immense theological problems, because if true it would mean that God purposefully designed a universe to deceive us. That does not square with everything else God tells us about himself in the Bible and so cannot make sense. Gosse's contemporaries clearly agreed: his Christian friend and correspondent Charles Kingsley, worried for his own children's faith if they read such nonsense, wrote to Gosse, 'I would not for a thousand pounds put your book into my children's hands,'[30] presumably not quite the response that the author had been hoping for, given that the intention of his book had been to defend biblical faith against the sceptics!

But of course the Bible is not a scientific textbook. Indeed, given all that has been discussed above about the provisional and changeable nature of science, it is a good job that it is not, because if it were, then it would not have stood the test of time over millennia. Rather, the Bible proclaims itself to be a vehicle by which God reveals himself to humankind, explaining his nature and his dealings with people. The purpose of the early chapters of Genesis appears to be to proclaim that the universe was created by a loving, personal God, in an orderly fashion, that he was pleased with it, and that one of his main objectives was to make it a place in which humans could live fruitful lives and have loving relation-

---

28. Psalm 8.

29. A. Thwaite, *Glimpses of the Wonderful: The Life of Philip Henry Gosse 1810–1888* (London: Faber & Faber, 2003).

30. Quoted by D. Alexander, *Science and Christian Belief* 16.2 (2004), p. 183.

ships with himself. From the earliest days of Christianity, the first chapter of Genesis has been interpreted as a theological essay in this way by such scholars as Origen in AD 231 and Augustine in AD 391.[31] Read in this light, Genesis gives meaning to the existence of the universe and of ourselves (*why* it exists), while our scientific investigations flesh out, albeit in a tentative, provisional way, *how* the material universe developed. God's revelation in Scripture tells us things that we cannot discover for ourselves. Scripture and science therefore provide complementary explanations of the world in which we find ourselves, and both are needed.[32]

That God chose to work his purposes through the vastness of the universe and the immensity of time should not surprise us: the Bible proclaims that God made everything,[33] that he upholds and sustains the universe moment by moment[34] and that nothing happens without his permission.[35] We can see through our scientific eyes that the seemingly profligate creation of stars (numbering in the whole universe an estimated million-million-million-million, or 10 with 24 zeros after it, which is more than the number of grains of sand in the entire earth), allows the creation of the very special conditions that allow life to exist on earth. Or that the long period before earth was formed – twice

---

31. For discussion of the interpretation of origins in Genesis and the evidence from science see D. Kidner, *Genesis*, Tyndale Old Testament Commentaries (Leicester: IVP, 1967); E. Lucas, *Can we Believe Genesis Today?* (Leicester: IVP, 2001); Alexander, *Rebuilding the Matrix*; D. Wilkinson, *The Message of Creation*, The Bible Speaks Today (Leicester: IVP, 2002).

32. Further discussion of the usefulness of the concept of complementarity in describing the interaction of the sovereign God with the material world is given by P. P. Duce, 'Complementarity in Perspective', *Science and Christian Belief* 8 (1996), pp. 145–155; and H. J. van Till, 'Response to Duce', *Science and Christian Belief* 8 (1996), pp. 157–161.

33. Genesis 1:2; John 1:3; 1 Corinthians 8:6.

34. See, e.g., Hebrews 1:3, '[Jesus] upholds the universe by the word of his power', ESV; Acts 17:28; Colossians 1:17.

35. See, e.g., Genesis 50:20; Job 42:2; Acts 2:23.

as long as the not inconsiderable age of the earth itself – was necessary in order to allow the very atoms of which our world and our bodies are made to be created in the nuclear reactions of stars. Or even that the long, slow evolution of life itself on earth took nearly 4,000 million years before God brought into being the first humans made 'in the image of God'. A robust view of God's providence and of his sustaining power would accept that God's hand was in the whole process from the moment he created the universe to the present day, a process sometimes termed 'theistic evolution'.[36]

Before we leave the topic of the age of the earth, it is interesting to note that if the Bible is used to estimate the period of time to the present since God breathed life into Adam and Eve, the dates are of the same order as the best scientific estimates. The Bible tells us that before the fall, Adam and Eve tended the Garden of Eden, and that after they were expelled due to their disobedience to God, they had to work the ground to grow food.[37] This suggests a clear reference to farming. It is also clear that after they were expelled from Eden, there were other people around of whom they were afraid,[38] which is consistent with God at a specific time having breathed spiritual life into particular individuals (either Adam and Eve alone, or possibly a wider group of people of whom Adam and Eve were a representative 'type', just as the one person Jesus was a representative for all redeemed people) from an existing evolved population. Archaeological evidence suggests that settled farming began to replace hunter-gathering in the Neolithic period, some 10,000–9,000 years BC.[39]

---

36. For a further discussion of theistic evolution and of scientific and religious views of the world see D. Alexander and R. S. White, *Beyond Belief: Science, Faith and Ethical Challenges* (Oxford: Lion, 2004).

37. Genesis 3:23; 4:2.

38. Genesis 4:14–15.

39. A. J. Day, 'Adam, Anthropology and the Genesis Record', *Science and Christian Belief* 10 (1998), pp. 115–143. See also the extensive data provided in S. Mithen, *After the Ice: A Global Human History 20,000–5,000 BC* (London: Weidenfeld & Nicolson, 2003).

So it is reasonable to suppose that Adam and Eve date from around this time. The Bible genealogies added up from that time to the present give a not dissimilar date to that arrived at by the archaeological methods outlined in this chapter, particularly if we bear in mind the possibility that much of the genealogical information represents compressed digests, rather than a detailed account of each generation.[40]

Some consequences for the Christian

I briefly outline below some of the consequences for Christians of the perspectives obtained from studies of the geological past.

1. *We should have a proper sense of awe at God's creation.* That the world is a habitable place for us is dependent upon the very special physical conditions at the time of the big bang, which formed the universe. If any of several physical constants were different by only a tiny fraction, then it would be impossible for us to be here. This is known as the *anthropic principle*, and is sufficiently striking that it is now the subject of secular scientific study. To the Christian it points both to God's creative power and to his care for us in that he created and has maintained through the ages a place fit for us to inhabit. The very coherency, consistency and fruitfulness of his creation point to the Creator.[41]

2. *We should acknowledge humankind's role as being made 'in the image of God'.* The Bible makes it clear that God has placed humans at the pinnacle of his creation.[42] When he created the material world, at every stage he proclaimed that what he had made was 'good'.[43] When he created humans, he said that was 'very good'.[44] He created the universe so that ultimately humans could have a loving

---

40. D. Kidner, *Genesis: An Introduction and Commentary* (Leicester: Tyndale, 1967), pp. 82–83.

41. Romans 1:20.

42. Psalm 8:4–8.

43. Genesis 1:4, 10, 12, 18, 21, 25.

44. Genesis 1:31.

relationship with himself. The whole of the Bible works through the consequences of this. Part of our responsibility to God, indeed part of our worship of him, is to strive to be good stewards of what he created. Christians are called to be God's representatives on earth, so in this sense we are 'imaging' God in his creation. In our generation, humankind by its activities is affecting the global system in an unprecedented way through pollution, through climate change and through economic and cultural globalization, and there is a strong imperative on Christians to understand and to take a lead in addressing these issues.

3. *We should learn to be better stewards of God's creation by striving to understand it better.* We rely on the earth system for our very life: the water we drink comes from its ground; the food we eat depends on its soil and its water; the energy on which we rely comes from its oil, gas and radioactive elements; the minerals on which our modern world is built are mined from the crust of the earth. Using the world's resources in a sustainable way must be an imperative of a Christian response to living in the world created by God. Understanding the geology of the earth, and the way in which humankind's activities are affecting it, underpins all of this. The geological record of the earth also contains a history of some of the major 'natural' disasters that remain one of the largest hazards to life: floods and global fires; meteorite impacts that on occasion have wiped out 95% of the species on earth; the effects of major volcanic eruptions; huge earthquakes and tsunami; extreme global climatic changes. In all these, the earth holds a record that, if we take the effort to understand it, can help us mitigate the effects of such hazards to our own and future generations.

4. *We should live our lives now in the light of the new heaven and new earth.* God has promised that one day he will renew the universe and recreate it in perfect relationship with him in the way he always intended it to be before it was spoilt by sin.[45] Throughout the Old and New Testaments, the Bible writers looked forward to this renewal both of creation as a whole and of humans in proper relationship with God.[46]

---

45. Revelation 21:1, 4.
46. See, e.g., Isaiah 65:17; 66:22; Romans 8:21; Hebrews 2:5–18; 2 Peter 3:13.

In the meantime, since heaven is to be a physical and not just a spiritual place, and since there is in some sense a continuity between this world and the next, we should behave in this physical world in a way that mirrors the life in that recreated, perfect world.[47] Our present-day toil in understanding and in caring for this world is part of our proper response in obedience and worship to God the Creator and will prepare us for the time all Christians look forward to when we shall be able to do the same in caring for the new heaven and earth[48] joyfully and without toil.[49]

© Robert S. White, 2005

---

47. For a helpful outline, see N. T. Wright, *New Heavens, New Earth: The Biblical Picture of the Christian Hope*, Grove Booklet B11 (Cambridge: Grove, 1999).
48. Revelation 21:4.
49. I am grateful to Denis Alexander, Christopher Ash, John Hilber and Stephen Walley for their comments on earlier drafts of this chapter.

11. HAWKING, DAWKINS AND *THE MATRIX*: SCIENCE AND RELIGION IN THE MEDIA

David Wilkinson

It has become somewhat common for both the church and the scientific community to view the media with suspicion and even a large degree of cynicism. Church leaders complain of bias against the Christian faith on television programmes, while scientists despair of a sound bite and headline culture that does not do justice either to the complexity or the tentative nature of scientific discovery. With such an attitude, it is easy to have nothing to do with those whose motive is commercialism, whose epistemology is relativism and whose ignorance of science and Christianity is legendary. We may not always articulate such a sentiment, but many of us within science and the Christian community seem to operate with this agenda towards the media.

Yet in our consideration of questions of truth in science and Christianity we should not ignore the way that such questions are communicated. While we may think we have control over truth in the pulpit or the lecture hall, the reality is that people are encountering questions of truth in science and Christianity in *Star Trek*, *The Simpsons* and the evening news. To opt out of such a world because we do not like the rules shows both a lack of courage and a lack of confidence in truth.

Fundamental to science and Christian faith has been communication. Christianity is based on the claim that God has communicated with us in many and various ways but supremely in Jesus in a particular culture at a particular time (Hebrews 1:1–2). Since that time the church has been charged with the mission of communicating the good news of Jesus to all nations (Matthew 28:19–20). Generations of preachers, evangelists and missionaries have therefore worked hard at the task of translating, explaining and embodying that good news into different cultures and times.

While the importance of communication is easy to demonstrate in terms of the history of the church, this is less obvious in terms of the history of science. Yet science does not proceed in a cultural vacuum. Michael Faraday's great achievements in electromagnetism were matched by his commitment to popularization, leaving the legacy of the Royal Institution Lectures.[1] Both Albert Einstein and Richard Feynman built a reputation for their ability to teach and communicate physics, while Stephen Hawking's *A Brief History of Time* has made him an iconic figure of our time. Science both delights in and has a responsibility to communicate the fruits of its labours to the society that funds its enterprises and marvels at its achievements.

To ask the question of whether we can be sure about anything we have to take this aspect of communication seriously. We do not need to go as far as to say that the message is only the medium, but we do need to see that the way we communicate is inextricably linked to the content of the message. For those who are concerned about science and religion, the media-dominated culture that we live in therefore gives us both opportunities and challenges.

---

1. C. A. Russell, *Michael Faraday: Physics and Faith* (Oxford: Oxford University Press, 2001).

Truth and the power of the media

In 1998 and 1999, cosmology, in terms of the end of the universe, experienced quite a revolution. Measurements on distant super-novae, in order to find out how the universe was slowing down, led to the claim that in fact the universe was accelerating in its rate of expansion. *Science* magazine called it the breakthrough of the year.[2] A subsequent BBC *Horizon* programme told the story of the discovery from the point of view of Saul Perlmutter and his team of astronomers. Yet Perlmutter was not alone in making the discovery. Brian Schmidt at the Siding Springs Observatory in Australia and Adam Weiss were part of groups whose work was as important in that respect.[3] But they did not get quite as much exposure. Therefore, in the general perception, Perlmutter was the one who became famous for the discovery. This is an example of the way the media act as a lens to shed light on certain discoveries or insights into science and indeed theology. It can go much further than simply highlighting certain personalities; it can shape truth claims.

It is easy to attack the media. As we have seen, some object to what they perceive to be a 'sound-bite culture' where information is presented in short stories or reports. This criticism is particularly interesting from Christian theologians whose founder actually told many sound-bite stories, or parables, as the theologians like to call them! Such criticism can be taken too far. While information is presented at terrific speed in a multimedia environment, many underestimate the variety of the mass media. The late-night shows in the US presented by David Letterman or Jay Leno may mix guests, music, comedy and stories but they both feature long introductory segments consisting simply of the host talking to the audience. Comedians such as Eddie Izzard can keep audiences enthralled for a couple of hours of stand-up comedy, and even *The Matrix Reloaded* intersperses its action with large chunks of

2. 'The Accelerating Universe', *Science*, 18 December 1998, pp. 2141–2336.

3. M. Livio, *The Accelerating Universe: Infinite Expansion, the Cosmological Constant and the Beauty of the Cosmos* (New York: Wiley, 2001).

philosophical dialogue. There is more to the media than a sound-bite culture, and quite detailed and complex issues can be communicated through television, radio or film.

A more valid criticism is that researchers, producers or journalists may not be specialists in the field of science or Christianity, and therefore lack a 'feel' for questions of truth in those subjects. I recently received a phone call from a journalist on a leading newspaper who told me that she had been asked by her editor to write an article on the existence of God, but she admitted that she did not know where to start. She had little background in science or theology, and she had been told by her editor to explore some of the issues around anthropic balances, intelligibility of the universe and quantum gravity, which is not an easy thing to do in a few days. However assiduously the reporter goes about her or his task, and however many experts are consulted, the final editing of the article or the television programme can shape the presentation of truth. In the BBC television series *Space*, presented by Sam Neill, the first programme seemed to indicate that most scientists believed that a comet impacting the earth seeded the origin of life. Indeed this is one theory but no sense of the weight of opinion in the scientific community against this view was given. In questions where there are different models or solutions it often needs an expert to communicate the strengths and weaknesses of different views.

Not only is this difficult for journalists or producers to grasp – they also have to work under severe constraints of time, budget and the need to entertain as well as to educate. BBC2's *Top One Hundred* greatest Britons picked out a number of scientists, but the brief pen pictures of some of them were quite interesting. To sum up Newton's contribution to the world in just two and a half minutes was very ambitious, yet that was all the time available. There is often not time to present the whole story.

The need to entertain often leads to the charge of sensationalism in presenting both science and religion.[4] It was interesting

4. N. Postman, *Amusing Ourselves to Death* (Harmondsworth: Penguin, 1985).

that in the *Top One Hundred*, a major part of Stephen Hawking's contribution was characterized by his debate with Homer Simpson on the structure of a doughnut. Peter Atkins was interviewed and put Hawking only in the 'B' team of cosmologists. Why was an Oxford chemist, who has written a couple of lay books on cosmology, shown giving an assessment of a professional cosmologist like Hawking? It was in large part because he was prepared to say something sensational about a cosmologist who has sold more books than the number of stars in a small galaxy!

All these are fair criticisms. Yet there is also a sense of jealousy and fear of the power of the media. Romanowski has pointed out that much of American Christianity dismissed pop culture because it saw it as a rival in terms of power within society.[5] For those faced with the reality of obtaining research grants or those who face declining congregations it is quite understandable that they should feel threatened by the power of the media, which so dominate the lives of so many people. When we remember that in the UK, a person over the age of 65 watches an average of 37 hours of television a week (twice as many hours as children watch) we see the power that it has. At the same time we can see that as an opportunity as well as a threat. The media have some of our most creative people in terms of storytelling, presentation and communication. At times the BBC soap *Eastenders* can attract 26 million viewers, which is roughly the number of car owners in the UK! The scale of this means that communication in terms of the media needs to be taken seriously by all of us.

In theology, communication needs to be central. Sometimes theology has not given communication the importance it should. The New Testament is largely a missiological document; that is, it is all about communicating good news. Indeed, the theology of the New Testament is worked out in the context of evangelism, preaching and ministry. Christians need to take communication seriously because God is fundamentally a God who

---

5. W. D. Romanowski, *Pop Culture Wars* (Downers Grove: IVP, 1996).

communicates. John 1:1–18 is a supreme picture of this communication: the Word of God becomes flesh and lives among us.
As the Methodist theologian Albert Outler once put it, the Word
made audible becomes the Word made visible. God communicates in word, image and deed in the life, death and resurrection
of Jesus. The nature of that communication is truth in vulner-
ability, for that Word was at times not recognized and at times
was rejected (John 1:10–11). Further, God communicates eternal
truths about himself to a particular people in a particular culture
at a particular time. Thus generations of preachers, evangelists
and missionaries have worked hard to bring together, in the
words of Phillips Brooks, 'truth and timeliness' in their presentation of good news. Therefore, the multimedia opportunities for
communication in radio, television and the printed media should
be welcomed by Christians. Apart from the option of the
Christian cable station where they can feel in control, Christians
are called to present truth in situations where they will feel vulnerable. The secular journalist or fast-moving television studio
are not a million miles away from the Areopagus in Athens (Acts
17:16–34).

Such commitment to the importance of communication
within the theological world is often missing. Church leaders
and leading theologians often have the attitude that because
they are good preachers or good academics, then they have
a natural ability to communicate in radio and television.
Unfortunately this is not always the case. The recent VOX
Project has surveyed training given to church leaders across the
UK denominations in over fifty colleges and courses. It shows
that little attention is given to media literacy or apologetics in
the context of the mass media.[6] The missiologist Hendrik
Kramer wrote, 'Communication involves a communicator
having somehow discerned which are the obstacles to the
receipt of the message in such a way as to be able to meet the

---

6. G. Stevenson, *The VOX Project 21st Century Communication: A Research Report
on the Provision of Training in Preaching, Apologetics and Media* (Durham:
Centre for Christian Communication, 2003).

listener on her or his own ground.'[7] If he were writing today he would probably say 'the obstacles to *and the opportunities for* the receipt of the message'. And understanding the media involves identifying those obstacles and opportunities.

In a similar way, science is an important area for communication. Donald MacKay used two models for the Christian who is a scientist. One was that of a mapmaker, someone who describes the lie of the land; the other a steward, someone who takes what is given and uses it responsibly under the lordship of Christ. To push the mapmaker analogy a little further, we could introduce a third model – that of the scientist as commentator.[8] When I watch soccer on the television I have my own prejudices about it, but in order to understand the technicalities of the game, I am reliant on those who know more about it who comment during half time or at the end of the match. Sometimes I agree and sometimes I disagree, but their analysis allows me to enjoy the game more. From the Christian perspective the scientist can be viewed as a commentator who looks at what is given and interprets it to a wider public. To fulfil such a role, then, communication skills become an essential part in the training of scientists.

Ian Barbour dedicates one of his recent books to his grandchildren with the hope that science and religion will continue to raise significant issues as they enter this new millennium.[9] I think they will do so only if we take the power of the media seriously. If we are to answer the question of whether we can be sure of anything we need to work hard at understanding the nature of the different media by which truth is presented, discussed and questioned. Only then will we begin to identify the opportunities and obstacles to hearing truth.

---

7. H. Kramer, *The Communication of the Christian Faith* (Surrey: Lutterworth, 1957).

8. D. Wilkinson and R. Frost, *Thinking Clearly about God and Science* (Crowborough: Monarch, 2000).

9. I. Barbour, *When Science Meets Religion: Enemies, Strangers or Partners?* (London: SPCK, 2000).

The continued dominance of the conflict hypothesis: science or religion

When 'Darwin's bulldog', T. H. Huxley, wanted to free science from the control of the church, he and the fellow members of 'The X Club' produced a model that became extremely successful. The model was one of *conflict* and indeed warfare between science and religion.[10] The model's popularity grew through its simplicity in communication. Books such as J. W. Draper's *History of the Conflict Between Religion and Science* (1875) and A. D. White's *A History of the Warfare of Science with Theology in Christendom* (1895) rewrote scientific and theological history, emphasizing controversy and conflict.

Today the conflict model is still widespread. It is sustained by the media because of its simplicity and its controversial nature, in spite of the evidence of the complex and fruitful dialogue between science and religion. Conflict makes good television and a lively conversation. The same applies to the world of publishing. Many of the best-sellers in the science field use this conflict model.[11] Supreme in all of this is Richard Dawkins, whose combination of superb science popularization and intense warfare with all things Christian has made him a media celebrity on both sides of the Atlantic.[12]

At the other end of the theological spectrum the conflict model is important in the growth of creation science, certainly in the US and increasingly in the UK.[13] Within the Christian subculture of

---

10. C. A. Russell, *Cross-Currents: Interactions between Science and Faith* (London: Christian Impact, 1997).

11. C. Sagan, *Cosmos* (London: Abacus, 1983); P. Atkins, *Creation Revisited* (New York: Freeman, 1992). E. O. Wilson, *Consilience: The Unity of Knowledge* (New York: Knopf, 1998).

12. R. Dawkins, *The Selfish Gene* (Oxford: Oxford University Press, 1989); *River out of Eden* (New York: Basic Books, 1995); *A Devil's Chaplain* (London: Weidenfeld & Nicholson, 2003).

13. L. Gilkey, *Creationism on Trial* (Charlottesville: University Press of Virginia, 1989); K. Ham, *The Lie Evolution* (El Cajon: Creation Life, 1990); H. M.

bookshops, creation science books sell extremely well. They also use the conflict model to pose the Bible against many of the widely held views of modern science concerning origins.

Of course the conflict model is not the only model of the relationship between science and religion. Barbour sets out the models in what has become a classic fourfold typology of the relationship between science and religion. In addition to the conflict model, the second model is that of *independence*, as demonstrated in Stephen J. Gould: 'The magisterium of science covers the empirical realm; what is the universe made of (fact) and why does it work this way (theory). The magisterium of religion extends over questions of ultimate meaning and moral value.'[14] This independence of science and religion is also demonstrated in certain theological schools stemming from Barthian neo-orthodoxy. Here God speaks by his word in the theological sphere and science has little to do with that.

The third model is that of *dialogue*. This is where the dialogue between science and religion explores the origin of the presuppositions of science, compares similarities and differences of method, uses concepts from science in analogies to talk about God's relationship to the world and notes that science raises questions it cannot itself answer. Since the 1990s such an approach has been demonstrated by Polkinghorne.[15] *Integration* is the fourth model that

---

Morris and G. E. Parker, *What Is Creation Science?* (San Diego: Creation-Life, 1982); R. L. Numbers, *The Creationists: The Evolution of Scientific Creationism* (New York: Knopf, 1992).

14. S. J. Gould, *Rocks of Ages: Science and Religion and the Fullness of Life* (New York: Ballantine, 1999), pp. 207–208.

15. J. C. Polkinghorne, *Faith, Science and Understanding* (London: SPCK, 2001); *Reason and Reality* (London: SPCK, 1991); *The Faith of a Physicist* (Princeton: Princeton University Press, 1994); *Beyond Science* (Cambridge: Cambridge University Press, 1996); *Belief in God in an Age of Science* (New Haven: Yale University Press, 1998); *Science and Theology* (London: SPCK, 1998); J. C. Polkinghorne and M. Welker (eds.), *The End of the World and the Ends of God: Science and Theology on Eschatology* (Harrisburg, PA: Trinity Press International, 2000).

features a revised kind of natural theology, or a theology of nature as in for example Peacocke's discussion of evolution and what that means for the Christian faith.[16] Barbour's own view is that of dialogue and a degree of integration. Within the overall typology, most evangelicals stress different aspects of the relationship but are opposed to conflict.[17]

The trouble is that however good the books are in discussing the third and fourth model, they do not sell in vast numbers compared to the conflict books, either from the atheistic camp or the creationist camp. Why is that? Why is this conflict model so attractive to the media? Conflict is attractive because it gives a simplistic view of philosophy, history, the nature of science and the nature of theology. That allows the media easy access to the subject.

This means that for those who want to take seriously both the media and questions of truth in science and theology we need to ask some questions. First, how do we represent truth in a way that is simple, attractive and faithful to the nature of both science and theology? That may not be an easy task. Einstein once cautioned that everything should be made as simple as possible but not any simpler than that. How do we communicate with simplicity but in a way that is faithful to the often complex nature of truth?

Secondly, there is a question concerning methods of education and in particular the need for cross-curricular education from an early age. At the Centre for Christian Communication in St John's College in the University of Durham, we have been surveying atti-

---

16. A. Peacocke, *Paths from Science towards God: The End of All our Exploring* (Oxford: Oneworld, 2001).

17. D. Alexander, *Rebuilding the Matrix: Science and Faith in the 21st Century* (Oxford: Lion, 2001); R. J. Berry, *God's Book of Works: The Nature and Theology of Nature* (London: Continuum, 2003); M. Jeeves, 'Changing Portraits of Human Nature', *Science and Christian Belief* 14 (2002), pp. 3–32; E. Lucas, *Can we Believe Genesis Today?* (Leicester: IVP, 2001); D. Wilkinson, *The Message of Creation*, The Bible Speaks Today (Leicester: IVP, 2002).

tudes to science and religion in a sample of UK sixth formers; that is, teenagers in the age group 16–18 years. The sample contains 1,824 responses. Figure 1 shows responses to the statement 'Science is in conflict with religion'.

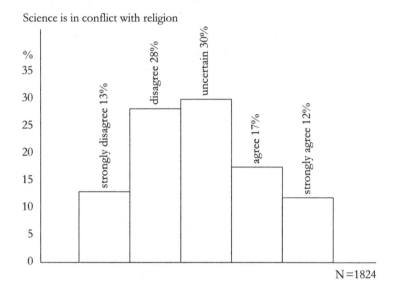

Figure 1: Survey of attitudes on science and religion in the 16–18-year age group

Such a distribution is in line with other surveys. But underneath it are some very interesting results. In 1995 Kay looked at a sample of five-and-a-half thousand 11–16-year-olds and found that 21% of boys agreed that science disproved religion, compared with only 11% of girls.[18] This demonstrates a clear gender difference in how science and religion are perceived. Kay further showed a correlation between boys interested in science and those who saw science and religion in conflict. That is, amongst males scientism is very strong for those

---

18. W. Kay, 'Male and Female Conceptualisations of Science at the Interface with Religious Education', in J. Astley and L. Francis (eds.), *Christian Theology and Religious Education* (London: SPCK, 1995), pp. 247–270.

who are interested in science. He argued that educationally girls have the ability earlier in life to hold together different views on the same subject (i.e. complementary descriptions of the same thing), whereas boys are not as intellectually developed at the same age.

In 1996, Kay and Francis, in a follow-up study, looked at over 700 16-plus-year-olds, and again found that scientism was stronger amongst males.[19] They then drew the following conclusions. They suggested that within mainstream education we were not paying enough attention to helping people understand the scientific method and its limits in an early stage; that there was not enough opportunity for cross-disciplinary dialogue in education. They also pointed the finger at the churches who were not affirming science sufficiently. Key to the continued popularity of the conflict hypothesis is that churches are breeding a culture where science is seen as a threat rather than as part of a God-given gift for the exploration of the world.

The third question we need to ask about the conflict hypothesis is how much we value and teach truth in the context of history. Brooke stresses how the history of science can be used both to attack religion and to defend it.[20] The conflict hypothesis is reinforced in people's minds by a biased telling of history, where Galileo and Darwin are presented as simple battles between the truth of science and the dogma of the church. Yet such a simplistic and biased view of history is often used in Christian apologetics. Preachers and evangelists repeat unsubstantiated stories such as Darwin's deathbed conversion. History is more complex than that. The Galileo affair was not simply the battle between the church and science. There were competing theories around at the time and Galileo's own personality was important in it all. Darwin's own religious position was influenced by deism, respect for his wife and the influence of emerging Old Testament critical scholarship alongside many

---

19. W. Kay and L. Francis, *Drift from the Churches* (Cardiff: University of Wales Press, 1996).

20. J. H. Brooke, *Science and Religion* (Oxford: Oxford University Press, 1991).

other things. A desire for truth in science and religion is a battle to be as true to the richness of history as we can and to teach and preach it with integrity.

Using the opportunities of the media

How might we use the media or learn from them in exploring questions of truth in science and Christian faith? Although there might be things to be cautious about, there are also many opportunities.

Focus on the person
Fame and celebrity are at the heart of the contemporary mass media where some people are just famous for being famous. Television, radio and newsprint tell their stories with reference to the personal, focusing on the individual at the heart of the story or the individual affected by the story, even if this is in the most trivial way.

This is strange to the culture of science where scientific reports are impersonal, and where, indeed, the personal element needs to be reduced to the lowest level. The trouble is that the media are not quite as interested in truth in the purely abstract: the person is important. Stephen Hawking's *A Brief History of Time* is the publishing phenomenon of our time, certainly in the area of science. It has sold ten million copies worldwide, been translated into 33 different languages and been reprinted 56 times in hardback. Part of its popularity is that it does engage with big questions, and ultimately, as Carl Sagan puts it in his foreword, is 'a book about God'.[21] However a major part of the appeal is Professor Hawking's own personal story. You cannot understand the phenomenon of *A Brief History of Time* without seeing the personal story coupled with excellent writing and an engagement with big questions. The media want to explore truth in the context of the person.

---

21. S. W. Hawking, *A Brief History of Time* (London: Bantam, 1988).

From the Christian perspective this is both an encouragement and a challenge. Christians may need to relearn the importance of the person. The Christian faith is based on incarnation; that is, the coming to earth of God in human form. The person is central to that communication. So the media, in focusing on the person, are not the Antichrist. They are picking up on something intrinsic to God's relationship with human beings and fundamental to the creation of the universe itself.

In practical terms, the centrality of the person in the media reminds us of the importance of testimony as part of the Christian proclamation and of the fact that some may be particularly gifted to communicate in the media. The outstanding theologian or public evangelist may not be the best media communicator. It may be the person who is more at home in front of a television camera, the person with the interesting personal experience or simply the person who was immediately available. This way of communicating truth should not be disparaged. It is in fact a recognition that all are called to bear witness and that we should all be ready to 'give the reason for the hope that you have' (1 Peter 3:15, NIV). The Christian community, then, needs to learn to give support, prayer and encouragement to those who work in the media, many of whom may not fit into the 'normal' timetables of church life.

Pop culture

Levine has suggested that Western culture has made a distinction between highbrow art, such as classical music, and lowbrow art such as television, films and pop music.[22] In education we have often exalted highbrow art and looked down on the lowbrow. American theologians such as Romanowski have built on this and argued that the churches have sanctified the highbrow arts and demonized the lowbrow arts.[23] Yet we need to take popular

---

22. L. Levine, *Highbrow/Lowbrow: The Emergence of Cultural Hierarchy in America* (Cambridge, MA: Harvard University Press, 1988).
23. W. D. Romanowski, *Eyes Wide Open: Looking for God in Popular Culture* (Grand Rapids: Brazos, 2001); *Pop Culture Wars.*

culture seriously because more and more it is the vehicle of the big questions.

For example, George Lucas's *Star Wars* is one of the most successful ever series of films, videos, games and merchandising. Why is it so attractive to so many people? Lucas talks about it as an ice-cream sundae, with lots of different ice cream, chocolate fudge brownies and all the rest. The 'ice-cream sundae' of *Star Wars* is then a combination of myth, the western, science fiction serials, the space race and samurai films. Into that religion is sprinkled, so that *The Empire Strikes Back* includes various Buddhist themes and in *The Phantom Menace* the virgin birth appears.

Looking at the sprinkles of religion, many have immediately claimed that the films are Buddhist or New Age, or indeed some have claimed that they are Christian allegories. In reality popular culture has more subtlety than that. There is something about an ice-cream sundae that you do not immediately see but which is very important. That is the glass that holds the whole thing together. If the glass were not there the whole creation would simply fall apart on your lap! The glass holds everything together and provides its structure. With the *Star Wars* films, I suggest that the glass is represented by a number of fundamental theological questions that underlie the films.[24]

This is relevant to questions of truth in science and Christianity. The whole *Star Wars* saga is about the hope of how the good, small people win over the powerful evil empire. In this context it is interesting that one of Lucas's early films was about the impact of science on a technological society. *THX1138* is very pessimistic as it shows the human spirit being crushed by the development of technology. After that film he wrote, 'I began to think that in order to do anything in film that would have social repercussions, you have to make an optimistic movie which gives hope, that way things can happen.'[25]

---

24. D. Wilkinson, *The Power of the Force: The Spirituality of the Star Wars Films* (Oxford: Lion, 2000).

25. J. P. Peecher (ed.), *The Making of Star Wars Return of the Jedi* (New York: Ballantine, 1983), p. 236.

Back in the 1970s there was not a lot of hope around, with the oil crisis, Watergate, Vietnam, our growing realization of the destruction of the environment, the stalling of the space programme and the decline of religion. Into that context not only does Lucas introduce a film about hope, but he also asks the question 'What is hope based on?' It could be escapism, or the cyclical nature of time, or the myth or dream of human progress.[26] Gene Roddenberry, the creator of *Star Trek*, bought into the myth of human progress: he believed that education, science and technology would deliver us into a new utopia. However, we know that the myth of human progress has in fact become not a dream but a nightmare. Films such as the Terminator ones of James Cameron or *The Matrix* paint a pessimistic picture of science out of control. How can we be sure of anything about the future?

Lucas provides an alternative picture, suggesting that hope should be based on transcendence, the belief that there is something greater to this universe than merely what science can describe and use. He does that by introducing the idea of the Force. Far from wanting to give a new philosophy or religion Lucas uses this mystical part of experience to pose questions about truth. These questions are not to say that technology is a bad thing, but to question what else is there apart from technology. The evil empire depends on its death star, the rebels depend on the Force and of course you can see the relationship of that to the science–religion debate as we have it in the last twenty or thirty years. Lucas himself says, 'I would hesitate to call the Force God – it's designed primarily to make young people think about mystery, not to say here's the answer. It's to say think about this for a second – is there a God, what does God look like, what does God sound like, what does God feel like, how do we relate to God?'[27] Embedded in the money-making enterprise and all of the

26. R. Bauckham and T. Hart, *Hope against Hope: Christian Eschatology in Contemporary Context* (London: DLT, 1999).

27. B. Moyers and G. Lucas, 'Of Myth and Men', *Time*, 26 April 1999, p. 90.

special effects is a fundamental question about the nature of God and its relationship to science and technology. Therefore to talk about truth in science, religion and the media, we need to take pop culture seriously and understand its nature and the kinds of questions it asks. So many people's understanding of truth and the important questions about truth is to be found in this medium.

Holding together intellect and imagination

Further, to explore questions of truth we need to hold together intellect and imagination in the discussion of science and Christianity. Laurence Krauss, a distinguished cosmologist wrote the fun book *The Physics of Star Trek* because '*Star Trek* is a natural vehicle for many people's curiosity about the universe'.[28] Stephen Hawking, in his introduction to that book, wrote, 'Science fiction like *Star Trek* is not only good fun but it also serves a serious purpose, that of expanding the human imagination.'[29]

In a similar way *The X-Files* creator Chris Carter engages the imagination. He explores UFO folklore in a contemporary setting and calls himself a person wanting to explore the realm beyond the rational. Some scientists have argued that in fact this kind of pseudoscientific stuff is detrimental to our understanding of the nature of science. The journal *Nature*, however, opposed this view, suggesting that series like *The X-Files* allowed people to explore their imagination, to be drawn to a world beyond what we know and to have that imagination stimulated. It is in this experience of wonder and curiosity that we can encounter truth.

The Christian tradition again needs to relearn this because often what is called Christian apologetics has relied heavily on the intellect at the expense of the imagination. We have often reduced God to an intellectual argument rather than the Lord who expands our imagination. McGrath helpfully defines apologetics: 'The chief goal of Christian apologetics is to create an intellectual

---

28. L. M. Krauss, *The Physics of Star Trek* (London: Flamingo, 1997), p. xvi.

29. Ibid., p. xi.

and imaginative climate conducive to the birth and nurture of faith.'[30] The holding together of intellect and imagination is a reminder that truth can be communicated through the visual as well as the spoken word, through art as well as through equation and through poetry as well as textbook. Such a renewed apologetics is more appropriate to contemporary culture.[31]

The mass media do give opportunities for both science and Christian apologetics to stimulate the imagination. NASA has been extremely good at using pictures from the Hubble space telescope to excite people about science and the exploration of the universe.[32] The vastness and the beauty of the universe can be communicated so powerfully through the visual image. The visual is very important in holding together imagination and intellect. Kepler spoke of his joy at creation and of his being ravished by it. How do we in presenting the relationship of science and religion use the visual in a way that stimulates people to think more, and does our communication of truth excite them and fill them with joy?

Imagination and intellect are also held together by the use of narrative. This occurs in many different elements of the relationship between science and religion; for example, in the discussion of the nature of time. Paul Ricoeur writes, 'Speculation on time is an inconclusive rumination to which narrative activity alone can respond.'[33] Philosophers such as Richard Swinburne and Sidney Shoemaker use stories to talk about the nature of time, while astronomers and physicists have often used stories to speak about time in terms of twin paradoxes. Of course a huge number of films, some good and others downright awful, have also explored the nature of time.

---

30. A. McGrath, *Bridge-Building: Effective Christian Apologetics* (Leicester: IVP, 2002), p. 9.

31. D. Wilkinson, 'The Art of Apologetics in the 21st Century', *Anvil* 19.1 (2002), pp. 5–17.

32. See the NASA website, http://www.nasa.gov/

33. P. Ricoeur, *Time and Narrative* (Chicago: University of Chicago Press, 1984), p. 122.

Narrative is an extremely important element in communication. *The Matrix* is a cult film amongst teenagers. There are numerous Christian interpretations of it, some seeing it as a Christian allegory. While in its plot there are very clearly themes such as a messianic hope, *The Matrix* is primarily about the future of technology and the nature of reality, asking in a fundamental way questions about both of those areas. For many it is the narrative that opens up these questions for an exploration that is open and engaging. The parables of the Kingdom use that same open and engaging exploration, drawing people into the story where they encounter truth.

Stories abound in the mass media. The Christian or scientific communicator will look for stories of value that are already exploring the questions of science and faith. The use of such stories brings questions of truth into the everyday world, and is able to communicate truth to those who think primarily in narrative rather than in prepositional logic.

The value of 'bottom-up'

By a 'bottom-up' approach, I do not mean using the media's interest in all things sexual! I mean it in the sense of the approach advocated and adopted by John Polkinghorne, who emphasizes the importance of the particular issue in the dialogue of science and religion, in contrast to a top-down model where one can become stuck in generalities.

Polkinghorne has been successful in his communication of that dialogue by taking a scientific insight into the way the world is, whether that of quantum theory, chaos, cosmology or the end of the universe and then working through the theology from that starting point.[34] Paul Davies has been even more successful in popularization by taking a series of issues as a way into the science and indeed his own speculations on religion.[35] At a much lower

---

34. J. C. Polkinghorne, *One World* (London: SPCK, (1986); *Science and Creation* (London: SPCK, 1988); *Science and Providence* (London: SPCK, 1988); *The God of Hope and the End of the World* (London: SPCK, 2002).
35. P. Davies, *God and the New Physics* (Harmondsworth: Pelican, 1983); *The*

level this approach has been fundamental to my own work. I have found that by concentrating on the specific, whether it be the cosmology of Stephen Hawking[36] or the search for extraterrestrial life, communication to a much wider audience is possible and indeed excites the interest of the media.[37] It ties into public interest in a current news story but also gives a sense of it being a manageable subject when for many people the vast vistas of both science and theology seem extremely daunting. Therefore, if the discussion of science and religion is earthed in specific instances, whether these be known historical characters or events or contemporary interest in the end of the world, cloning, genetic medicine, planetary exploration or quantum gravity, then the media will naturally pick these up and communicate them to a wider audience. Much very good work in science and theology relates very badly to the media because it is not earthed in specific issues.

The nature of science and theology

In the previous section, I have made a plea to take the opportunities presented by the media seriously and to learn from them. Focusing on the person, on pop culture, on the importance of the imagination and on specific instances all help in exploring questions of truth in science and Christian faith. Indeed, such things have often been relegated to secondary importance compared with the primacy of the impersonal argument, Greek philosophy and general principles in the exploration of truth. Yet in all of this, it is important to affirm the overall arguments presented in

---

Cosmic Blueprint (London: Unwin Hyman, 1989); *The Last Three Minutes: Conjectures about the Ultimate Fate of the Universe* (London: Weidenfeld & Nicolson, 1994); *About Time* (London: Penguin, 1995); *Are we Alone?* (London: Penguin, 1996); *The Fifth Miracle: The Search for the Origin of Life* (London: Allen Lane, 1998).

36. D. Wilkinson, *God, Time and Stephen Hawking* (Crowborough: Monarch, 2001).

37. D. Wilkinson, *Alone in the Universe? The X-Files, Aliens and God* (Crowborough: Monarch, 1997).

the other chapters of this book. In the media it is essential to continue to be true to the nature of science and Christian theology. That is that science is a critical realist activity which explores in a complex impersonal way objective truth, while Christian theology is an exploration of the objective truth of a personal God who created the universe and reveals himself within it.

Often the representation of the nature of science and theology in the media is very far from this. For the sake of simplicity it is presented in stereotypes. Science is represented by Mr Spock, the cool logical Vulcan, the epitome of the 'fascinating' and confident power of science. Christianity is represented very differently. Richard Dawkins sums it up for many people when he writes, 'What has theology ever said that is the smallest use to anybody? When has theology ever said anything that's demonstrably true and is not obvious?'[38]

The challenge is to communicate the nature of science and theology with integrity. The world of the visual or the personal story can never do justice to the whole truth. For example, the colour photograph of Hawking on the UK hardback edition of *A Brief History of Time* shows him in front of a number of equations on a blackboard. It gives the impression that science is about a great mind and a few equations. If only it were that simple! Another popular impression of science is of the picture of Galileo pointing his telescope at the moons of Jupiter while underneath a computer printout says that the sun is at the centre of the solar system. These are popular impressions of science and the nature of science but how do we convey the messy nature of science, the interplay of theory and observation, the competing theories refereed by the scientific community, and the role of human judgment?

In a similar way how do we represent with integrity the truth claims of the Christian faith. The graph below shows how 16–18-year-olds in our survey responded to the statement that Christian faith is based on evidence.

---

38. R. Dawkins, 'Writer donates £1m to strike blow for theology',
    Independent, 18 March 1993, p. 7.

Christian faith is based on evidence

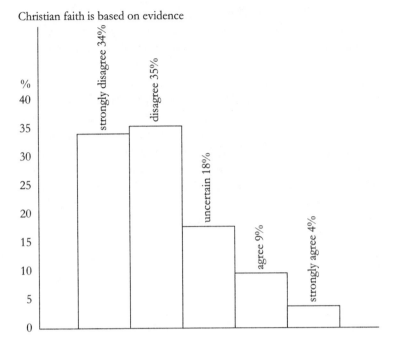

Figure 2: Survey of attitudes on science and religion in the 16–18-year age group

Although Christians of different traditions might disagree on the balance of evidence and experience, it is interesting that teenagers in our survey discounted evidence so strongly. In part this is because of the way that faith is presented in our media culture; that is, in the old school definition that 'faith is believing things you know aren't true'.

On this basis it is easy to set up a conflict between the 'fact' of science and the 'faith' of being a Christian. Of course Christian theology is a subtle interplay of evidence and experience, of models, of a community together under God's word. It is ultimately based on what Francis Schaeffer called 'brute facts'; that is, of a God who in Jesus walked in the space-time history of the universe. But the brute facts are only part of the story, for that personal God now invites us to experience and live truth in a relationship with the risen Jesus by the power of the Holy Spirit. The challenge before us as Christians is therefore to resist the relativism, the sensationalism and the stereotypes of the media, but to communicate in the media environment with faithfulness and integrity.

Luke's description of Paul in Athens is helpful at this point (Acts 17:16–34). Paul spent time in the marketplace before taking the risk of going into the hostile environment of the Areopagus. There, using the images, quotations and ideas of his audience, he proclaimed the good news of Jesus. He was bold and was true to the gospel, but he did show respect to his hearers. The media are a risky place for science and the Christian faith. But if we are concerned for truth, then we need to respect them, understand them and use the opportunities they present.

12. BSE, MMR AND GM: WHO'S TELLING THE TRUTH?

Derek Burke

Working scientists like to believe that uncertainties in science are resolved primarily by the accumulation of ever-clearer evidence and that what we discover tells us something about realities in the world 'out there'. But how reliable is the evidence that scientific enquiry yields? It is a striking fact that science does eventually reach a consensus on disputed issues, which is not the usual rule in human endeavours, and that the answers obtained from quite disparate lines of inquiry are consistent rather than contradictory: for example, in medicine evidence from physiology, biochemistry, genetics and clinical observation can be drawn together to give a single consistent picture. It is difficult for me to conceive how this could be so unless there was a reality 'out there' to which we are successfully gaining access by our enquiries. The flawed nature of our understanding does not contradict the brute fact that there is a reality that is independent of ourselves. It might be argued that there are other explanations for this consistency, such as social pressures within the scientific community, but it seems to me difficult to believe that so many different persons in so many different cultures at so many different times should produce data that are self-consistent and scientifically coherent, unless there was a deep order in the structure of matter about which we in the scientific community can agree.

Now everyone who has done scientific research knows that the process is usually much less ordered than we would usually admit: muddle and conflicting results are commonplace. How often have we suddenly stumbled on the explanation through a series of ill-conceived experiments and then written the scientific paper as if we had had the bright idea right at the beginning! Peter Medawar, the Nobel prize-winning immunologist, wrote a classic paper entitled 'Is the Scientific Paper a Fraud?'[1] Of course Medawar did not really mean that scientific papers were fraudulent per se, only that it is well-known and well-accepted 'poetic licence' within the scientific community that scientists describe their published results in a more logical and orderly way than the research was carried out in practice (if that were not so, scientific journals would be considerably larger than they in fact are!). However that point is very different from saying that our understanding of everything 'out there' is determined by social factors. Such a philosophy is not only very damaging to the scientific enterprise, but also has disturbing implications for religious faith, for what is believed and what is being studied systematically in theology is then no more than the product of social attitudes. So scientists are more comfortable as 'critical realists'; realists because we believe that there is a real universe 'out there' which can be understood by the combined use of reason and empiricism, and critical because we realize that our descriptions of the world are never exhaustive and will always fall short of complete objectivity.

Coupled with this declining faith in the reliability of scientific evidence has come a greatly increased emphasis on an individual's 'right to choose'. So in the consumer movement, it has become a basic right, and whether the consumer's choice is seen by others to be rational or irrational is irrelevant; that choice must be respected.

---

1. P. B. Medawar, 'Is the Scientific Paper a Fraud?' in P. B. Medawar, *The Threat and the Glory* (New York: HarperCollins, 1963), pp. 228–233.

There is a similar attitude to scientific evidence; it is often maintained that people have the right to believe, or not to believe, a
particular piece of scientific evidence, particularly if the evidence
is disputed in any way. Whether to accept or reject religious faith
also becomes a matter of purely personal inclination, for there is
no absolute truth out there, and to assert that there is, either in
science or in Christianity is 'judgmental'. In the extreme, evidence
is weighed equally with opinion. After all, authorities are no longer
trusted as they were, and sometimes with good reason; individuals
do have rights, and we live in a democracy where every individual
has equal standing. But does this mean that there is now no such
thing left as an authoritative statement? Can anyone, everyone,
make up their minds as to what is 'true'? Has opinion overtaken
knowledge? Obviously at the extreme, that way lies social chaos, so
in current politics we have to find a compromise between evi-
dence-driven policy and what is acceptable to an electorate, and
electorates do of course have the final veto. But how should
electorates inform themselves? That is the question. What sort of
communication is needed?

So if scientific evidence is no longer the rock-hard indisputable
set of ideas we once thought it was, how can we trust its findings?
Does it matter for science? Certainly a recent House of Lords
report thought so and said:

> Society's relationship with science is in a critical phase. Science today is
> exciting, and full of opportunities. Yet public confidence . . . has been
> rocked by BSE [Bovine Spongiform Encephalopathy] and many people
> are uneasy about the rapid advance of areas such as biotechnology and
> IT [information technology] . . . This crisis of confidence is of great
> importance both to British society and to British science.[2]

It also matters for our faith, for the same mindset slides easily
over into our thinking about Christian faith and poses us believers

---

2. 'Science and Society'. A report from the House of Lords Select
   Committee on Science and Technology (London: HMSO, 1999),
   p. 5.

a particular problem, for Christianity is a historical religion; Christ has died, Christ has risen and Christ will come again.

So let us look at three case studies where the public now mistrusts scientists, and see if we can see a pattern, see if we can understand what lies behind the caution, even cynicism, that is common and then relate it to our faith.

Bovine spongiform encephalopathy

I shall start with Bovine spongiform encephalopathy (BSE). We know only too well the extent of this disaster: hundreds of thousands of cattle infected, well over 100 people already dead and the numbers likely to go on rising for a number of years. No one is prepared to give a number for the number of deaths that might ultimately result from the transfer of this new agent from cattle to humans,[3] although it does look as if the numbers of human deaths will be lower than predicted at one time. What went wrong? Why did this happen? The answers are many and varied, but let me quote just a few words from a speech by Lord Phillips, who chaired the BSE inquiry. He said, 'Perhaps the most important single lesson we learned is of the importance of the open communication of information to the public. In the months after BSE was first identified, there was an embargo on the disclosure of any information about this new disease.' And then he goes on:

> There was in government a deep-seated culture of confidentiality. It was
> dangerous to keep the public too well informed because they were
> bound to over-react. And so, through the period up to 1996, the way that
> information was put before the public was weighted. There was a
> campaign of reassurance, if not of sedation. There was no
> misinformation or concealment of information, but a failure to admit to
> the public that there was uncertainty, that there was risk and that the

---

3. For a general review, see Robert J. Maxwell, 'An Unplayable Hand? BSE, CJD and British Government' (London: Kings Fund, 1997).

early reassuring conclusion that BSE was scrapie was less and less convincing. The public was repeatedly assured that it was safe to eat beef, and that there was no evidence that BSE was transmissible to humans.[4]

But BSE was transmissible to humans. So who was telling the public the complete story over BSE? Not the government or its scientists, it appears. The damage that this episode has done to trust in the scientific integrity of government scientists and politicians will take years to put right. The government's style has certainly changed in response, with the welcome change in style of the new Food Standards Agency, while the formation of two new Commissions, one concerned with human genetics and the other with agriculture and the environment, is novel because both contain advocates of all points of view – both for and against the new technologies. So government is feeling its way to a new form of decision-making, and not finding it easy. All such commissions have to be 'inclusive', and that has meant, for example, that the former Chairman of Greenpeace UK, who is a professor at Lancaster University, is a member of the Agriculture, Environment and Biotechnology Commission. Yet Greenpeace has a non-negotiable position over many aspects of genetically modified food and crops! How can consensus be reached? I have a feeling that in a post-BSE era, the UK Government has decided to avoid difficult decisions and has passed them down to the commissions, trusting that a consensus solution will emerge. I fear that is an abdication of responsibility. And can governments really tell the 'truth'? No-one expects government to be completely open about everything, so where do you draw the line? As a start, I suggest that it is never ethical to withhold information that affects human health, and that full information must be given, even if the story is not straightforward – and it rarely is.

But there is another, related problem that is often raised: Can

---

4. Lord Phillips of Maltravers, 'Lessons from the BSE Enquiry', *Journal of the Foundation for Science and Technology* 17.2 (2001), pp. 2–5.

the public completely trust any scientist who either works for the Government, or, in the most extreme case, has just a research grant from a government agency? My judgment is that this case is very much overstated; I have found the overwhelming majority of my colleagues to be rigorous in resisting such pressures, but it is obviously not a black and white situation; there are some things that any state will want to keep secret. However, experience tells me that confidentiality agreements are overused, and that there is an instinctive tendency for civil servants and for commercial managers to err too much on the side of secrecy. So our being cautious about signing such agreements is wise and discretion remains an underrated virtue, while all of us need to avoid the temptation to gossip. Openness and honesty are essential if we are to be trusted, and we scientists have a lot of work to do to rebuild trust, to earn it again in fact. For though we are trusted more than politicians and journalists, we are not trusted nearly enough! It is almost a truism to say that trust is easily lost and very slowly regained. I suggest that we should always work as if everything we do *might* become public. That is certainly a lesson that those who have been following the Hutton enquiry, undertaken in the summer of 2003, into the death of the Government scientist Dr David Kelly will have noted.

Measles, mumps and rubella

What about my second example? The measles, mumps and rubella (MMR) vaccine has been used virtually to eliminate measles, mumps and rubella in both Europe and North America. The vaccine has been used extensively, and safely, around the world since the 1970s, and is normally given as a single vaccination containing antigens for all three viruses. However, a paper published in the *Lancet* in 1998[5]

---

5. A. J. Wakefield et al., 'Ileal-Lymphoid-Nodular Hyperplasia, Non-Specific Colitis, and Pervasive Developmental Disorder in Children', *Lancet* 351 (1998), pp. 637–641. The arguments for a link between MMR and inflammatory bowel disease and autism are summarized in Angus

described how twelve children had developed autistic disorders shortly after being given the MMR vaccine, and suggested a causal connection, although the authors themselves state, 'We did not prove an association between MMR vaccine and the syndrome described.' The interpretation of this work has since been heavily criticized, and a number of reports have failed to confirm the link. Finally this issue went to the Court of Appeal when three appeal court judges dismissed the evidence of a link between autism and the MMR vaccine as 'junk science' when it ruled that two girls should be immunized against their mothers' wishes,[6] and families trying to prove that the vaccine caused autism were told 'that they did not have the medical evidence to fight the claims in court'.[7] The same newspaper article reported that 'it would be wrong to spend a further £10 million of public money funding a trial on top of the £15 million already invested'. So this report in the *Lancet* has already cost £15 million, but that is not all by any means. Inevitably, because of the scare, a decline in the number of vaccinations followed with the very likely outcome of a nationwide measles epidemic.[8] For example, it has been reported that the decline in uptake of the MMR vaccine has led to an increasing number of cases of measles in South London, which is putting vulnerable children at risk with any immuno-compromised children at severe risk.[9]

Nicholl, 'MMR: The Vaccine Is Safe', *Science and Public Affairs* (August 2002), pp. 18–19. A recent review of two books, both published in 2004, on the controversy, with a commentary by an internationally respected figure with the title 'Immune to the Facts: A Flawed Paper on Autism Compromised MMR Vaccination and Public Health', can be found in *Nature* 432 (2004), pp. 275–276.

6. Oliver Wright, 'Judges Call MMR Link to Autism "Junk Science"', *The Times*, 31 July 2003.

7. Oliver Wright, 'Legal Aid Blow to Families in MMR Battle', *The Times*, 2 October 2003.

8. Anthony Browne, 'Jab Fear "Makes Measles Epidemic Inevitable"', *The Times*, 8 August 2003.

9. Nigel Hawkes, 'Doctors Link Illness to Fall in MMR Jabs', *The Times*, 6 September 2003.

So illness and deaths will inevitably result from what is almost certainly an unwarranted scare. How can parents make informed decisions? Not easily is the answer.

One result is that there has been growing pressure for parents to have the choice to have the vaccine delivered as individual doses at four-month intervals, on the assumption that this would avoid the putative link to autism. Vaccination is compulsory in the US and France and there are a number of good medical reasons why a protracted procedure is unwise, but I'm more interested in the basis for the rejection of the conventional approach. What leads to this widespread suspicion? One element is the existence of conflicting scientific reports, and we who are used to such controversy at the growing edge of science do not realize quite how disturbing such conflicting reports are to the general public. A second factor must be a lack of parental choice,[10] though offering choice is fine in theory but complicated in practice. A recent article titled 'Should the MMR Vaccine Be Compulsory?' concluded as follows:

> We live in a society with a National Health Service that values personal choice. But personal choice can only be made in the light of the facts. Perhaps the answer lies in easy access to presentable information and an emphasis on relative risks. The scare about autism and the MMR focuses our need to understand the causes and development of autism. Similarly, efforts need to be made to discourage public misunderstanding that science is exact, rather than having defined limits with scope for error within those limits. Maybe we should step back from the suggestion that the MMR vaccine itself should be compulsory and combine reading of the current NHS literature with a compulsory short verbal or written test, before we are made to choose whether to vaccinate or not?[11]

---

10. Eileen Rubery, 'MMR: We Should Be Able to Choose', *Science and Public Affairs* (April 2002), p. 7.

11. C. Derry, 'Should the MMR Vaccine Be Compulsory?' *Biologist* 50 (2003), p. 244.

A third factor is the effect of the media; for example, in 2001 the BBC Radio 4 *Today* programme ran a headline about the 'research' it had done showing that parents wanted a public enquiry as to how the MMR vaccine should be administered to their children. Their research, reported in *The Times* of 30 August 2001, found that 'Four out of five parents questioned in an ICM poll for BBC Radio Four's *Today* programme wanted a public inquiry into the combined MMR vaccine, but 73% of the 1004 people asked considered it safe. Nearly two-thirds of them would like the option of separate vaccines.' 'What sort of research is this?' we might ask. Asking people whether they would like a public inquiry is a very simple way of getting a 'yes' answer, and I feel the programme has been mischievous here, especially when the same poll showed that 73% of the people asked said that the vaccine was safe. How can we possibly make decisions on this sort of basis?

But there is another issue here. How do you ever prove that the people who say that the vaccine is unsafe are wrong? Indeed, they might be right! They start from a different premise: that new developments have to be proved to be totally safe, while we can only ever say that we have no evidence that they are unsafe. So who is right? Where does the truth lie? Scientists are very cautious about non-rigorous, anecdotal information, but this is not a view shared by everyone, and the MMR vaccine story shows that, despite the lack of any clear evidence, the public can choose a conclusion driven by a deep-seated suspicion of 'official' attitudes, preferring their own judgment to those of scientists. That is very postmodern and has profound implications for the way we present our conclusions.

Genetically modified foods

Finally, what about genetically modified (GM) foods and crops? These are widely grown in North and South America, with China and South Africa also making up a significant portion of the world's GM crops. In 2003 GM crops were being grown in 18 countries across six continents, with Argentina alone accounting

for 21% of the world's GM crops.[12] Most will be familiar with the
introduction of GM foods in the late 1990s, of the storm that
arose, initially based on claims that GM foods caused cancer in
rats, the public rejection of these foods and the withdrawal of
such foods from the supermarkets. There is now general agreement that there is no evidence that any current food derived from
genetically modified organisms is unsafe, and I personally have no
hesitation in eating such foods. I notice, for example, that much of
the cheese on sale in supermarkets is made by the use of an
enzyme produced in genetically modified bacteria. Few seem to be
worried. The problem has arisen in the aftermath of the BSE epidemic, in the absence of any demonstrable benefit to consumers,
and with a product from a major US multinational, for all multi-
nationals are now suspect. But setting these aside, what exactly is
the risk of harm from eating a GM food? Again science can only
show no evidence of risk, while the consumer often wants evidence of no risk. And how does the consumer assess risk? Look at
the following, and see how different it is from the way that a scientist might assess risk

Risks are generally more worrying if perceived:

- To be involuntary (e.g. exposure to pollution) rather than
  voluntary (e.g. smoking),
- As inequitably distributed,
- As inescapable by taking personal precautions,
- To arise from an unfamiliar or novel source,
- To arise from man-made rather than natural sources,
- To cause hidden and irreversible damage,
- To pose some particular danger to future generations,
- To threaten a form of death or illness/injury arousing
  particular dread,
- To damage identifiable rather than anonymous victims,
- To be poorly understood by science,

12. Clive James, 'Preview: Global Status of Commercialized Transgenic
    Crops', *ISAAA Briefs* 30 (2003).

As subject to contradictory statements from responsible sources.[13]

So are these fair concerns? And if yes, where is the truth? With the scientist or with the consumer? Surely with both, but we are having real trouble determining how to handle such debates. People tend to talk past each other. The media, of course, have had a field day. On 18 February 1999 the *Express* ran the headline 'Mutant crops could kill you', where the unproven possibility that antibiotic resistance could be transmitted to human pathogens through genetic modification of food crops was presented in the most lurid terms. The editor of the *Express* did admit to the House of Lords that this particular headline was 'probably pushing it quite far'. But of course the message had gone home. Indeed the headlines of many newspapers from that period stagger the imagination:

- Are we at risk from mutant make-up? *Express on Sunday* 21/02/99
- Scientists warn of GM crops link to meningitis. *Daily Mail* 26/04/99
- Scientists raise the fear of GM foods triggering new allergies. *Express* 30/04/99
- Lifting the lid on the horror of GM foods. *Express* 12/05/99
- The GM pollen that can mean a cloud of death for butterflies. *Daily Mail* 20/05/99
- Mutant porkies on the menu. *News of the World* 23/05/99
- GM risk in daily food of millions. *Guardian* 24/05/99
- Charles: my fears over the safety of GM foods. *Daily Mail* 01/06/99
- GM food 'threatens the planet'. *Observer* 20/06/99
- Meat may be tainted by Frankenstein food. *Daily Mail* 06/07/99
- M&S sells genetically modified Frankenplants. *Independent on Sunday* 18/07/99

---

13. P. Bennett, 'Understanding Responses to Risk: Some Basic Findings', in P. Bennett and K. Calman (eds.), *Risk Communication and Public Health* (Oxford: Oxford University Press, 1999), p. 6.

Does this overdramatization of risk tell us anything about getting at the truth? Not much really will be the reaction of any informed scientist; for whatever one thinks about the future of GM food and crops these headlines do not reflect the complexity of the issues fairly, nor is their style a sensible way forward for a sophisticated democratic society to make decisions. But when newspaper editors were admonished for not telling what scientists regard as the truth, they responded by saying that 'our job is to sell newspapers'. It is also true that during the period of maximum coverage in early 1999:

- No news articles on GM foods were written by science journalists; 45% were written by political journalists.
- 50% of features were written by news journalists and only 17% by science journalists.
- Commentary came largely in letters to the editor, editorials and opinion columns; none came from science writers.

We scientists have to face the fact that this is the way the news is made. The issues have not gone away by any means, for as I write in October 2003, we are in the middle of a full-blown scare about the dangers of sowing GM crops. My scientific colleagues are near despair about the way in which any cautious comment of theirs is misinterpreted and the way in which the NGOs are allowed to make rash statements without any editorial control. One famous newspaper used to say of itself 'All the news that is fit to print' and another 'News is sacred; comment is free'. These moral distinctions – and it is a matter of morals – seem to have been lost by newspapers that continually run campaigns to maintain circulation in a very competitive market.

Conclusions

But enough of case studies; what conclusions can we draw? I suggest that there are three distinguishable types of response to the case studies I have described. The first comes from those who see science as socially constructed and lacking objective 'truth'.

Most scientists take a highly realistic attitude towards scientific findings; they believe that there is a reality 'out there'. In contrast, many supporters of organic agriculture, for example, seem to doubt that an objective proven scientific truth can exist. They seem to believe that natural systems are more than the sum of the parts, that the reductionism widely used in the natural sciences does not see the whole picture, and so fails as a political or social tool of analysis. For these people the 'natural' has a very special meaning.

But what do we mean by 'natural'? Perhaps the most basic meaning of the word 'natural' is captured in the titles Natural History or Natural Philosophy. Then there is another meaning of the word, and that is 'natural' as opposed to 'supernatural'. There is yet a third meaning and that is 'natural' as opposed to 'artificial' or 'deliberate', and that is the way in which it is being used in these debates. Indeed I suggest that the word 'natural' has become not a description of the world around us, but a value in itself. I also suggest to you that in our postmodern Western world, which has largely abandoned conventional religion, the 'natural' has become the 'Good'. So *The Times Higher Educational Supplement* of 27 July 2001, under the title 'Protective clothing', carries a picture of a student putting 'finishing touches to clothes made from her award-winning fabric, which is filled with microscopic medicine beads. They contain natural cures for conditions such as arthritis, eczema and even depression and are released by body heat.' This looks to me to be a form of pantheism, and I recall some wise words of John Stott's,[14] arguing that we must avoid the deification of nature, and pointing out that this is the mistake of the panthe-ist, who identifies the Creator with his creation, of the animist, who populates the natural world with spirits, and especially of the New Age's Gaia movement, which gives nature its own self-perpetuating mechanism and leaves no room for God. It seems that for many British people a concern about the natural world, and especially the animal kingdom, now fills the gap occupied for

14. John Stott in the foreword to R. J. Berry (ed.), *The Care of Creation* (Leicester: IVP, 2000), pp. 7–9.

most of human history by faith in God. Creation has taken over from Creator, and we are in danger, as a society, of worshipping 'nature'.

This view goes back to the beginnings of the Romantic movement, whose early poets Coleridge and Wordsworth were so influential. They wrote in blank verse and in all sorts of free forms; their objects were drawn not from the closed and ordered life of man in society, but from a limitless world in which all things were possible to the spirit and will of the individual. The literature was no longer judicial and objective; it was enthusiastic and expressive of the inmost soul of the poet. The poets became aware of the life of the remote and primitive past; of simple persons, who were regarded with tender and pitiful emotion, and finally these poets began to discover in nature an inexhaustible source of inspiration. The movement came to fruition only after the turbulence driven by the ideas and events of the French Revolution. From France came the notion that the central fact of existence was the individual who was essentially good. The evils of life were due to the perversion of that natural virtue by pestilent social institutions; humanity was to be liberated and allowed to remake the world into a fit home for all. Using his or her own feelings as a guide, undreamed of happiness would result.

Other poets, such as George Crabbe, writing 250 years ago in a poem called 'The Village', have no such romantic view of nature:

> I grant indeed that fields and flocks have charms
> For him that grazes or for him that farms;
> But, when amid such pleasing scenes I trace
> The poor laborious natives of the place,
> And see the midday sun, with fervid ray,
> On their bare heads and dewy temples play;
> While some with feebler heads and fainter hearts,
> Deplore their fortune, yet sustain their parts:
> Then shall I dare these real ills to hide
> In tinsel trappings of poetic pride?

And further on, after giving a firm 'No' to that question, he continues:

> Rank weeds, that every art and care defy,
> Reign o'er the land, and rob the blighted rye:
> There thistles stretch their prickly arms afar,
> And to the ragged infant threaten war.

I submit that a Christian view is closer to this attitude; we are not romantics; we do not have to assume that nature as we find it is ideal, but we do have responsibilities as stewards for this world, even though perfection is not going to be found here.[15]

There is a second, quite different position, which is held by Richard Dawkins and others, who argues that science is the only way to get at 'truth', and what we discover in science displaces other human ideas, including those of religion. So, Dawkins would say, can anything be called 'true' if there is no scientific proof that it is 'true'? Richard Dawkins often makes the point that in the nineteenth century people read novels because this gave them an insight into the book of life, but in our own century we read the book of science, because this contains all we need to know. Dawkins himself says in the preface to his very readable account of the theory of evolution, 'I want to persuade the reader, not just that the Darwinian world view *happens* to be true but that it is the only known theory that *could*, in principle, solve the mystery about existence. This makes it a doubly satisfying theory.'[16]

And of course it excludes all other theories.

Dawkins's central concern is with a famous argument for the existence of God, classically expounded by William Paley, the argument from biological design. Dawkins admits that the impression

---

15. See, e.g., an interesting discussion in S. R. L. Clark, *Biology and Christian Ethics* (Cambridge: Cambridge University Press, 2000), especially pp. 94–104.

16. Richard Dawkins, *The Blind Watchmaker* (Harmondsworth: Penguin, 1991), p. xiv.

that animals were designed is hard to escape, because they have so many different parts precisely organized and intricately arranged to help them live. Dawkins calls this feature of living things 'organized complexity'. He writes:

> This [appearance of design] is probably the most powerful reason for the belief, held by the vast majority of people that have ever lived, in some kind of supernatural deity. It took a very great leap of the imagination for Darwin and Wallace to see that, contrary to all intuition, there is another way and, once you have understood it, a far more plausible way, for complex 'design' to arise out of primeval simplicity.[17]

Dawkins, following Charles Darwin himself, admires Paley for his 'passionate sincerity' and for putting the argument more clearly and more convincingly than anyone before. However, Dawkins thinks Paley's explanation for the appearance of design is as follows:

> Paley's argument [that the complexity of the world argues for a creator God] is made with passionate sincerity and is informed by the best biological scholarship of his day, but it is wrong, gloriously and utterly wrong. The analogy between telescope and eye, between watch and living organism is false. All appearances to the contrary, the only watchmaker in nature is the blind force of physics, albeit deployed in a very special way. A true watchmaker has foresight: he designs his cogs and springs, and plans their interconnections, with a future purpose in his mind's eye. Natural selection, the blind, unconscious, automatic process which Darwin discovered, and which we now know is the explanation for the existence and apparently purposeful forms of all life, has no purpose in mind.

Now if all that Dawkins meant by this was that Paley's idea of separate creations was wrong in view of the current understanding of the origin of species, then there is nothing more to say. But it is

---

17. Ibid., p. xvi.

his claim in many different places that religious explanations are displaced by scientific ones that is open to criticism. His position admits only of physical explanations: 'The kind of explanation we come up with must not contradict the laws of physics. Indeed it will make use of the laws of physics, and nothing more than the laws of physics.'[18]

Of course scientific explanations must use the laws of physics, but he excludes, without argument, the possibility that creation could have any other meaning but that described by physics and chemistry. So he does not just think that Paley's suggestion of miraculous creation by God is wrong. He argues that the Darwinian explanation undermines God *completely*, that the emergence of animals can be explained by the action of physical laws alone and that these physical laws and objects need no further explanation.

The Blind Watchmaker strives to convince us that Darwinian evolution is not just blind chance or sheer fluke. Rather, small, helpful changes automatically accumulate through natural selection as millions of generations of animals live, reproduce and die. Dawkins uses computer programmes to illustrate how something that would never happen all at once might be broken down into many small steps. 'Natural selection' means that helpful changes are more likely to survive and be reproduced, so that each small step toward improvement tends to be passed on to later generations, while harmful changes are weeded out. In this way the improvements add together, until, given the colossal stretches of geological time, really huge improvements can result, all by natural, blind processes.

Crucially, Dawkins maintains that such a process does not require a creator God; he maintains that no breaks in natural processes are necessary to explain organic life and he presents this as a powerful argument for atheism. He maintains that the appearance of design is an illusion, that religion is false, and that we have to look elsewhere for the basis of our morals, hopes and fears. I think that this influence has been a powerful force on all of us; Dawkins

---

18. Ibid., p. 15.

expresses articulately and clearly the pervading secularist philosophy of the Western World. But is he right?[19]

The first thing to say is that his assumption, for example, that if one can describe a process by which life arose, then there is no God, although self-evident to Dawkins himself, is very obviously a 'faith' statement – albeit of course of a secular 'faith'. His conclusion is not at all obvious; how could he show that God did not intend an evolutionary process to happen? Dawkins's belief is part of his metaphysics, not his science; science does not demand that conclusion, and many scientists, like I do, reject it.

Dawkins also assumes that, because Darwinian evolution offers a cogent explanation of the living world, there is no room for any other *complementary* explanation, nor can we assume there *is* a purpose to our existence. Surely the existence of fine-tuned lawful nature itself invites explanation? It is obvious that we can ask more than one question about the world; asking 'How?', what science is about, but we ask other questions too. We ask 'Why'? Why are we here, is there any purpose to life, and in particular is there any purpose for my life? I put it to you that science cannot answer these questions, because it is not what science is about.

This reductionist philosophy is implicit in much of the current public understanding of science programmes, and I think there is a danger of these programmes being counter-productive, for it is not just Christians who find this bare reductionist world both uninviting and threatening. Anyone with an artistic or literary sensitivity will reject it, and maybe reject science too, as a useful way of looking at the world. I submit that scientific naturalism is not just uninviting and threatening, but it is also less able than Christianity to explain why there is a lawful, comprehensible universe and why we can trust our brains to unlock the secrets of the universe.

There is a third, the Christian, position; for we worship not the

---

19. See the article by Michael Poole, 'A Critique of Aspects of the Philosophy and Theology of Richard Dawkins', *Science and Christian Belief* 6 (April 1994), p. 41; the reply by Richard Dawkins and a response by Michael Poole, in *Science and Christian Belief* 7 (April 1995), pp. 45, 51.

creation but the Creator. We do not fear the discoveries of science, for what we discover is God's handiwork in the first place. Philosophically we are critical realists, with a firm theological basis for regarding the world as 'real', but aware too that our fumbling attempts to understand it are error prone, and that we work by a series of approximations, some of which are conditioned by the society we live in. But in the end we find a coherent, intellectually satisfying position that reflects the glory of God.

To sum up. There has been an attack on the concept of truth in science, which at its most extreme reduces science to a mere discourse, socially determined and of no more than social significance. For if 'truth' is just a social construct, then there is no longer any role for the 'expert', and everything, for example how the MMR vaccine is to be used, will be settled by public vote. As Prince Charles once said about GM foods, 'Let's just ask the public what they want.' Of course there is a major role for the consumer but there is also a role for the expert and specifically for the scientist, who must listen, inform, honestly evaluate, and stay involved in the public debate. But we also have to recognize that we scientists no longer hold the high-priestly role we held back in the 1950s!

But we are not just defending science; for how can we argue for the 'truth' of Christianity if we do not even agree on what counts as 'truth'? For if those who deconstruct science are right, then there is little point to science, and it is no more than phenomenology. Indeed if they are right, there will soon be no science left, because science is not a worthwhile activity, while the social scientists of science themselves will have nothing left to study and will have destroyed their own field! There is a circularity in their argument too, as many have pointed out, for their criticism that the sciences are socially determined can be applied with equal force to their own work, and if their arguments are themselves socially determined, we slide into an infinite regress.

So this is an attack upon both science and upon Christian faith, for it denies that there is a reality outside our own minds. We who are Christians and scientists have a special role to play, for both our profession and our faith are under attack. Historically, you will recall, it is generally accepted that in the seventeenth century it was the Judaeo-Christian faith in a world created by a rational God and in man made in his own image that gave scientists the confidence to regard the world as real, accessible to minds that could comprehend, at least partially, what was going on out there.

We in our new century, as Christians and scientists, now have a responsibility to preserve this tradition, on the one hand avoiding the subjectivity of the social scientists and on the other, the reductionism of Dawkins and his friends.